Praise for *Immigration in the 21st Century*

A brilliant, comprehensive textbook on the comparative politics of immigration—a *tour de force*. Easily accessible and highly readable, this book sets the standard for the field and will be used in classes across the globe.

James F. Hollifield, Southern Methodist University and Global Fellow, Wilson Center

International migration is one of the most contentious political issues of the 21st century, especially in wealthy democracies that are the preferred destinations for millions of migrants each year. Givens and her colleagues focus on the politics of immigration control in these countries, with an emphasis on electoral politics, including the role that migrants themselves play in the political system. The authors bring a comparative approach to their presentation, allowing students to understand the variation in policy choices across countries. This will be the text of choice for students as it describes the centrality of political decisions in governing international migration flows today.

Jeannette Money, University of California—Davis

For students and scholars interested in the politics of immigration, this is the place to begin. The three core chapters on the histories of immigration provide a rich foundation for understanding both policies and the differences of policy outcomes that are outlined and analyzed in this excellent book.

Martin A. Schain, New York University

Immigration in the 21st Century provides an engaging and comprehensive introduction to immigration politics and policy. Taking readers from North America to Europe and Australia, this book is impressive in its sweep, clarity, and insight.

Daniel J. Tichenor, University of Oregon

IMMIGRATION IN THE 21ST CENTURY

This text provides students with an introduction to the politics of immigration policy in the U.S., Australia, Canada, and Europe. The book gives students an overview of the theoretical approaches used by political scientists to analyze immigration politics and provides historical background to the policies and politics that affect democracies today. A comparative politics approach develops the context that explains how immigration and politics interact in different types of countries. Covering topics including party politics, labor migration, and citizenship, students gain an understanding of the complexities of immigration politics and how immigration policies are affecting the world today.

Terri E. Givens is the former provost at Menlo College and Professor at the University of Texas at Austin. She has written extensively on immigration politics, the radical right, and antidiscrimination policy in Europe, and is a Senior Fellow with the Center for the Analysis of the Radical Right (CARR). She is most recently the author of *Legislating Equality: The Politics of Antidiscrimination Policy in Europe* (2014) and is a regular blogger and commentator for a variety of outlets. She has been teaching courses and speaking on the politics of immigration policy for over 20 years.

Rachel Navarre is Assistant Professor of political science at Bridgewater State University in Massachusetts. She received her PhD from the University of Texas at Austin in Government and specializes in the fields of comparative politics and public policy. After completing her degree, she was a post-doctoral fellow at the Center for Inter-American Policy at

Tulane University in New Orleans. Her research focuses on comparative public policy, specifically issues of framing and issue definition; immigration policy and politics; regional governance; populism; and content analysis.

Pete Mohanty is a data scientist at Google. He was previously a science, engineering & education fellow and lecturer in the Department of Statistics at Stanford University. He holds a PhD in Government from the University of Texas at Austin where he studied comparative immigration politics in Europe and where he was advised and mentored by Terri E. Givens. Pete's research adapts recently developed statistical methods and models to the challenges of comparative research, especially how xenophobia affects political behavior.

IMMIGRATION IN THE 21ST CENTURY

The Comparative Politics of Immigration Policy

Terri E. Givens, Rachel Navarre, and Pete Mohanty

Routledge
Taylor & Francis Group

NEW YORK AND LONDON

First published 2020
by Routledge
52 Vanderbilt Avenue, New York, NY 10017

and by Routledge
2 Park Square, Milton Park, Abingdon, Oxon, OX14 4RN

Routledge is an imprint of the Taylor & Francis Group, an informa business

Library of Congress Cataloging-in-Publication Data
Names: Givens, Terri E., 1964- author. | Navarre, Rachel,
author. |
Mohanty, Pete, author. | Routledge (Firm)
Title: Immigration in the 21st century : the comparative politics
of immigration policy / Terri E Givens, Rachel Navarre, Pete
Mohanty.
Other titles: Immigration in the twenty-first century
Description: First Edition. | New York : Routledge, 2020. |
Includes bibliographical references and index.
Identifiers: LCCN 2019053712 (print) | LCCN 2019053713
(ebook) | ISBN 9781138932241 (Hardback) | ISBN
9781138932258 (Paperback) | ISBN 9781315660554 (eBook)
Subjects: LCSH: United States–Emigration and
immigration–Government policy. | United States–Emigration
and immigration–Political aspects. | Australia–Emigration and
immigration–Government policy. | Australia–Emigration and
immigration–Political aspects. | Canada–Emigration and
immigration–Government policy. | Canada–Emigration and
immigration–Political aspects. | Europe–Emigration and
immigration–Government policy. | Europe–Emigration and
immigration–Political aspects.
Classification: LCC JV6483 .G58 2020 (print) | LCC JV6483
(ebook) | DDC 325/.1–dc23
LC record available at https://lccn.loc.gov/2019053712
LC ebook record available at https://lccn.loc.gov/2019053713

ISBN: 978-1-138-93224-1 (hbk)
ISBN: 978-1-138-93225-8 (pbk)
ISBN: 978-1-315-66055-4 (ebk)

Typeset in Sabon
by Integra Software Services Pvt. Ltd.

This book is dedicated to the thousands of students who have taken Terri Givens' Comparative Immigration Politics course over the years. It was your experiences in that class that guided the development of this book.

CONTENTS

ILLUSTRATIONS

Figures

Tables

1

INTRODUCTION

The Complex Landscape of Immigration Policy and Politics

Give me your tired, your poor,
Your huddled masses yearning to breathe free,
The wretched refuse of your teeming shore.
Send these, the homeless, tempest-tossed, to me:
I lift my lamp beside the golden door.

(Emma Lazarus, 1883)

These words that grace the Statue of Liberty have animated the mythology of the United States, which prides itself on its history as a country of immigrants. Many Americans came to this country from other lands, but what is less well known are the complicated politics that determined the flows of people that came to this country since it became independent in the late 1700s.

Someone in the 1880s could hardly imagine that the U.S. would become a country mostly closed off to immigration within the next 40 years. Although many people in the United States are proud of the fact that we are a country of immigration, policy in the U.S. has not always been as welcoming to immigrants as our national understanding implies. Even as the words of Emma Lazarus were being written, politicians in California were concerned about the flow of immigrants from China and looking at ways to limit their entry. Soon, one of the first restrictions on immigration into the U.S., on immigrants from China, would be passed by Congress. The politics of immigration began with a focus on control that would continue through the 1920s.

In the 19th century, immigration was a critical component to the development of countries like the United States, Australia, and Canada. However, by the turn of the 21st century, these countries, and newer countries of immigration, like France, Germany, and Spain, were look-ing at ways to limit the immigration flows that had once been important to their economic development. Political parties on the left and right agreed on the need to control immigration, and some on the far right were arguing for complete halts to immigration and even the return of many who were living in their countries temporarily or as undocu-mented immigrants.

The United States became more open to immigration after the passage of the 1965 Immigration Act, but the focus has been on more restrictive policy since a series of economic downturns in the 1980s, the 1990s, and in 2008, when the most recent fiscal crisis began. Perhaps more dra-matically, the politics of immigration restriction came to the fore again in a string of elections in 2016. In both the U.S. and Europe, populist, anti-immigrant parties gained votes and seats, and in the U.S., a president was elected on a promise to restrict immigration, particularly for Muslim immigrants. Immigration policy varies tremendously over time and place. Nevertheless, there are key patterns in the politics of immigration that underpin the policymaking process examined in detail in this book.

Since immigration policy varies substantially between countries and changes dramatically over time, this book intends to provide an under-standing of those differences. Specifically, this book focuses on the politics of immigration that underlie the policymaking process.

What Are the Politics of Immigration?

Immigration is complex. Immigration is a function of geography, eco-nomics, international pressures, and various factors like family connec-tions that lead people to move from one place to another. The policies developed to regulate immigration are no simpler: They may be impacted by electoral politics, public opinion, and other factors like international law. The combination of these political and economic fac-tors often leads to major policy shifts.[1] This book focuses on the politics and history of immigration control and management, with a focus on the ways that policies are impacted by immigration, and the way that politics impacts immigration. We do not focus directly on the issues of immigrant integration like immigrant rights, immigrant benefits, and immigrant responsibilities, although these issues are often intertwined with the politics of control. Our main focus is electoral politics and the way that policymakers have dealt with immigration, but we will also look at the way some interest groups and public opinion have impacted policy. Ultimately, the goal of this book is to provide students with an understanding of the complex factors behind immigration, how politicians make the decisions that can have an impact on immigration, and how immigrants themselves impact politics and policymaking.

Why Does Immigration Matter?

Human history is made up of the movements of peoples. In the last few centuries, as borders have been drawn and redrawn, some migrants have fled war and famine, while others have simply sought a better life. Immigration is important for four key reasons: (1) historical formation of nation-states, (2) economic development, (3) globalization, and (4) state sovereignty. In the U.S., Canada, and Australia, all originally British colonies, immigration was the main form of nation-building going back to the 18th and 19th centuries even though these countries had indigenous populations (which were often decimated when Europeans came along). Nonetheless, these countries encouraged immigration and celebrated the mythology around their beginnings as countries of immigration. The reality is much more complicated, as these countries went through periods of being more open, or less open, and although immigration continues in each of these countries, at rates much higher than most industrialized countries, anti-immigrant sentiment has often defined politics and policy.

Beyond nation-building, many other countries have also seen immigration as a source of labor. Labor migration, however, often impacts host populations and policies far beyond economic development. For countries like France and Germany, immigration became an important issue for policymakers after World War II. In order to rebuild after a devastating war, these countries had to import workers, initially from other parts of Europe, but eventually from places like Turkey and Northern Africa. Although they were considered temporary, in the end, many of these immigrants would stay and become residents and ultimately citizens of these countries, creating the need for new policies to recognize new issues like discrimination.

More recently, countries that had been more likely to send emigrants to other countries until recent years have become the "newer" countries of immigration. Countries like Spain, South Korea, and South Africa have more recently begun to deal with significant in-flows of migrants wanting to take advantage of economic opportunities. As these countries have developed economically and politically, they have become more attractive, but these countries have also been caught up in the wave of globalization.

In this era of globalization, people are on the move. The percentage of foreigners in the U.S. at the beginning of the 21st century is as high now as it was at the beginning of the 20th century. The percentage of foreign born in the U.S. hit close to 15 per cent in the first decade of the 21st century – very similar to the percentages at the beginning of the 20th century, a time when nativists and progressives were pushing for restrictions on immigration. Since at least the 1600s, the part of the world that would become the United States developed as a country of immigration. Migrants from Spain, Portugal, France, Britain, and many other countries sought refuge and/or their fortune in what was seen as a new land, with little regard for those who already lived there.

The history of immigration is often forgotten even though many countries owe their growth and development to various influxes of people over the years. Today when you turn on the news, you often hear reports talking about a "flood" of immigrants heading to a county. Politicians speak about the need to reinforce borders and to provide resources to support refugees feeling wars or political persecution. The politics of asylum depends not just on whether refugees meet the legal criteria ensuring refugee status but on who is meant to provide safe haven.

The ability to control a country's borders is at the heart of sovereignty. The nation-state is defined by its borders and the people who live within those borders. This makes immigration a potentially serious challenge to a country, particularly in homogenous countries or if immigrants are perceived not to fit the national mold. As noted by Castles, de Haas, and Miller (2014), "[i]n this sense international migration is intrinsically political and is almost inevitably an imagined or real challenge to the state sovereignty" (p. 313). Although the main focus of the study of immigration is often around the reasons that people may migrate to another country, the policy and politics of the receiving states have received less attention. In an era of globalization, the politics of immigration are highly salient and relevant to domestic and international politics.

Immigration from a Comparative Perspective

The politics of immigration has become a very salient issue since the end of World War II. Though there may be a tendency to focus on the U.S., the politics of immigration in one country are intrinsically intertwined with politics in others. Immigration policy often has an impact far beyond the borders of the country that makes it. This book takes a comparative approach to the study of the politics of immigration in order to understand the broader context of immigration, how different countries have addressed and been impacted by these issues, and to examine the impact of different institutions. There are four main questions central to the study of comparative politics:

- How do countries vary in their political institutions?
- What is the relationship between political development and economic development?

- How do countries vary in the outputs of government, that is, in their public policies?
- How do policies impact outcomes and behavior?

Comparative politics focuses on the domestic policy level and policy-making in a country, using a variety of approaches to understand differences across countries. Although we will also touch on relationships between countries, for the most part, this book examines internal politics and policies that have been impacted by immigration. When comparing policy, it is useful to understand historical differences, governmental structures, geographical issues, and other factors that will impact policy-making and the outcomes that we see over time.

As an example, the discourses around immigration policy in the U.S. have had a tendency to alternate between strict control at particular junctures, to more open policies over our long history of being a country of immigration (Tichenor 2002). Although the Democratic party is currently seen as the proponent of policies that would potentially lead to legalization (often referred to as "amnesty"), it was often Republican presidents who were champions of more open policies.

Scholars take different approaches to understanding how immigration policy is made, as we describe in Chapter 2. It is important to keep in mind that there are contending theories for explaining the development and outcomes of immigration policy, particularly when comparing countries. As noted by Rosenblum and Tichenor (2012), international migration "has ebbed and flowed with shifting economic forces, new social and cultural linkages that transcend borders, innovations in communication and transportation, warfare, natural disasters, and numerous other sources of dislocation" (p.1). For our purposes, immigration flows are also impacted by policy, which in turn are impacted by politics, such as ideological competition between political parties. Policies range from Germany's claim that it not a country of immigration (at least up through the late 1990s) to those of the U.S., Canada, and Australia, which use visa preference systems to try to control the flows of immigrants, with particular policies for family reunification and skilled workers.

Many studies of migration focus on the economic and personal factors that influence people to move from one country to another. However, in this book we examine how policies are made and how these policies impact the numbers and types of flows into receiving countries.

Immigration Policy and Security

It is striking that immigration is often described as a security issue, which focuses on the border, but there are somewhere between 10 and

12 million undocumented immigrants living in the United States, which the U.S. can neither document nor track. Which is the greater security issue? Many critics of American immigration policy argue that illegal immigrants should be deported and made to "stand in line" in order to get back into the country. However, as advocates of comprehensive immigration reform often point out, there is no line to get into. This is why the majority of illegal immigrants come into this country on a valid (usually tourist) visa and then overstay that visa because they are able to get a job, housing, and live well in the United States despite their status.

In recent years, new strategies have emerged to deal with undocumented immigration. These include systems to track workers such as e-verify and focusing on making life in the U.S. untenable for those without legal status. As Tom Wong (2015) has found in his research, "What has emerged in recent years is a concerted strategy of attrition through enforcement... In practice, the strategy... is designed to create for unauthorized immigrants conditions of life that are so harsh that the benefits of 'self-deportation' exceed those of remaining in a country without authorization" (p. 10). These tactics have also been used on the border with asylum seekers, with families separated and placed in detention, then agreeing to return to their country of origin in order to be reunited, in some cases.

A major turning point for immigration policy in the U.S. followed the 9/11 terrorist attacks. A group of terrorists, some of whom had trained to fly airplanes in the U.S., launched attacks on the Twin Towers of the World Trade Center (WTC) in New York City, the Pentagon, and what was presumed to be the U.S. Capitol (the fourth plane crashed in a field in Pennsylvania).[2] The attack on the WTC led to the collapse of the two massive buildings, while the Pentagon was severely damaged, and nearly 3,000 lives were lost. This event impacted not only the U.S., but it reverberated around the world. It led to major changes in policy for screening airline passengers, students, and a focus on security for immigration policy. The attacks also had a major impact on American political culture and have changed the ways politicians in both parties talk about immigration.

Since 9/11, in the United States, Canada, Australia, and Europe, immigration policy has shifted to an increased focus on security, particularly at airports and land borders (Givens, Freeman, and Leal 2008). Though there have been considerable political efforts, especially on the right, to conflate immigration, Islam, and terrorism, the reality facing policymakers is far more complex. Though research consistently shows few Muslims living in the West are sympathetic to terrorism, many subsequent Islamic radical attacks, such as the 7/7 bombings in London, were carried out not by immigrants but their children. The notion that seemingly well-integrated immigrants would turn into homegrown terrorists has confounded policymakers on both the left and the right.

Political Science and Immigration Politics

The politics of immigration has only become a serious focus of study for political science in the last 30 years. Though political science is at least a century old, it developed into its maturity only after World War II. As such, many of the major research concerning international relations reflect the Cold War. But, with the fall of the Berlin Wall in 1989 and the increasing contentiousness of immigration politics, political science has increasingly focused on immigration. For example, California became a flashpoint in the mid-1990s when Proposition 187 was on the ballot, a citizens' initiative that would have limited access to education and health benefits for undocumented immigrants.[3]

As renowned political scientist Hollifield noted at the turn of the century, "only recently, in the 1980s and 1990s, the field of study has begun to emerge, which we might call the *politics of international migration*; and theorists are scrambling to see how we can 'bring the state back in' to social scientific analyses of migration" (Hollifield 2000, 137). Since that time there has been a strong growth in the number of scholars focusing their research in this area. By the second decade of the 21st century, a literature had developed that focused on immigration control, immigration and security, and immigrant integration (Hollifield and Wong 2014). These are areas that we explore throughout this book.

Is opposition to immigration driven primarily by economic or cultural concerns or, more recently, security? Are immigration politics distinct from the politics of left and right? Why do most advanced democracies consistently admit more immigrants than the public seems to want? In the 21st century, political scientists in the U.S. focused on issues beyond migration from Mexico, shifting to Muslim migrants, immigration as a security issue, and the major bureaucratic changes that would come into play after 9/11.[4] Immigrant integration – policies aimed at integrating immigrants into the host society – at both the national and local level – became an important topic of study as researchers sought to understand which policies, if any, are effective.

Immigration, Migration, and Sovereignty

In order to understand many of the political issues around immigration, it is important to understand the role of borders. The ability to control a country's borders is at the heart of sovereignty. The nation-state is defined by the people who live within its borders. In this section, we examine some of the terms that are used to define migrants and immigrants, as well as the factors that lead people to move across borders.

What Is Immigration Versus Migration?

The *Oxford English Dictionary* defines **immigration** as "the action of coming to live permanently in a foreign country" and **migration** as "movement of people to a new area or country in order to find work or better living conditions," making the two terms indistinguishable. However, in political science, we tend to look at people who are moving from one country to another and have the potential to become settlers as immigrants and the people who are moving to another region or area of a country as migrants that includes a broader range of factors that cause the movements of peoples. Immigration and the policies related to it are generally the focus for political scientists studying people who move across borders. Particularly in the U.S., it is the norm for politicians and the media to use the term immigration when discussing policy and the movement of people into the United States (see Figure 1.1).

Immigration is often seen as an issue of demographics or economics. Examining the history of immigration, it is also clearly a political issue. Politicians are the ones determining policy through legislation, and those

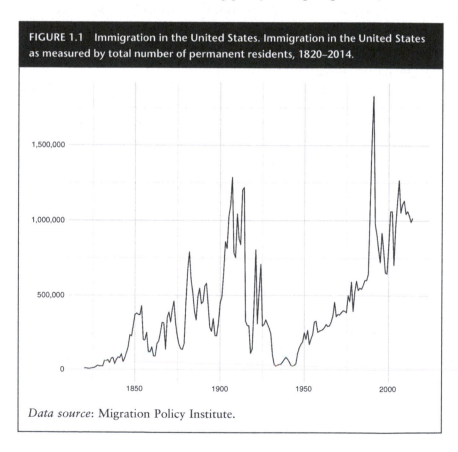

FIGURE 1.1   Immigration in the United States. Immigration in the United States as measured by total number of permanent residents, 1820–2014.

Data source: Migration Policy Institute.

policies are often driven by ideology, not just economics, or demographics. Although geography clearly plays a role in the movement of people, it is a surprisingly small factor in the overall movement of people.

There are a variety of factors which impact whether people want to leave their country of origin, and which country they chose to migrate to. These are known as "push and pull factors" and these include the following:

- Population growth
- Industrial revolutions
- Economic opportunity
- Diasporas and family reunification
- War, natural disasters
- Political/personal repression.

As populations grow, this puts pressure on resources in a particular region, leading people to leave for better opportunities, or the opportunity for land, as in the case of the early years of the United States. Industrial revolutions may lead to new opportunities in urban centers, but fewer opportunities for people in rural areas, causing them to move to the urban centers, or to other regions where they may have better economic opportunities.

The entry of Europeans was relatively unregulated at the federal level until after the Civil War, when immigration stations were built at ports of entry.[5] Although a form of passport, that is a letter of introduction or identity papers, did exist prior to the early 20th century, and they did not become formalized and standardized until around 1914 when Britain introduced their passport as a result of the Nationality and Status Aliens Act 1914[6] and other countries soon followed suit, including the United States. Prior to this time, border agents had a great deal of leeway in determining who could enter a country. Going forward, consulates and embassies became responsible for determining the suitability of applicants for entry into a country, leading to the development of bureaucracies to deal with a wide range of issues related to immigration, adding to the importance of entities like the U.S. State Department.

In Europe, most countries have only recently begun to see themselves as countries of immigration. After World War II, countries like France and Germany imported labor to help them recover from the war and redevelop their economies. By the early 1970s, economic downturns led to the end of labor importation, but immigrants continued to arrive through family reunification and as refugees. The politics of immigration came more into play in the 1980s with the rise of anti-immigrant political parties, but also the acknowledgement that immigrants were needed to maintain labor markets. Political scientists have focused on the ways that immigration has played a role in electoral politics, particularly with the rise of anti-immigrant populist parties and the influence of attitudes towards immigrants and immigration on electoral outcomes (Art 2011; Givens 2005; Hampshire 2013; Mudde 2019).

The politics of immigration has also become an important issue at the subnational level. With an increase in refugee flows in particular, states, provinces, and local municipalities have come to play an important role in determining policies which impact the settlement and even the entry of immigrants, particularly from Muslim dominant countries, in recent years. In the U.S., many states have attempted to pass laws that would impact immigration policy, including policies that would impact access to benefits such as healthcare and education. This was exemplified by the passage of Proposition 187 in California, which would have limited undocumented immigrants' access to non-emergency healthcare, public education, and other services. It was eventually declared unconstitutional, but other localities have attempted to pass other restrictive measures, such as rules that require landlords to report undocumented migrants, often leading to costly legal battles.[7]

Types of Flows

Here we briefly outline major immigration flows, though who belongs in which one is often fiercely contested in public debate as well as various legal proceedings.

- **Forced Migration/Slavery:** Forced migration played a major role in the flow of people in the 16th and 17th centuries. Millions of people from Africa were forced into slavery and sold to plantations in the Caribbean, South America (particularly Brazil), and the American South. Although forced migration is not a central focus of this book, it was an important component to the flow of people during a time of national development in the Western hemisphere.
- **Legal Immigrants:** Legal immigrants follow visa regimes in order to migrate from their home country to their desired destination. Typically, a person must apply for a visa at a consulate of the country they wish to migrate to, which often requires the payment of fees and submission of many documents. The emphasis often on the migrants' ability to support him or herself, whether they have family or a sponsor in the destination country, and more recently a focus on an ability to speak and read the language of the destination country.

    An important component of legal migration is skilled migration. This type of immigration has come to the fore with the rise of high-tech companies like Intel, Microsoft, and Apple who had high demand for engineers and use H1B visas to bring in high-skilled workers from countries like China, India, and Russia.

- **Refugees:** Refugees tend to come from war-torn regions, places where there have been natural disasters, and other factors that cause large numbers of people to leave their homes. Since the creation of the United Nations, countries have worked together to designate groups as refugees, giving them the opportunity to be resettled in a new country, or at least to be placed in a camp where they can receive services. Refugee regimes vary by country, despite international agreements, and the numbers of refugees entering particular countries varies dramatically. Refugees may or may not be able to seek asylum.

- **Asylum Seekers:** Asylum seekers must demonstrate a "well-founded fear of persecution" in the native country. They may be part of a targeted group (e.g., LGBTQ individuals) or an individual like a journalist who has run afoul of the government or armed groups in a country.

- **Undocumented Immigrants:** Illegal or undocumented immigrants are those who enter the country without a proper visa, but a person can also become undocumented after entering a country legally. Many people enter a country on a tourist visa and then decide to stay without getting a proper visa, thus overstaying their visa. Others may come on a student visa or other type of short-term visa that expires including tourist visas. These people are often referred to as visa "overstayers," since they entered the country legally but stayed in the country after their visa had expired. Others may become undocumented after losing a work or residence permit.

Range of Policies

Immigration policies can range from being very open and expansive, as in the U.S. from its founding to the early 1900s, or they can be very restrictive, as the U.S. was from the 1920s through the mid-1960s. Expansive policies encourage migrants to come to a country and put few hurdles in place to keep them from being able to enter. Certain types of visa programs can be considered expansive, including programs to encourage the entry of agricultural or high-skilled workers. Naturalization regimes which provide easy paths to citizenship can also be considered expansive, and encourage immigrants to stay in a country, but some regimes discourage naturalization which can leave immigrants without access to many of the rights of citizenship.

Restrictive policies can make it difficult or impossible to get a visa to enter the country, and many island nations are able to effectively restrict flows both in and out of their countries. When countries have more restrictive policies, it can often encourage migrants to stay in a country without documentation. When the population of undocumented immigrants gets high, countries may consider amnesty programs which allow those who are undocumented to pay fines to regularize their status and get a visa to remain in the country legally.

Policy Types

- **Visa** – a document or stamp in a passport that allows entry and temporary or permanent residence in a country. Some visas allow an immigrant to transition to a naturalization process, such as an H1-B guest worker visa.

  - Temporary
    - Tourist visas
    - Guest worker visas
    - Asylum or refugee status
  - Permanent visa or green card

- **Quotas or Preferences** – define who may enter the country and the number each year, usually defined by category or skill, or from a particular region of the world, or by status, such as asylum seekers and refugees.
- **Naturalization regimes** – citizenship is determined by each country as a function of whether a person is born on that country's soil (*jus soli*) or born to parents who are citizens (*jus sanguinis*). Naturalization can be complicated, and we go into more detail on citizenship and naturalization regimes in Chapter 8.
- **Immigration enforcement** – this issue of enforcement touches on a variety of policy areas, and countries have generally maintained border controls to enforce policies to keep out undocumented immigrants. At various times, countries have used amnesty or regularization policies to give undocumented immigrants the opportunity to legalize their status. This has been an issue with Deferred Action for Childhood Arrivals (DACA) and how to manage a political stalemate on the status of young people who entered the country as children.[8]

Most countries tend to shift between more expansive immigration policies and more restrictive politics. As we will describe in this book, there are many political factors which play into these policy changes. Since the 1960s, many countries have shifted their focus from quotas either from particular countries or for workers to a focus on family reunification and/or skilled workers. Concerns about migrants' ability to integrate has also played a role in policy, as we will describe later in this book.

Country Cases

Different political systems impact the nature of politics, but the following countries have similarities in their approaches to immigration historically. The cases outlined here will be considered throughout the book, along with other relevant cases as we examine specific policy areas.

Settler Countries: United States, Canada, Australia

In general, settler countries based their nation-building on the influx of immigrants, mainly from Europe. As former colonies of the British Empire, the U.S., Canada, and Australia still consider themselves countries of immigration. Each country had indigenous communities that it dealt with in various ways, for the most part, taking land and encouraging settlers from Europe to come and expand their claims. These countries maintained open immigration policies until the early 1900s. Australia, Canada, and the U.S. all pursued policies to restrict non-immigration, beginning with Chinese exclusion in the U.S. in 1872. More restrictive policies became codified with the implementation of National Origins Quotas in the 1920s. Australia passed the Immigration Restriction Act of 1901, or the White Australia Policy, in order to restrict non-white immigration, whereas Canada also placed restrictions with the passage of Chinese exclusion in 1885 and broader restrictive legislation in 1910. The U.S. became more open to immigration from non-European countries with the passage of the 1965 Immigration and Naturalization Act, which shifted the country from a policy based on quotas to one based on family reunification, while Canada and Australia also became less restrictive after World War II.

Figure 1.2 shows that though volatile, immigration into the U.S. has grown steadily over the last few decades. Immigration into Canada and Australia, by contrast, has been much more stable. Note that the population of the U.S. is almost ten times that of Canada, which has a larger population than Australia. So, relative to population size, the U.S. is currently receiving the least immigration.

Postwar Immigration Countries: France, United Kingdom, Germany

Germany was mainly a country of emigration until after World War II, when many Germans moved to the U.S. and South America. There were many refugees in Europe after World War II, but most of them remained in Europe, given the difficulty with entering the United States.

Signaling the end of the Cold War, the Berlin Wall came down in 1989. In the years that followed, Germany considered increased migration (which was also driven by those fleeing the ethnic wars in Yugoslavia). Germany, however, largely stabilized its immigration flows

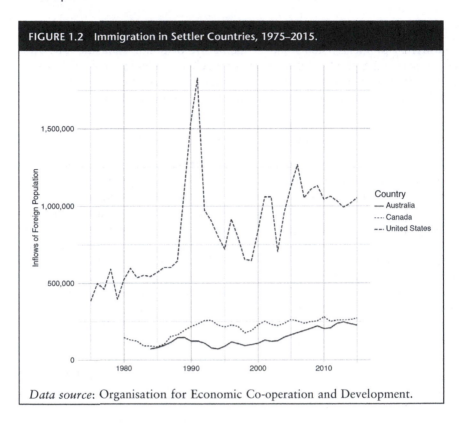

FIGURE 1.2   Immigration in Settler Countries, 1975–2015.

Data source: Organisation for Economic Co-operation and Development.

by the 2000s until the Arab Spring and civil war in Syria sent huge numbers of refugees to Germany. Immigration into France and the U.K., by contrast, started this time period at a lower level which grew more steadily over time, as shown in Figure 1.3.

Immigration in Globalizing Countries: Spain, Italy

All these countries have in common that they are democracies, they have market-drive economies, and they are open to globalization. However, with Spain and Italy, immigration takes on particular challenges in the context of "Europe without Borders." Otherwise, they have very different histories on immigration, as we will explore in more detail in Chapter 3. They also have some major variation in their political systems, as described below. As shown in Figure 1.4, migration into Spain and Italy clearly follows the economic "boom bust" cycle in that it was very strong during the late 1990s and 2000s but declined sharply with the onset of the euro crisis, which started shortly after the onset of the financial crisis in the U.S. in late 2008.

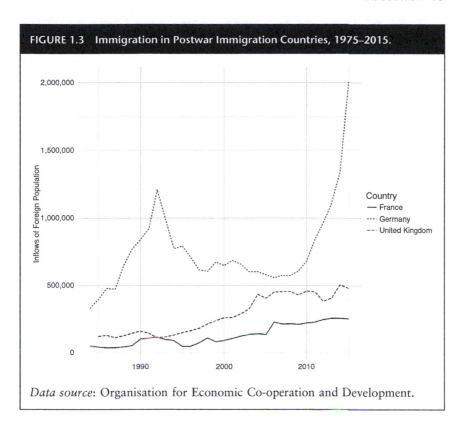

FIGURE 1.3   Immigration in Postwar Immigration Countries, 1975–2015.

Data source: Organisation for Economic Co-operation and Development.

Book Chapter Outline

This book examines the development of immigration policy and the role of political actors in that development. The results of those actions have major implications for the demographic and political structure of a country. We will begin by looking at immigration flows over time, in countries with a long history of immigration and countries that have only recently begun to experience immigration flows, for example, the United States, Canada, Australia, France, Germany, Italy, and Spain. Chapter 2 begins with an examination of migration/immigration theory and how political science has approached the development of policy. Chapters 3, 4, and 5 cover the history of immigration politics in our cases. We focus on party politics in Chapter 6, followed by the politics of labor migration in Chapter 7. In Chapter 8, we focus on the politics of citizenship and the impact on immigration policy. The politics of immigrant integration are covered in Chapter 9, and we conclude with a discussion of the dynamics of the politics of immigration and the possibilities for regional or global governance.

For blog posts, news updates, and ancillary materials, please visit www.terrigivens.com/immigration.

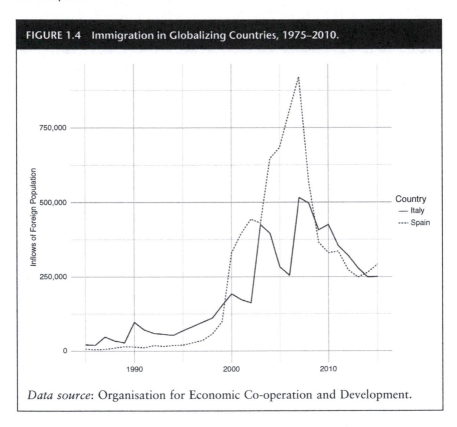

FIGURE 1.4   Immigration in Globalizing Countries, 1975–2010.

Data source: Organisation for Economic Co-operation and Development.

KEY TERMS

Globalization   International trade agreements, the greater flow of products and capital, as well as the development of multinational corporations, are all components of globalization.

Immigration Enforcement   Enforcement processes cover a wide range of activities, including border patrol, customs enforcement at ports of entry at airports and at border crossings, and activities of agents within a territory that can lead to deportation of undocumented immigrants.

Immigration Versus Migration   Individuals who are entering a country and have the potential to become settlers are considered immigrants, and people who are moving to another region or area of a country are considered migrants. Migration is a more general term for the movement of people (or birds and other animals).

Naturalization   Immigrants can become citizens through a naturalization process. These processes vary from country to country and over time, as described in Chapter 8.

Quotas or Preferences   Quotas define the number of people from a specific country that may enter a country as immigrants on an annual basis. Preferences tend to focus on types of individuals, such as family members or skilled workers, and can allow unlimited entry for certain family members, while putting caps on other types of individuals, for example, skilled technical workers.

Sovereignty   The authority and power of a state. In the context of immigration, sovereignty focuses on the ability of a state to control its borders and enforce related policies such as visas.

Visa   Visas are documents which are provided by a sovereign power to an individual, allowing them entry and to remain in the country for a specified amount of time.

NOTES

1 In general, we take *policy* to refer to laws, rules, and administrative procedures. *Politics*, by contrast, is a much broader term that involves public opinion, elections, and so on.
2 See "9/11 Timeline." History.com. http://www.history.com/topics/9-11-time line, accessed 9/21/2019.
3 However, California was also an important flashpoint for immigration in the late 1800s, when Chinese immigration became a contentious issue and led to the rise of the anti-immigrant "Know Nothing" party. White Californians were concerned that Chinese immigrants would take away jobs and resources – similar to concerns raised about Mexican migrants in the late 1900s.
4 See "9/11 forever changed the concept of immigration in the US." *Quartz* published 9/11/2015. http://qz.com/499481/911-forever-changed-the-concept-of-immigration-in-the-us/, accessed 9/21/2019.
5 See "Origins of the Federal Immigration Service." https://www.uscis.gov/his tory-and-genealogy/our-history/agency-history/origins-federal-immigration-ser vice, accessed 9/21/2019.
6 See "A brief history of the passport." *The Guardian* published 11/17/2006. https://www.theguardian.com/travel/2006/nov/17/travelnews, accessed 9/21/2019.
7 See "Kobach promised cities help. It cost them millions – and powered his political rise." *Kansas City Star* published 8/21/2018. https://www.kansascity.com/news/politics-government/article215374130.html, accessed 9/21/2019.
8 See "Federal judge refuses to shut down DACA program." *NBC News* published 8/31/2018. https://www.nbcnews.com/news/us-news/federal-judge-refuses-shut-down-daca-program-n905586, accessed 9/20/2019.

REFERENCES

*References marked with an asterisk are sources that can be used for further research and information

Ciment, James and John Radzikowski, Editors. 2014. *American Immigration* (2nd ed.). Armonk, NY: M.E. Sharpe.
*Foblets, Marie-Claire and Jean-Yves Carlier, Editors. 2020. *Law and Migration in a Changing World* (*Ius Comparatum* – Global Studies in Comparative Law). Heidelberg, Germany: Springer-Verlag.

Givens, Terri. 2005. *Voting Radical Right in Western Europe*. New York: Cambridge University Press.

Givens, Terri, Gary Freeman, and David Leal, Editors. 2008. *Immigration Policy and Security*. New York: Routledge.

Hampshire, James. 2013. *The Politics of Immigration: Contradictions of the Liberal State*. Boston: Polity Press.

Hollifield, James F. 2000. "The Politics of International Migration: How Can We 'Bring the State Back In'?" In Caroline B. Brettell and James F. Hollifield, Editors, *Migration Theory: Talking Across Disciplines* (1st ed.). New York: Routledge.

Hollifield, James F. and Tom Wong. 2014. "The Politics of International Migration: How Can We 'Bring the State Back In'?" In Caroline B. Brettell and James F. Hollifield, Editors, *Migration Theory: Talking Across Disciplines* (3rd ed.). New York: Routledge.

*Koning, Edward A. 2019. *Immigration and the Politics of Welfare Exclusion: Selective Solidarity in Western Democracies*. Toronto, Ontario, Canada: University of Toronto Press.

*Mainwaring, Cetta. 2019. *At Europe's Edge: Migration and Crisis in the Mediterranean*. New York: Oxford University Press.

Mudde, Cas. 2019. *The Far Right Today*. Boston: Polity Press.

Rosenblum, Marc and Daniel Tichenor, Editors. 2012. *The Oxford Handbook of the Politics of International Migration*. New York: Oxford University Press.

*Sitkin, Lea. 2019. *Re-thinking the Political Economy of Immigration Control: A Comparative Analysis*. New York: Routledge.

Tichenor, Daniel J. 2002. *Dividing Lines: The Politics of Immigration Control in America*. Princeton, NJ: Princeton University Press.

*Triandafyllidou, Anna, Editor. 2016. *Routledge Handbook of Immigration and Refugee Studies*. New York: Routledge.

*Weinar, Agnieszka, Saskia Bonjour, and Lyubov Zhyznomirska, Editors. 2018. *The Routledge Handbook of the Politics of Migration in Europe*. New York: Routledge.

Wong, Tom K. 2015. Rights, Deportation, and Detention in the Age of Immigration Control. Palo Alto, CA: Stanford University Press.

2

IMMIGRATION AND POLITICS

Explaining Outcomes

Introduction: How Do We Use Theories?

Political scientists use theories so that we are able to focus on deeper, recurring patterns in policy development rather than focusing on the particular groups and individuals involved in any given political conflict. In this chapter, we explain the main approaches that political scientists take to explain immigration policies and policy outcomes. Many authors have developed theories about the types of policy outcomes we have seen over time, and the way that politicians have dealt with immigration policy. Why are policies more expansive at particular times and more restrictive at other times? Factors such as economics certainly play a role in the development of immigration politics, but we point out that the politics of immigration must be understood through the lens of factors like electoral politics, the role of key interest groups, including immigrant voting blocs, and the development of coalitions for or against immigration. The role of the judiciary must be included as well, since policy is often determined by judges who must interpret the laws and the constitution of a country to determine if policies are in line with existing law and are being properly implemented.

Until the second decade of the 21st century there was a lack of focus on the politics that were impacting immigration policy. In spite of the fact that voters consistently listed immigration as a top issue, political scientists generally lumped immigration together with other issues (such as economic or labor market dynamics). Penninx, Spencer, and Van Hear (2008) have examined the state of research on migration and integration in Europe. They found that "[a]nalysis of the mismatch between policy evaluation and advice and actual political processes is lacking and it is not clear how political processes originate and develop in the field of immigration and integration as well as what is the role of different actors (governments – central, regional, local, trade unions, NGOs, individuals, etc.)" (p. 7). In the U.S., there has been a focus on immigration as a labor issue, and immigrant integration has been a focus for sociologists, but the literature on the politics of immigration is still developing.

In 2004, Zincone and Caponio came to a similar conclusion regarding the study of migration policy. They saw the study of migration policy as a "young" research area and divided it into four "generations."

> *First generation* studies were essentially concerned with the demographic composition and evolution of migration flows into and immigrant stocks within European countries. *Second generation* research has focused primarily on immigrants' economic integration and their social behaviours [sic]. The *third generation* has dealt mainly with integration policies and political participation. Lastly the *fourth generation* has tackled the problem of understanding how immigrant and immigration policies are decided upon and carried out. Even more recently, a sort of *fourth and a half* generation type of studies has emerged. This new generation is starting to carry out research on the issue of the multilevel governance of immigrants and immigration (Zincone and Caponio 2004, p. 2).

As the study of immigration policy has progressed in the last 15 years or so, these categories may not be as relevant, but the study of immigration politics is still in development. Hollifield and Wong (2014) noted that "[o]nly recently have political scientists begun to formulate hypotheses about the political dimension of international migration and specifically the role of the state" (p. 234). They go on to argue that the state does matter and formulate a politics of migration which they feel allows political scientists to empirically test the political determinants of migration politics and policies (Hollifield and Wong 2014).

In the second decade of the 21st century, we can see that the study of immigration politics has matured, and a more complex set of approaches has developed. Scholars are examining a wider set of concerns that include security issues, a specific focus on Islamophobia in both Europe and the U.S., and the impact on electoral politics. As anti-immigrant parties have become fixtures in party systems, more recent studies have focused on the normalization of the rhetoric and policy approaches that have impacted government approaches to immigration policy. It is also clear that subnational government structures, for example, state and local governments in the U.S., are having an important impact on policy developments.

We begin with a brief explanation of the legislative and judicial processes that affect policy outcomes, and how electoral politics impact legislators and their approach to immigration policy. We then examine two approaches that have been developed to explain the politics of immigration: the historical institutional approach and the migration management approach, which focuses on the limited ability of states to control immigration.

How Is Policy Made?

Since the U.S. Supreme Court ruled on plenary powers, immigration policy has been generally made at the federal level. This is also true of most other federal systems like Germany, although some aspects of policy can be handled at the state level. Policies are generally proposed by the executive and then legislation is developed and passed by the legislature. The political aspects of policymaking tend to come into play when policy impacts different groups, from business interests to native workers and immigrants themselves. Each of these groups will try to impact policy outcomes so that they work in their favor, but it is not always clear whether business interests are the same or that workers will favor a particular policy approach, as we will see when we examine the histories of policymaking.

Political Systems

When looking at the impact of different political systems, it is important to understand that differences in government type impact the way that politicians approach issues. Federal systems tend to devolve certain powers to states and/or regions. However, even in federal systems, immigration tends to be dealt with by the central government, but states may have a voice in the legislature or parliament. Centralized systems tend to have unicameral, or one chamber legislatures, while federal systems usually have two chambers. In the U.S., we have the House of Representatives and the Senate, while Germany has its Bundestag and Bundesrat. Countries like the U.K. and France are more centralized, and while they have more than one chamber, the second chamber has limited powers. In the following sections, we describe examples of the two types of systems and their impact on immigration policy.

Federal Versus Centralized Systems

One of the issues that impacts the formation of immigration policy in the U.S. is the fact that we are a federal system. In the early years of the country, immigration policy was managed at the state level, but by the end of the 1800s, the Supreme Court ruled that immigration policy was in the domain of the federal government, and this became part of the plenary powers doctrine. This issue has impacted many state-level attempts at passing laws on immigration, with the Supreme Court regularly calling on the plenary powers ruling to strike down laws related to immigration at the state level.

Another country that has a federal system is Germany. Most immigration policy is also handled at the federal level, but other areas of policy, like citizenship, are administered at the state level. Most other countries have centralized systems and policymaking is handled by the central government.

France and the U.K. are examples of more centralized systems. In France, the president tends to dominate policy, with the legislature (i.e., the Assembly) generally supporting policies pursued by the government. There are situations, called *cohabitation*, where the president must work with an assembly with a majority from a different party, but then the prime minister tends to take the lead on domestic policy, like immigration. In the United Kingdom, the prime minister leads a majority in the parliament and generally has little difficulty passing legislation, although there are divisions within the main parties that lead to conflicts over policy, as we describe in Chapter 5.

Another important factor in understanding the politics of immigration is the role of veto points. Veto points vary in different political systems. As Tichenor (2002) noted, "decisive triumphs and non-incremental immigration reforms have been hard to achieve due to the abundance of 'veto points' in American government, thus often biasing the process in favor of existing policy patterns" (p. 8). Federal systems like the U.S. and Germany tend to have more veto points than centralized systems like the U.K. and France. One example that impacts both types of systems is the courts. Often the judiciary will act as a veto point when legislation or policy goes against the constitution. Other veto points include the legislature, the executive (including regulators), and in rare cases, the people in popular referenda.

Citizenship

What does it mean to be a citizen? The question of citizenship has been pondered since at least the writings of Aristotle, who wondered if it was possible to be both a good citizen and a good person, and the answers have been varied and complex. Thus, it is beyond the purpose of this chapter to fully discuss the nuances of citizenship in this introduction. Nonetheless, we can generally regard citizenship as being recognized as a member of a state and not recognized as a member of another state. As Hansen and Weil (2001) asserted, citizenship gives formal "institutional expression to the state's prerogative of inclusion and exclusion" and it is thus an institutional device that defines membership in a political community, with all the attended rights and responsibilities in that community (p. 1).

Much of the early comparative literature on citizenship has focused on various national models of citizenship, or ideal types of approaches to the question of citizenship. Within this macrohistorical perspective, different states developed different national models of incorporating foreigners into their polities. Although a number of different scholars have developed theoretical frameworks for understanding these models (Brubaker 1992; Castles, de Haas, and Miller 2014; Favell 1998; Koopmans et al. 2005; Schain 2019), four different approaches to incorporation and citizenship developed over time: the imperial, republican, multicultural, and ethnic models.

The early imperial model, used by those states with vast multinational empires like Great Britain or Austria, permitted the incorporation of foreigners on the basis of their subjecthood. Citizenship designated a certain status and membership for those living within the empire itself but often meant little in terms of ethnonational identity, cultural assimilation, civic rights or loyalty.

The republican model, traditionally associated with France, is both assimilationist and universalistic in its approach to citizenship. Political identity and belonging within the state are based not on subjecthood within a territorial empire but adherence to the laws, values, and national culture of the republic. Those willing to adopt and assimilate into the state and the national culture that it represents are considered citizens, while those that do not are excluded. Thus, this model is not based on race or ethnicity. In France the republican model is also coupled with a very strong form of separation of church and state (i.e., *laïcité*).

The third model, the multicultural model, is similar to the republican model in its emphasis on adherence to the laws and civic values of the state but differs on the necessity of shared national culture. As the name suggests, the multicultural model accepts and fosters ethnic and cultural difference rather than requiring integration or assimilation. This model has been traditionally associated with the settler countries like the United States, Canada, and Australia, as well as with European countries such as the Netherlands and Sweden.

In contrast to these three models, the fourth and final model, the ethnic model, is much more restrictive and limiting in its conception of political community. The ethnic model defines political belonging on the basis of ethnonational characteristics. This may entail shared language, religious beliefs, culture, or racial characteristics. This nearly always implies citizenship by means of common descent, and non-citizenship for those individuals who do not share in the ethnic or cultural heritage of the nation so defined. The ethnic model has been historically associated with Germany but would also apply to countries like Italy or Greece.

It is important to bear in mind that these models are archetypes, and that in any given country it is usually not hard to find proponents of another model or elements of a different system. For example, in the United States the push to make English an official language might be seen as a preference for a more assimilationist, republican model of citizenship. When others argue that America is a Christian nation, they advocate an ethnic model. And though the United States never had the type of empire that the United Kingdom did, Puerto Rico's status as an American territory is arguably more typical of the imperial model. Thus, though these models may be primarily associated with particular places, we can use them as theories to analyze politics at a more nuanced level as well.

The Asylum System

Asylum and refugee seekers are another important stream of immigration. Owing to the distinct history of this type of immigration, this stream follows a different logic which is more heavily influenced by international laws, organizations, and norms. However, actual enforcement and implementation of safeguards still rests primarily with individual nation-states. After briefly introducing that history in this chapter, we discuss those politics throughout the remainder of the text.

Genocide (the intentional destruction of a people) was recognized for the first time as a legal concept in the aftermath of World War II alongside the creation of the United Nations. The International Refugee Organization (IRO) was formed in 1946 to manage the "repatriation of the millions of Europeans displaced by World War II," that is, the return of refugees to their countries of origin (Mavroudi and Nagel 2016, p. 123). The activities of the IRO led to the creation of the United Nations High Commission for Refugees (UNHCR).[1] The 1951 United Nations Convention Relating to the Status of Refugees defines the term refugee, which "focused exclusively on persons who were unable or unwilling to avail themselves of the protection of their home countries because of a 'well-founded fear of persecution based on their race, religion, nationality, political opinion or membership in a particular social group'" (Martin 2012, p. 57). The UNHCR stated that the "core principle is non-refoulement, which asserts that a refugee should not be returned to a country where they face serious threats to their life or freedom. This is now considered a rule of customary international law."[2]

World War II ended with the U.S. as a global superpower and Europe trying to recover from devastation. The domestic politics of immigration would run headlong into the politics of international relations, as Cold War rivalries led the U.S. to become a haven for asylum seekers and refugees from communist countries. Large numbers of Jewish refugees resettled in New York after World War II. After the Vietnam War, many refugees migrated to Los Angeles and Houston. To take a more recent example, many fleeing Somalia settled in the Twin Cities and Detroit.

Globally, the total number of refugees grew exponentially throughout the Cold War. According to the UNHCR, there were only 1.7 million refugees in 1960. By the end of the Vietnam War, that figure had doubled. By the time the Berlin Wall fell in 1989, which heralded the end of the Cold War, there were almost 15 million refugees. That figure climbed as the Soviet Union disintegrated but began to fall by the mid-1990s, leading West Germany to tighten its asylum policy. For the first decade of the 21st century, there were about 10 million refugees. That figure began to climb starting in 2012 and reached an all-time high in 2018 at 20.3 million.[3] However, it is worth noting that only 3.5 million are actively seeking asylum.

Although the main source of refugees in the current era is the "Global South" forced movement of people across borders was a regular feature in the "Global North." "European history, in particular, has been punctuated by massive forced migrations" (Mavroudi and Nagel 2016, p. 120) due to the persecution of religious groups and major wars. In fact the motivation for the development of a global approach to the management of refugees came from, "[t]he massive destruction and dislocation of the first half of the 20th century provided the impetus for the creation of the United Nations as an international organization designed to foster stability and cooperation in the interstate system" (Mavroudi and Nagel 2016, p. 123).

The terror attacks by Islamic extremists on 9/11 in the United States and in several western European countries in the following years complicates refugee policy both in terms of administrative challenges to verify the authenticity of asylum claims and in terms of public support. Europe and the European Union has played an important role in dealing with refugee crises in the Middle East, for example, after the Arab Spring, and during conflicts and natural disasters in Africa. Large numbers of people fled Syria following the onset of civil war in March 2011. The conflict is brutal as it is complex – those loyal to the dictator Assad, Islamic extremists including (but not limited to) Isis, Kurds, Iran, Russia, France, and the United States have all been involved in the conflict to some extent. Neighboring countries, notably Turkey and Jordan, have accepted large numbers of refugees. In particular, Turkey has struggled to meet the humanitarian challenge while maintaining stability due to its own security challenges from terrorists and ongoing tensions with the Kurds, an ethnic minority that is present in Iraq, Syria, and Turkey. Though, like Turkey, the Kurds have been a steadfast ally of the United States in the region, the Turks and the Kurds do not get along due to a century of Turkish nationalist policies which do not tolerate minority languages and (at times violent) Kurdish separatism.

Against this inhospitable backdrop, many Syrian refugees did not stop in Turkey but instead travelled onwards to Europe, often by unsafe or illegal means. Though in principle refugees in Europe are meant to request asylum status in the first country they arrive at, most countries in southern and eastern Europe (like Greece) are struggling economically in the aftermath of the euro crisis.[4] Many refugees headed north to Germany and Sweden, in some cases aided by local law enforcement.

By 2014, the influx had reached the level of a political crisis. Angela Merkel, the chancellor of Germany who is widely considered to be the most important politician on the European continent, was forced to walk a tightrope. On the one hand, Merkel leads the Christian Democrats, which has long favored European integration and open borders. On the other hand, like most conservative voters in Europe, many German conservatives are skeptical of immigration and particularly adverse to further Muslim influxes, as pressure mounted to suspend the provision of the Schengen agreement that allows people to travel between most European countries without being subjected to border controls.

The United States under President Trump challenged a number of international norms related to the asylum process in an attempt to control immigration from Central America. Trump's "zero tolerance" at the Mexican border, which controversially involved family separation, reflected in part a legal argument about the asylum process. Critics noted that it is permissible to enter the United States and claim asylum. Attorney General Jeff Sessions, however, argued that the definition of refugee should be interpreted more narrowly so as not to include those fleeing domestic or gang violence, which would exclude most of those coming from Central America.[5]

Whereas many countries struggle to find solutions that are humane and fair in regard to those seeking asylum, few industrialized countries' policies in this area have come under as much criticism as Australia. Its policies of mandatory offshore detention have come under attack from international organizations, domestic groups, and the courts.

The current asylum policy regime can trace its roots back to the mid-1990s, where there was an increase in the numbers of refugees seeking asylum in Australia. Coming by boat from Southeast Asia and the Middle East, the issue of what to do with these refugee seekers burst onto the agenda when the Norwegian freighter MV Tampa rescued 400 from a sinking boat in the Indian Ocean. The Australian military intercepted the freighter and government refused to allow the ship to offload the rescued migrants. After this incident, legislation was passed which created offshore detention and processing facilities in Papua New Guinea and Nauru.

The Australian government also passed new legislation relating to asylum seekers, commonly known as the "Pacific Solution." This solution allowed for the "excision" of Australia's island from its migration zone, which had the practical effect of denying asylum seekers that landed in these areas the right to apply for asylum (known as the "Tampa Affair"). The Pacific Solution ended in 2007, but the Rudd Labor government kept key elements of the plan, including the excision area, mandatory detention, and offshore processing. In 2011, the Prime Minster attempted to negotiate a settlement that would allow Australia to send refugees to Malaysia for processing; however, the High Court of Australia held that this contravened the country's obligations under the 1951 UN Refugee Convention. In 2013, Operation Sovereign Borders placed the military in control of asylum operations; this resulted in sending migrants back to Indonesia and not permitting them to land, regardless of the state of their vessels.

As for the detention camps, the Papua New Guinea Supreme Court ruled the detention center located in Manus Island was unconstitutional in April 2016. Later that year, the Australian government announced that the Manus Island center would indeed be closing; however, the Nauru center would remain open.

This decision has not lessened criticism of the camps or the process governing asylum seekers. Human rights groups have continuously criticized the country for violating asylum seekers' human rights and argued that the camps were unsafe and overcrowded. In 2016, the day before the Australian government announced the closure of the Manus Island camp, 103 current and former camp staff signed a letter detailing abuse in the camps, especially sexual assault and child abuse.[6] It remains unclear what will happen to those that remain at the Manus Island center.

Theories on the Politics of Migration

Within political science, the main approaches to the study of immigration politics break down into two general approaches. The first approach, historical institutionalism, exemplified by Daniel Tichenor, Ari Zolberg, and Martin Schain, uses a political development approach to explain immigration policy over time, focusing on the states' ability to control immigration through policy, and the positions that different actors take at different points in time. This approach focuses on explaining policy change and why policy may have been expansive at one particular time period and more restrictive at other time periods.

The second approach can be called migration management or as Hollifield calls it, the liberal state thesis (Cornelius et al. 2004; Freeman 1998; Hollifield 2014). This approach focuses on immigration policies that are designed to control flows and labor migration but also takes into account domestic politics and international factors, and their impact not just on the policies pursued by governments, but the actual outcomes in terms of immigration flows. Some authors have noted that the outcomes may not jibe with the expectations or preferences of voters.

Although we will focus on our two main theoretical approaches through most of this chapter, it is also important to examine some of the economic issues related to immigration. As noted in the introduction, some argue that immigration hurts natives by driving down wages. Others have argued that immigration is a boon to the economy. The reality, as usual, is complicated. In September 2016, a panel formed by the National Academies published a report on "The Economic and Fiscal Consequences of Immigration" (National Academies 2017). The report was written by a group of high-profile academics in economics, sociology, demography, public policy, and international studies. The report focused on the U.S. but also had implications for the broader impact of immigration flows. They note that,

> Economic theory provides insights into the mechanisms whereby immigration may impact wages and employment in a receiving country. By increasing the supply of labor, an episode of immigration is predicted to reduce the wages of workers already in the labor market who are most similar to the new arrivals; the incomes of others may increase, either because immigrants' skills complement their own or because the returns on capital increase as a result of changes to the labor force. The mix of skills possessed by arriving immigrants – whether manual laborers, professionals, entrepreneurs, or refugees – will influence the magnitude and even the direction of wage and employment impacts.
>
> (National Academies 2017, p. 4)

The main conclusions of the report were as follows:

- Viewed over a lengthy time horizon (75 years in our estimates), the fiscal impacts of immigrants are generally positive at the federal level and negative at the state and local levels. State and local governments bear the burden of providing education benefits to young immigrants and to the children of immigrants, but their methods of taxation recoup relatively little of the later contributions from the resulting educated taxpayers. Federal benefits, in contrast, are largely provided to the elderly, so the relative youthfulness of arriving immigrants means that they tend to be beneficial to federal finances in the short term. In addition, federal taxes are more strongly progressive, drawing more contributions from the most highly educated. The panel's historical analysis indicates that inequality between levels of government in the fiscal gains or losses associated with immigration appears to have widened since 1994. The fact that states bear much of the fiscal burden of immigration may incentivize state level policies to exclude immigrants and raises questions of equity between the federal government and states.

- Today's immigrants have more education than earlier immigrants and, as a result, are more positive contributors to government finances. If today's immigrants had the same lower educational distribution as immigrants two decades ago, their fiscal impact, expressed as taxes paid minus expenditures on benefits received, would be much less positive or much more negative (depending on the scenario). Whether this education trend will continue remains uncertain, but the historical record suggests that the total net fiscal impact of immigrants across all levels of government has become more positive over time.

- An immigrant and a native-born person with similar characteristics will likely have about the same fiscal impact. Persons with higher levels of education contribute more positively to government finances regardless of their generational status. Furthermore, within age and education categories, immigrants generally have a more salutary effect on budgets because they are disqualified from some benefit programs and because their children tend to have higher levels of education, earnings, and tax paying than the children of similar third-plus generation adults (National Academies 2017, pp. 11–12).

Margaret Peter's (2017) book, *Trading Barriers: Immigration and the Remaking of Globalization*, examines the relationship between international trade and immigration policy. In an in-depth exploration of lower trade barriers and the impact on the need for low-skilled workers, she finds that many businesses in wealthy countries have closed or moved overseas, reducing the need for low-skilled immigrant workers. This has led to a decline in support for immigration by businesses, who had traditionally supported more open immigration policies. As she noted in her conclusion, "the book helps explain why greater migration is not on the development agenda by focusing on the shrinking business-based pro-immigration coalition" (Peters 2017, 240).

There are clear limitations to economic models, Hollifield and Wong noted that "[a]s Freeman puts it, the drawback of these economic models of politics is their extreme parsimony. They leave us with generalizations about labor, landowners and capitalists; useful abstractions, surely, but probably too crude for the satisfactory analysis of immigration politics in particular countries, especially highly developed ones" (Hollifield and Wong 2014, p. 239).

Hollifield and Wong went on to note that "These economic and sociological factors were the necessary conditions for continued migration; but the sufficient conditions were political, legal, and ideational" (Hollifield and Wong 2014, p. 242). This leads us to a larger understanding of the factors that lead to trends in immigration and Hollifield's formulation which he calls the "liberal state thesis," which is described in more detail below.

Historical Institutionalism and Path Dependency

Historical institutionalism is often described as an approach, rather than a theory. Political scientists use this approach to understand how institutions, especially government structures, have impacted policy development over time. Path dependency considers the fact that outcomes are dependent upon the actions that were taken previously. Policymaking is often reactive and policymakers may go in a particular policy direction because of actions that were taken previously, but also within the context of the institutional structures within which they are working. Context matters.

One of the most comprehensive studies of immigration politics in the U.S. is Daniel Tichenor's *Dividing Lines*. Tichenor traces the politics of immigration from the founding of the nation through the beginning of the second millennium. He argues that "the organizational biases of governing institutions can favor the capacities and policy designs of specific political actors, while disadvantaging others" (Tichenor 2002, p. 29). He focuses on four interlocking processes:

1. Dynamism of national governing structures
2. Changing coalitions of organized interests
3. Professional expertise
4. International pressures

The role of national governing structures, or institutions, is a key component to understanding the development of immigration policy. Legislative processes tend to be the focal point of policy development, however, there are other institutions that play just as critical a role: "the organizational biases of governing structures can favor the capacities and policy designs of specific political actors while disadvantaging others" (Tichenor 2002, p. 29).

In general, each institution has its opportunity points or institutional openings and veto points. Some actors have the ability to keep policy from moving forward, but this may also change over time. As Tichenor (2002) noted, "The internal development of legislative, executive, and judicial structures each has presented immigration activists with distinctive institutional opportunities and constraints as they pursue their goals" (p. 31).

Structural veto points such as the Supreme Courts don't change over time, because they have constitutional authority. However, shifts in power balances can lead to different party leaders, such as particular committee chairs, having power at one point in time, but not at another. There can also be the development of new political institutions, new committees that focus on a specific topic, that can have a dramatic impact on policy development, and these committees are influenced by professional expertise on the various sides of an issue. Beyond the role of legislators, the judiciary is a key player in determining policy outcomes, and the constitutionality of policy.

Electoral politics are another key factor in Tichenor's typology, impacting both the dynamism of national governing structures and the changing coalitions of organized interests. Parties and individual candidates' positions on policy are dependent upon a variety of factors, but their main goal is to be elected and to remain in power. Ideology plays a role in this as they pursue the interests of their constituencies and that of the national party. Interest groups attempt to influence politicians and form coalitions in order to maximize their influence. Over time this has led to immigrants developing their voting power, the rise of anti-immigrant groups, and the growth of think-tanks devoted to research to support various sides of the issue.

Tom Wong brings the politics of immigration into the 21st century with his analysis of partisanship and the impact of the demographics on policymakers and electoral politics. Drawing on Tichenor, Wong (2015) pointed out that "placing too much emphasis on the causal role of governing structures, which are undoubtedly important in explaining major policy shifts, can obscure the fact that immigration policy changes both incrementally as well as in waves..." (p. 6). Wong also pointed out that a fundamental shift occurred in 2006 with the mobilization of undocumented youth as well as the political mobilization of immigrant communities in the wake of the introduction of H.R. 4437, the Border Protection, Antiterrorism and Illegal Immigration Control Act of 2005 which "sought to criminalize unlawful *presence* in the United States which is currently a civil offense" (Wong 2015, p. 7). Millions of immigrants protested this bill and voter registration in immigrant communities increased. Wong argued that this mobilization and the shift in demographics (a significant increase in naturalized citizens) has led to less support for restrictive immigration measures, but an increase in partisanship has meant that policy proposals are more likely to end up in stalemate at the federal level and an increase in policymaking at the state and local level.

Controlling Immigration and Migration Management

The ability to control a country's borders is at the heart of sovereignty. The nation-state is defined by its borders and the people who live within those borders. This makes immigration a potentially serious challenge to a country, particularly in homogenous countries or if immigrants are perceived not to fit the national mold. As noted by Castles, de Haas, and Miller (2014), "In this sense international migration is intrinsically political and is almost inevitably an imagined or real challenge to the state sovereignty" (p. 313). Although the main focus of the study of immigration is often around the reasons that people may migrate to another country, the policy and politics of the receiving states have received less attention.

Borders are an important component of immigration control. In *The Border*, Martin Schain (2019) argued that borders have become increasingly important, politicized, and divisive in both Europe and the United States. As the focus of immigration has shifted to issues related to demographics and growing minority communities, borders have become the focus for immigration control, but there are historical precedents for the current approach to immigration control, with the focus on specific groups, such as Muslims.

Immigration control has been an issue since the first laws controlling Chinese immigration were passed in the late 1800s. Political scientists have focused on the ability of states to control immigration flows over time as well as the relationship between public opinion and government policy. Policy outcomes are also often in conflict with the stated aims of policy. This issue was highlighted in particular by authors like James Hollifield, who developed the "liberal state hypothesis." Hollifield's research found that most developed countries, although espousing strict immigration control policies, allowed relatively high numbers of immigrants to enter the country by various means. He and his co-author Tom Wong found that, "[a]lmost by definition, the more liberal and democratic a society is, the greater the likelihood that migration control will be an issue; and that there will be some level of 'unwanted migration' (Hollifield and Wong 2014, p. 236). Thus, in the formulation of Hollifield's work, international migration can be seen as a function of (1) economic forces (demand-pull and supply-push), (2) networks, and (3) rights (Hollifield and Wong 2014, p. 242).

Other authors have focused on the issue of how states, particularly newer states of immigration, have developed their immigration policies, and the ways they try to manage labor migration and the rights that are accorded migrants by the judiciary. They argued that "[m]igration management emphasizes organization and optimization over restriction, and it revolves around 'best practices' that pursue several goals simultaneously: the circulation of flexible labor; respect for migrant's human rights; and the protection of state sovereignty" (Mavroudi and Nagel 2016, pp. 159–160).

As a liberal democracy, the United States has always allowed immigration, but restrictions on the types of immigrants allowed to enter the country came into play in the mid to late 1800s when the majority of immigration shifted from Northern to Southern Europe. Concerns also began to arise about Chinese immigrants, particularly in California, during the time. Some of the first immigration restrictions were placed on Chinese immigrants, and eventually country-based National

Origins Quotas became the law of the land in the late 1920s. Policy changed dramatically in the 1960s with the shift from quotas to preferences, but the focus on immigration control remained, with new legislation in the 1980s designed to slow legal immigration and stop illegal immigration. Britain began to restrict immigration in the 1960s when immigrants began to flow in from former colonies like Jamaica, India, and Pakistan. Germany had inflows of guest workers during the 1950s and 1960s, but ostensibly had a policy of no immigration beginning in the early 1970s. Despite these policies, all these countries have had a significant flow of immigrants since the 1970s.

One of the most cited theories in the study of immigration politics has been Gary Freeman's work on client politics and the difficulty of controlling immigration in the context of liberal democracies. Freeman explained client politics as follows:

> Freeman (1995) argued that the typical mode of immigration politics in the liberal democracies is client politics in which policymakers interact intensively and typically out of public view with groups having direct interests in immigration. Client politics develops, according to the model, because the benefits of immigration tend to be concentrated while its costs are diffuse. This gives those who expect to gain from migration stronger incentives to organize than those who anticipate bearing its costs. Client politics should be associated with expansive policies. The limits of Wilson's simple typology become apparent as it is applied to particular cases. In a recent paper Freeman employed the model in the context of post-1994 immigration policy in the United States. Although the client mode is dominant, he finds new elements which he calls "populist," a category not part of Wilson's framework (Freeman 1998). Populism shares characteristics with Wilson's entrepreneurial mode, including high levels of conflict and a penchant for restrictionism, and with interest group politics to the extent that opponents of immigration gain additional voice. It typically entails the activities of entrepreneurial politicians of the sort represented by Jean-Marie Le Pen in France, Joerg Haider in Austria, Preston Manning in Canada, Pauline Hanson in Australia, and Patrick Buchanan in the United States who engage in the mobilization of resentment among groups whose members believe they are adversely affected by immigration. Successful entrepreneurs may succeed in institutionalizing competition between pro and anti-immigration groups, leading to the emergence of a more stable interest group mode.
>
> (Freeman 2005, pp. 3–4)

In both the U.S. and Europe, immigrants were recruited after World War II, whether through the Bracero program in the U.S. or guest worker programs in Germany and France. Particularly in the 1990s, inflows were much higher in the U.S., Britain, and Germany than policymakers desired. Hollifield explains that this is because liberal democracies are required to accept refugees and asylum seekers, and that illegal immigration is difficult to control.

Joppke weighed in on this issue as well, in his article "Why Liberal States Accept Unwanted Immigration," arguing that "accepting unwanted immigration is inherent in the liberalness of liberal states" (as cited in Messina and Lahav 2006, 547). He makes this argument as a response to a series of articles that focused on the external factors that influence states and expansionist immigration policy. He noted that it is "self-limited sovereignty" which leads countries to maintain more open immigration regimes, partly due to respect for human rights and the rule of law, rather than external factors, which he finds play a limited role. Joppke agreed with Freeman's model of client politics with two modifications that play more of a role in the European cases, first that "the legal process [is] a second source of expansiveness toward immigrants in liberal states" which was particularly true in countries like France and Germany when courts affirmed family reunification rights for immigrants. The second is "that there are important variations in the processing of unwanted immigration...within West European states" noting that Germany's guest-worker regime had a different logic for not disposing of them after ending their importation, as compared to Britain where immigration was "tolerated for the sake of a secondary goal – the maintenance of empire" (Joppke as cited in Messina and Lahav 2006, p. 530).

Others, such as Cornelius, Martin, and Hollifield (2004), argued that continued and perhaps increasing labor migration is desired and that policymakers may pass legislation to control immigration but won't fund or implement policy once it is in place. This can be related to particular interests that want to maintain the status quo, for example, of having access to low-skilled, undocumented immigrants. Business interests may influence regulations or enforcement in a way that keeps policies focused on immigrant workers, rather than the employers who hire them.

Illegal immigration has become a much more salient issue for the general public than in the past, leading to the dominance of a more populist approach to immigration policy in recent years. This shift has led to a more restrictive approach to the issue at both the state and federal level. Even President Obama placed an emphasis on securing the border and increasing deportations early in his term.

This shift in focus by the general public has meant that issues like comprehensive immigration reform faces an uphill battle. One thing that counteracts this push is the role of pro-immigrant interest groups and the Hispanic voting bloc. Candidates from both parties have had to consider the preferences of Hispanic voters, particularly in states where these populations have grown, such as Colorado, Ohio, and other states where the Mexican diaspora has spread in the last decade. In a liberal democracy, politicians must remain aware of their constituencies and the latest census showing a strong growth in the Hispanic population in many states. In June 2012, Philip Wolgin of the Center for American Progress noted,

> [i]n some key battleground states, the number of eligible but unregistered Latino voters runs into the hundreds of thousands or even millions. On top of these millions of potential voters, the Department of Homeland Security estimates that there are 8.1 million legal permanent residents, or green card holders, that are eligible to become citizens and vote in the fall election.[7]

These numbers have only increased, with Pew Research Center indicating that "[s]ince 2012, the number of Hispanic eligible voters has increased by 4 million, accounting for 37 per cent of the growth in all eligible voters during that span. The Hispanic share of eligible voters in several key battleground states has also gone up."[8] However, these increasing numbers were not enough to tip the election in favor of a more pro-immigration congress, nor president in the 2016 election.

Conclusion

Immigration has been one of the most important factors impacting the development and demographics not only of the U.S. but also of many countries around the world. In the coming chapters, we will examine the history and politics of immigration through the lens of the theories and approaches we have described in this chapter. The politics of immigration are complex, particularly from a comparative perspective. We begin by examining the history of the politics of immigration in the U.S. in Chapter 3 and then go on to the comparative cases in Chapters 4 and 5.

KEY TERMS

Asylum   The concept of asylum is often connected to refugees from war or conflict, but in the context of this book, we tend to refer to these people as refugees. We use the term *asylum seeker* for people who ask to remain in a country other than their own because they have a well-founded fear of persecution in their home country.

Federal Systems Versus Centralized Systems   Federal systems like the United States and Germany have state and regional level governments that share sovereignty with the central government. They tend to have bicameral legislatures (two chambers) and state level legislatures. Centralized systems like France and Britain have a strong central government, and second chambers tend to have more limited powers than in federal systems.

Historical Institutionalism   A theoretical approach that examines political development over time to explain immigration policy, focusing on each state's ability to control immigration through policy, and the positions that different actors take at different points in time.

Migration Management or the Liberal State Thesis   This approach focuses on immigration policies that are designed to control flows and labor migration, but also takes into account domestic politics as well as international factors, and their impact not just on the policies pursued by governments, but the actual outcomes in terms of immigration flows.

Plenary Powers   In the United States, the "plenary power doctrine" holds that the political branches – the legislative and the executive – have sole power to regulate all aspects of immigration as a basic attribute of sovereignty and that the states have no role in this policy area.

Political Development   Political development in political science tends to be a historical approach to understanding the capacity of a political system, and the changing roles of governmental organizations. Other factors can be taken into account, such as economic development, social issues, modernization, etc.

Veto Points   Veto points or veto players are important institutions or actors in a political system, like the judiciary or legislative committee chairs, that can stop the passage of legislation.

NOTES

1 The UNHCR remains the most important international body for refugee policy and is also a vital source of data on several categories of displaced persons, including refugees.
2 See "The 1951 Refugee Convention," UNHCR, http://www.unhcr.org/en-us/1951-refugee-convention.html, accessed 1/6/2020.
3 The last year for which data are available is 2018 (at the time of writing) at http://popstats.unhcr.org/en/overview, accessed 7/14/2019.
4 Also known as the "euro sovereign debt crisis," the euro crisis was triggered by the financial crisis which hit the United States in late 2008; unstable markets revealed unmanageable levels of government debt and, in some cases, financial fraud. These pressures almost destroyed the euro, which is the multinational currency that most EU countries use.
5 See "Sessions Says Domestic and Gang Violence Are Not Grounds for Asylum." https://www.nytimes.com/2018/06/11/us/politics/sessions-domestic-violence-asylum.html, *The New York Times*, published 6/11/2018, accessed 7/01/2018.
6 See "Australia to Close Manus Island Detention Center" https://www.cnn.com/2016/08/17/asia/nauru-former-workers-statement-australia/index.html, *CNN*, published 8/17/2016, accessed 10/05/2016.
7 See "Interactive Map: The Untapped Electoral Power of Latinos and Citizens-in-Waiting," http://www.americanprogress.org/issues/2012/06/latino_voters_map.html, accessed 10/12/2019.
8 See "Key Facts About the Latino Vote in 2016," http://www.pewresearch.org/fact-tank/2016/10/14/key-facts-about-the-latino-vote-in-2016/, accessed 1/30/2018.

REFERENCES

Castles, Stephen, Hein de Haas and Mark J. Miller. 2014. *The Age of Migration: International Population Movements in the Modern World* (5th ed.). New York: Guilford Press.

Cornelius, Wayne, Philip L. Martin, and James F. Hollifield. 2004. *Controlling Immigration: A Global Perspective* (2nd ed.). Palo Alto, CA: Stanford University Press.

Freeman, Gary P. 1998. "The Decline of Sovereignty? Politics and Immigration Restriction in Liberal States." In Christian Joppke, Editor, *Challenges to the Nation-State*. New York: Oxford University Press.

Freeman, Gary P. 2005. "Political Science and Comparative Immigration Politics." In Michael Bommes and Eva Morawska, Editors, *International Migration Research: Constructions, Omissions and the Promises of Interdisciplinarity*. New York: Routledge/.

Hansen, Randall and Patrick Weil. 2001. *Towards a European Nationality: Citizenship, Immigration and Nationality Law in the EU*. London: Palgrave Macmillan.

Hollifield, James F. and Tom K. Wong. 2014. "The Politics of International Migration: How Can We 'Bring the State Back In'?" In Caroline B. Brettell and James F. Hollifield, Editors, *Migration Theory: Talking Across Disciplines* (3rd ed.). New York: Routledge.

Koopmans, Ruud, Paul Statham, Mario Giugni, and Florence Passy. 2005. Contested Citizenship: Immigration and Cultural Diversity in Europe. Minneapolis: University of Minnesota Press.

Martin, Susan. 2012. "War, Natural Disasters, and Forced Migration." In Marc Rosenblum and Daniel Tichenor, Editors, *The Oxford Handbook of the Politics of International Migration*. New York: Oxford University Press.

Mavroudi, Elizabeth and Caroline Nagel. 2016. *Global Migration: Patterns, Processes and Politics*. New York: Routledge.

Messina, Anthony M. and Gallya Lahav, Editors. 2006. *The Migration Reader: Exploring Politics and Policies*. Boulder, CO: Lynne Rienner.

National Academies of Sciences, Engineering, and Medicine. 2017. *The Economic and Fiscal Consequences of Immigration*. Washington, DC: The National Academies Press.

Penninx, Rinus, Dimitrina Spencer, and Nicholas Van Hear. 2008. *Migration and Integration in Europe: The State of Research. Commissioned by the ESRC.* Available at https://pdfs.semanticscholar.org/beec/e4dd6619962f9eb7e623 b450ea194aad7dba.pdf, accessed 10/12/2019.

Peters, Maggie. 2017. Trading Barriers: Immigration and the Remaking of Globalization. Princeton; Oxford: Princeton University Press.

Schain, Martin. 2019. *The Border: Policy and Politics in Europe and the United States*. New York: Oxford University Press.

Tichenor, Daniel J. 2002. *Dividing Lines: The Politics of Immigration Control in America*. Princeton, NJ: Princeton University Press.

Wong, Tom K. 2015. *Rights, Deportation, and Detention in the Age of Immigration Control*. Palo Alto, CA: Stanford University Press.

Zincone, Giovanna and Tiziana Caponio. 2004. "The Multilevel Governance of Migration," *State of the Art Report*, Cluster C9, https://pdfs.semanticscholar. org/bedd/9056daa8e48a6940c945e35429d4c56b59d0.pdf, accessed 10/12/2019.

3

IMMIGRATION POLITICS

U.S.

Introduction: Policy Development in Settler Countries

The history of immigration to what would become the United States began long before it became an independent country. It is important to remember that immigrants were coming to a land that already had a longstanding indigenous population. The slave trade and forced migration also factored into the populations that would inhabit this new country. Overall, the growth of the country and the varied flows into it would lead to conflicts, but ultimately, the U.S. has relied on immigration to maintain its vibrancy over a long history of expansive and restrictive policies.

As noted in Chapter 1, there has been great variation in immigration flows over time, and much of that can be explained by policies that have developed since the government began regulating immigration in the 1800s. Countries like the U.S., Australia, and Canada have fairly open regimes now, but they have had more restrictive regimes in the past, which limited immigrants by race and nationality. This chapter focuses on the political factors which influenced policies to become more restrictive or more expansive over time, using process tracing and focusing on specific cases that exemplify the variance in policy processes that lead to different policy outcomes.

This chapter relies heavily on the work of Daniel Tichenor (2002) who wrote the first comprehensive book on the politics of immigration, *Dividing Lines: The Politics of Immigration Control in America*. Several other books have also had an important impact on the study of immigration politics since then, such as Zolberg's (2008) *A Nation by Design: Immigration Policy in the Fashioning of America*. The main focus of these books is the development of not only immigration policy, but also how that development impacted party politics and the role of other institutions like unions and other interests.

This chapter describes the history of U.S. immigration policymaking, examining how politics often plays a role in making policy change difficult. Major shifts in policy are often decades in the making. Immigration policymaking has often shifted between the legislative and executive branch in the U.S. government. Whereas most think of legislative bills as the main movers of policy, presidential action was often a source of major policy changes, typically occurring when Congress acted as a veto point to expanding immigration (Tichenor 2002). Starting in the post-war era, Congress rejected expansive immigration policy due to fears of communist infiltration and a desire to maintain the character of American society. At the same time, the executive came to see Congressional immigration policy as contradictory to national foreign policy goals and the quota system as overly constraining.

The competition between the two branches over the purpose of immigration policy led to the executive bypassing Congress to issue regularizations of migrants, especially in response to foreign policy initiatives such as addressing refugees from Cuba, Latin America, and Indochina (i.e., the former French colonial territories that are now Vietnam, Cambodia, and Laos). Although presidents issued "amnesties" or used prosecutorial discretion that addressed specific groups when Congress would not act, the largest changes to the U.S. immigration system were overseen by Congress. These include the 1965 Hart–Celler Act, the 1986 Immigration Reform and Control Act (IRCA), and the Illegal Immigration Reform and Immigrant Responsibility Act of 1996 (IIRIRA).

Immigration in the United States

The history of immigration to the United States stretches back to before its founding in the 1700s. Early settlers from Europe pushed out Native American populations, and the British colonies that developed ultimately gained independence, forming the United States of America. Even before the Declaration of Independence, the need for labor had led to forced migration, mainly from Africa.

One of the things that characterized immigration to the United States up until the mid-1800s was a lack of social disruption, partially due to the economic vitality of the country and the push to open more lands to the West. With a relatively small number of immigrants and geographic dispersal, there was relatively little opposition to immigration. The politics of immigration, particularly in terms of restriction, began in the late 1800s with legislation limiting Chinese immigrants.

It is difficult to understand the current situation for immigration policy without understanding the past. In particular the period from late

1800s to early 1930s was a critical period for immigration regulation. The first major step toward limiting immigration into the U.S. came with the passage of the Chinese Exclusion Act in 1882. In many ways, the situation for Chinese immigrants can be compared with the situation for Hispanic immigrants today. For the U.S. case, as noted in the preceding text, I draw mainly on the work of Daniel Tichenor and Aristide Zolberg, but much of the legislative history is drawn from Edward P. Hutchinson's (1981) book *Legislative History of American Immigration Policy 1798–1965*.

The United States has traditionally seen itself as a country of immigration. However, the history of immigration policy is much more complicated. There have been times when immigration policy was expansive and times when it was restrictive. Table 3.1 lists the most important legislation impacting U.S. immigration policy since the late 1800s. In general, there are three clear shifts in immigration policy, the first being a shift from an expansive policy to a more restrictive policy beginning in the 1860s and culminating in the passage of strict national origins quotas in 1924. The next shift from restrictive to expansive policy occurred in the 1960s with the passage of the 1965 Hart–Celler Act which ended national origins quotas. The next shift began in the 1990s with a greater focus on border enforcement, although we are currently in a relatively expansive period in terms of numbers, the rhetoric, and numbers of deportations, and limited

TABLE 3.1

Key Immigration Legislation in the United States

Year	Legislation
1882–1888	Chinese Exclusion Acts
1891	Immigration Act, creation of federal immigration bureaucracy
1907	Immigration Act creates Dillingham Commission
1917	Immigration Act, literacy test, Asians, including Japanese, excluded
1921	National Quota Law limits based on 1910 census
1924	National Origins Act limits based on 1890 census
1940	Immigration Act, Immigration and Naturalization Service transferred from Labor to Justice as national security measure
1943	Bracero Program – recruitment of guest workers (mainly from Mexico)
1965	Hart–Celler Act dismantles quotes, starts preferences
1975	Indochina Refugee Act, Indochinese resettlement
1980	Refugee Act adopts UN definition of *refugee*
1986	IRCA Amnesty and watered-down sanctions
1990	Immigration Act adds employment-based and "diversity" visas
1996	IIRIRA strengthens border enforcement and employer sanctions – exceptions for noncitizen access to public benefits

Note. Data compiled from Tichenor 2002 and Hutchinson 1981.

legislative activity has turned into a case of deadlock as described in Chapter 1.

One constant throughout the history of immigration policy in the U.S. is the rise of nativist groups that push for immigration restrictions, initially for particular groups, and more recently for general restrictions on immigration. The rise of nativism became clear during the Civil War, as noted by renowned historian Erika Lee (2019) in her book *America for Americans*. Professor Lee describes the sentiment, such as Americans' anxiety over the arrival of Irish Catholics, that turned xenophobia into a national political movement. She demonstrated that an irrational fear, hatred, and hostility toward immigrants has been a defining feature of our nation since the colonial era. As the nature of immigration began to change, with more Irish, Southern, and Eastern Europeans entering the country, resentment toward new arrivals, many of whom were Catholic and destitute, was on the rise.

Between the Civil War and WWI, the United States shifted from a relatively open country of immigration to one with restrictions, particularly on immigrations from countries that were considered undesirable. Immigration policy shifted from the state level to the federal level, making national-level politics important in the direction of policy. In New York and on the East Coast, the focus was on Irish, Southern, and Eastern Europeans. The initial focus at the state level was on poor immigrants, as explained by award-winning historian Hidetaka Hirota. In his book *Expelling the Poor: Atlantic Seaboard States and the Nineteenth-Century Origins of American Immigration Policy*, Hirota (2016) argued that American immigration control was rooted in cultural prejudice against the Irish and concerns about their poverty in 19th-century New York and Massachusetts. However, another impetus for immigration restriction at the federal level would truly begin on the West Coast of the United States. California would become the focal point for immigration restrictions as Chinese immigrant laborers came to fill jobs in the gold fields and mines and building the transcontinental railway.

Chinese immigrants presented a dilemma for the industrialists in California. On the one hand, they needed the labor to build the railroads that would open up the riches of the West and get them quickly to the markets on the East Coast. On the other hand, they represented a new foreign influence that did not fit into the Anglo-Saxon ideal, described by Hutchinson as "the violent anti-Chinese reaction to Oriental immigration on the West Coast" (Hutchinson 1981, p. 83). Anti-immigrant groups on the West Coast, including the Workingmen's Party, were joined by Southern Democrats who called for a "political alliance of the South and the West dedicated to white supremacy and defeat of Northeastern 'radicalism'" (as cited in Tichenor 2002, p. 104).

As seen with the rise of the Workingmen's Party in California, laborers were concerned about competition from Chinese workers.

As Zolberg (2008) noted, "[f]rom the late 1860s on, demands for Chinese exclusion were voiced in the annual congresses of various state and national labor organizations, including a convention of Negro workers, and in 1873 it was endorsed by the International Workingman's Association as well" (p. 184). Chinese workers were brought in as strike breakers, and the completion of the transcontinental railroad in 1869 led to conflict between an influx of recent mostly white immigrants and surplus Chinese workers who "were being dumped on the urban industrial labor market" (Zolberg 2008, p. 182).

California was an important state for national electoral politics. With a strong grassroots movement of anti-Chinese clubs, including the Chinese Exclusion League, and weak support for pro-Chinese groups, there was little to stop the tide of anti-Chinese sentiment. Chinese were limited in their ability to gain citizenship and weren't going to be able to become a reliable voting bloc. Party politics played an important role in these developments. On the Democrats' side, they were supportive of European migration but hostile to racial minorities. The Republicans were conflicted – California Republicans supported Chinese exclusion, whereas much of the National party (particularly Radical Republicans) opposed racial discrimination.

A coalition of unions, Southern Democrats, exclusionists like the Anti-Coolie clubs, and pragmatic Republicans supported Chinese exclusion. After many years of political wrangling and rewriting of the Burlingame Treaty with China, the Chinese Exclusion Acts of 1882, 1888, and 1892 effectively suspended the flow of Chinese immigrants, consolidated federal control of policy (particularly through the Immigration Act of 1875), and would ultimately lead to broader restrictions at the beginning of the 20th century.[1]

From Chinese Exclusion to the Dillingham Commission: 1902–1905

When Theodore Roosevelt became President in 1901, he faced a Congress that was primed to be more restrictive on immigration.

> We cannot have too much immigration of the right kind, and we should have none at all of the wrong kind. The need is to devise some system by which undesirable immigrants shall be kept out entirely while desirable immigrants are properly distributed throughout the country... (President Roosevelt after passage of 1903 Act, Congressional Record, 38:3; as cited in Hutchinson 1981, p. 134).

At this point in time, Asian immigration was still on the agenda, although Chinese immigrants were already excluded from both entry and citizenship. An increase in Japanese migration led to what became known as the "Gentleman's Agreement" in 1907. Japan agreed to limit labor emigration, and the U.S. government agreed to avoid discrimination of Japanese, including exempting Japanese students from segregation in San Francisco and a prohibition on Japanese entering continental U.S. from Hawaii. The U.S. government was concerned about Japanese military power and was concerned about getting into a conflict over the treatment of Japanese in the United States.

In the meantime, Southern and Eastern European migration continued. Polish, Italian, and others, particularly from Catholic countries, were clearly seen as different "races" than Western and Northern Europeans. These migrants did not fit in with the desire of many groups to maintain Anglo-Saxon dominance and to increase the homogeneity of the United States. In 1905, President Roosevelt was calling "for more effective protection from unwanted immigration" due to the increasing volume of immigrants entering the country, although he argued that "admission should be based not on creed or nationality but on individual quality" (Hutchinson 1981, p. 136).

While immigration restrictionists and many legislators were calling for a literacy test, President Roosevelt did not support it, and Congress passed the Immigration Act of 1907 that required a new head tax on immigrations and replaced the provision which called for a literacy test with the creation of a new commission, which would come to be known as the Dillingham Commission. In true progressive fashion, the commission was designed to conduct an expert investigation into the need for any new policies. House Speaker Joseph Cannon was the key player in ensuring that the literacy test did not pass in the House version of the bill, and support from President Roosevelt helped to ensure final passage.

The Dillingham Commission is often seen as coming at a major turning point in U.S. immigration policy. The Commission went to great lengths to gather information, including a fact-finding tour of Europe to determine why some immigrants were returning to their home countries as well as conditions at ports of departure to the United States. As noted by Tichenor, "The work of the Dillingham Commission was unprecedented, even by the standards of the Progressive era fact gathering and social engineering. The Commission conducted investigations for more than three years, spent more than a million dollars, employed a staff that reached three hundred and ultimately published a hefty forty-two-volume report" (Tichenor 2002, p. 129).

The Commission's lengthy report – in the end proposed a literacy test and increased head taxes and national origins quotas – is the last of these proposals that started the United States on its way to the policy that would dominate U.S. immigration until the mid-1960s.

The Commission did not start out as a strongly anti-immigrant group, although it is often characterized that way. Several of the commissioners were pro-immigration, some were open-minded, and others were for restrictions. However, as Tichenor noted, "[t]he recurrent theme of its forty-two reports was the vast contrast between immigrants from traditional European source countries and those from southern and eastern Europe" (2002, p. 129). These immigrants were seen as less skilled and being the source of various social problems. The reports were embraced by groups like the Immigration Restriction League (IRL) and labor unions like the American Federation of Labor (AFL), who supported immigration restriction.

World War I and the "Red Scare"

The Dillingham Commission completed its work in 1910, and the new decade would be filled with major political shifts as well as World War I, which would lead to an increase in isolationism and protectionism in the United States. The war led to a decline in political activism based on country of origin as immigrants feared a backlash against those who were considered aggressors in the war. There was also a major push for "Americanization," which was focused on getting rid of the hyphenated American and creating an assimilated immigrant who did not rely on group identity but identified as an American citizen. Many states and federal agencies had Americanization programs, and these were embraced by Progressives. Immigrants were urged to naturalize and to take English and civics lessons; however, often the motivation for supporters of the movement was an "implied pressure to conform to a white Anglo-Saxon ideal that submerged other ethnic identification" (Motomura 2006, p. 40).

Getting to Quotas – 1913

The Immigration Acts of March 3, 1891, March 3, 1903, and February 20, 1907 were all steps toward a more racially based approach to immigration restriction. As noted by Hutchinson (1981),

> [c]omparing this series of acts, we can see the development of more and more excludable classes; reinforcement through deportation provisions that extended longer and longer after entry; greater and greater elaboration of the wording of the laws in an attempt to cover every conceivable case and aspect of the labor contract, the immoral classes, the anarchist or subversive classes, and others...
>
> (p. 155)

Another important step along the way to immigration quotas was the passing of the literacy test in 1917, which was an attempt to keep less-educated immigrants from outside of Western Europe from entering the country. However, these measures were not enough to stop Southern and Eastern European immigration. The Passport Control Act of 1918 also added the important requirement that potential immigrants had to obtain a visa from a consulate or qualified representative, allowing representatives in embassies and consulates to screen applicants before they left for the United States. These policies were reinforced by the 1924 National Origins Act that required European immigrants to obtain entry visas and pass consular inspection. These two measures in effect moved our borders to the countries of origin.

It is important to see both the **Immigration Act of 1921** and the **Reed–Johnson Act of 1924** (i.e., **National Origins Quotas**) in the broader context of an isolationist United States that was wary and weary of war after World War I. Although the concerns about immigration had begun with a focus on Chinese immigrants, the increase in flows from Southern and Eastern Europe in the late 1890s and early 1900s raised concerns about a flow that would be difficult to assimilate. Many of these immigrants were considered to be less educated and of ethnic stock that was not desirable. These were hallmarks of the **eugenicist** belief that there is a hierarchy of races. Also, many of these immigrants were Catholics, who were also discriminated against by some Protestant, nativist groups.

The 1921 Act had already created quotas based on the 1910 census that limited immigration to three per cent per year of each European nationality already residing in the United States. Some felt that this still allowed too many Southern and Eastern Europeans. The 1924 Act limited immigration to two per cent per year of each nationality, based on the 1890 census when there were fewer immigrations coming from Southern and Eastern Europe. The annual ceiling from the 1921 Act of 387,803 was reduced to 186,437 by the 1924 Act. This was a huge reduction in levels of immigration from approximately 700,000 per year. By 1925, Japanese exclusion was also phased in along with the already existing Chinese exclusion policies (Tichenor 2002, p. 145).

The result of the 1924 Act was the institutionalization of racial bias in U.S. immigration policy, which would have a major impact on refugees, particularly Jewish refugees who were denied entry to the U.S. before and during World War II and the Cold War. This would also have an impact on labor flows, given the ongoing need for workers, including during the war. The ultimate outcome was a very restrictive immigration policy, with the exception of the Western Hemisphere.

Not all legislation was restrictive, particularly those related to policy in the Western hemisphere. The government ran the Bracero Program from 1942 to 1964 with the idea that immigrants from Mexico would want to or could easily be returned. In general, Mexicans were not considered a threat by nativists and were considered necessary for agriculture in the Southwest: "More than 80,000 braceros pass through the El Paso Center annually. They're part of an army of 350,000 or more that marches across the border each year to help plant, cultivate, and harvest cotton and other crops throughout the United States."

The end of WWII saw a resurgence of pro-immigrant groups, with Jewish groups vowing that "never again" would Jewish refugees be turned away from foreign shores. This was also the time period when organizing of farm workers and the fight for Hispanic rights began. American academics disavowed the impact of Nazi racist theory on race, and the newly started Cold War between the U.S. and the Soviet Union led the government to be concerned about racism that would reflect badly on the United States' moral authority in the world. President Eisenhower viewed national origins quotas as impediments to his foreign policy goals, including welcoming Hungarian refugees. On the other hand, the Eisenhower Administration also pursued "Operation Wetback," which focused on deporting undocumented farm workers and Mexicans along the border.

From Quotas to Preferences – 1965

With the death of President John F. Kennedy in 1963, President Lyndon Johnson faced a series of challenges. To pursue a legacy for President Kennedy, Johnson decided to push for "New Frontier" Civil Rights reform. Johnson linked immigration reform to foreign policy and civil rights goals to move the country away from national origins quotas toward a more balanced policy that was based on a series of categories that were no longer race-based. For the most part, Congressional resistance was neutralized through President Johnson's negotiating tactics. Also, expectations were that the new "preferences," particularly for family reunification, would limit immigration from Asia and Africa.

The 1970s saw major changes in U.S. immigration flows with fewer people coming from Europe and more from Asia, Africa, the Caribbean, and Latin America. The government began to focus on immigrants coming from Mexico, particularly illegal immigrants. As noted by Tichenor (2002), "the illegal immigration problem assumed new prominence during the Ford presidency. In 1975, Ford created a special interagency committee, the Domestic Council on Illegal Immigration, to investigate the scope of the problem and formulate a policy response" (Tichenor 2002, p. 229). Policy proposals included **employer sanctions**, which would have imposed fines on employers who knowingly employed undocumented immigrants. Many **labor unions**, including the **United Farm Workers** (UFW) opposed illegal immigrants because they felt that they could be used by employers to depress wages. However, they also opposed employer sanctions because it could give employers an excuse to avoid hiring Hispanics – regardless of legal status. A plan proposed in 1977 by then President Jimmy Carter was unsuccessful, with a deadlock between groups opposed to illegal immigration, such as the UFW, AFL-

CIO, LULAC (League of United Latin American Citizens), and those supporting employer sanctions, including the National Association of the Advancement of Colored People (NAACP) and other African American groups. With a major divide, President Carter and Congress were unable to agree on a way forward.

Overall there was little policy change during the 1970s. First there was a lack of consensus on dealing with illegal immigrants, including divisions in the Democratic party and sympathetic groups over employer sanctions and how to deal with illegal immigrants, particularly whether there should be employer sanctions. There was in the end no move to restrict legal immigration.

1980s – 1990s

During the 1980s, legal immigration soared, despite a restrictionist mood in the country. Organizations like the **Federation for American Immigration Reform** (FAIR) pushed for new restrictions based on issues of overpopulation and the environment, as compared with the more racist approaches to restrictionism from the past. However, a continued coalition of liberal and conservative legislators continued to resist change. The resulting immigration flows, based on the 1965 Act, led to a huge change in policy regime from the post-WWII era. However, the basis of a new reform agenda was being put into place.

One of the more important developments was the creation of the **Select Committee on Immigration and Refugee Policy (SCIRP)** in 1979. As noted by Zolberg (2008), "[b]y the time SCIRP submitted its report in February 1981, Ronald Reagan had been elected to the presidency; but despite the change of administration, hailed as the dawn of a new era in American politics, the commissioners set the legislative agenda for an entire decade, leading to the enactment of major legislation in 1986 and 1990" (p. 354).

The 1981 staff report *U.S. Immigration Policy and the National Interest* placed emphasis on civil rights values, and the makeup of the commission was drawn from leaders in civil rights and legislators. The report emphasized that immigration was a positive force in the national interest but also focused on illegal immigration as a serious problem. The commission members wanted to "close the back door and open the front door." The report also affirmed the three-track system of legal admissions: family reunification, skilled migration, and refugee admissions. The Commission also "voted unanimously on behalf of the legalization of a substantial portion of the undocumented/illegal aliens now in the country," while emphasizing the need for border control (Zolberg 2008, p. 355).

The first major piece of legislation to be developed after the SCIRP report was the 1986 IRCA. The Act built on the SCIRP recommendations by dealing with illegal immigration first, including legalization of approximately three million undocumented immigrants. President Reagan argued that the law's provisions would "remove the incentive for illegal immigration by eliminating the job opportunities which draw illegal aliens here" and that the bill's legalizations would "go far to improve the lives of a class of individuals who now must hide in the shadows"[2].

The passage of the bill required overcoming gridlock in the House of Representatives and closed-door negotiations to negate the influence of special interests. Another important component of the legislation was **employer sanctions**, which were theoretically designed to help cut off the demand for illegal immigrants, whereas beefing up border security would focus on the supply. Business interests were against sanctions, but their opposition was blunted when the employer sanctions provisions weren't given any teeth during legislative negotiations.

A measure designed to discourage immigration ended up having little impact on the U.S.'s expansionist immigration policy. As Zolberg (2008) noted, "IRCA contributed to the further growth of illegal movement as well: not only did the loosely enforced employer sanctions have little deterrent effect, but the newly legalized millions also provided a stronger and more stable community base to sustain and protect unauthorized newcomers" (p. 383). Although the bill's provisions did improve the situation for those immigrants who met the qualifications for legalization, it did little to reduce the incentives for illegal immigration, since employer sanctions were not enforced. Stuart Anderson (2011) also argued that "[t] he 1986 law failed because it did not include a well-designed temporary worker visa system" (p. 1).

The Immigration Act of 1990 focused on legal immigration, with a modest expansion of family-based visas and an increase in visas based on education and job skills. A diversity program placated politicians, like Senator Edward Kennedy, who were concerned about allowing more immigration from Europe, particularly Ireland, and also including Central and Eastern Europeans, who no longer qualified as refugees (Zolberg 2008).

The Commission on Immigration Reform, also known as the Jordan Commission, was established by the 1990 Act. The Commission focused on making employer sanctions more effective and called for modest cuts in annual visa numbers and family preferences (Tichenor 2002, p. 278).

By the mid-1990s, anti-immigrant sentiment was growing, particularly because of the flow of undocumented immigrants into California. In 1994, Kathleen Brown was poised to follow her father and brother as the next governor of California. However, her opponent Pete Wilson's embrace of ballot measure Proposition 187, which was designed to cut benefits to undocumented immigrants, gave him a boost in the polls. Wilson ultimately won, but Proposition 187 was short-lived because several groups immediately filed lawsuits, leading a judge to impose an injunction. The ballot measure was never implemented, but it did lead to the mobilization of eligible Hispanic voters.

The focus on illegal immigration in California and other parts of the country led the Clinton Administration to endorse some of the more restrictionist components of the Jordan Commission, taking a hard line on mass asylum from Cuba and Haiti. During this time, formation of the Center for Immigration Studies, a think tank focusing on immigration restriction, was formed to try to the continued focus on expansive legal migration (Tichenor 2002, p. 279).

The next major legislative action was the 1996 Illegal Immigration Reform and Immigrant Responsibility Act (IRIRA). In line with a more restrictive approach to legal migration, the legislation enhanced border security and limited access to public benefits (Tichenor 2002, p. 284). Although the bill was limited in its impact, along with the Personal Responsibility and Work Opportunity Act of 1996, "the immigration and welfare reform laws marked a retrenchment of the legal protections and social entitlements that legal and undocumented aliens could claim" (Tichenor 2002, p. 284).

Although President Clinton supported measures to limit legal immigration and immigrant access to welfare benefits, he also encouraged naturalization – and for those who were in the country legally, citizenship would give them better access to benefits as well as the opportunity to vote. Many Latinos, in particular, were angered by the anti-immigrant measure and took advantage of a streamlined naturalization process with the Citizenship USA Initiative of 1995. By the time of the 2000 presidential campaign, it was clear that Latinos were going to be playing an important role in the election results, particularly in states like California. Both Al Gore and George W. Bush worked to reach out to new voters, decrying measures like California's Proposition 187 that would have restricted state benefits.

U.S. Immigration Policy in the 21st Century

Perhaps the most important policy shift in the U.S. after 9/11 was the change from the Immigration and Naturalization Service (INS) to the Department of Homeland Security (DHS). On March 1, 2003, INS enforcement and service functions and responsibilities transitioned into the Department of Homeland Security (DHS). Prior to the 9/11 terror attacks, studies had been done to look at the possibility of dividing the customer service component of INS from the enforcement/border patrol sides of INS. It was felt that these two components of the organization could be in conflict. The attacks provided the imperative to move forward with these changes and emphasize security for the "homeland."

The main functions of the former INS were divided into three bureaus under the Department of Homeland Security: U.S. Customs and Border Protection (including the U.S. Border Patrol), U.S. Immigration and Customs Enforcement (ICE), and U.S. Citizenship and Immigration Services. The INS had been under the Department of Justice, and DHS became its own cabinet-level department. Several other entities, including the Federal Emergency Management Agency (FEMA), the Coast Guard, and the Secret Service also became part of DHS. To improve security at airport terminals, which had mainly been under the control of contractors, the Transportation Security Administration was formed to ensure consistent approaches to security at airports.

The shift from the INS to DHS has been lauded as allowing each of the components of the department to focus on their particular aspect of security and/or immigration policy. However, there have been many critiques of DHS, with an initial focus on the fact that this created one of the largest bureaucracies in the government, which could be slow to respond to threats that weren't foreseen, "on the two years since the 9/11 terrorist attacks on New York and Washington, some say the new Department of Homeland Security, led by Secretary Tom Ridge, is little more than a sprawling and unwieldy reaction to crisis" (Lytle 2003).[3]

Other areas of concern included the experience of its employees. The bureaucratic shifts have led to morale issues for employees.

> Poor morale has been a problem for DHS throughout its history. DHS consistently has been identified as one of the worst places to work in the federal government. According to the Department's most recent survey, employee morale and satisfaction continued to decline in 2014. Overall, only 41 per cent of its employees were satisfied with DHS. The survey data reveal some alarming findings, including that only 22 per cent of DHS employees believe that "steps are taken to deal with a poor performer who cannot or will not improve" On the positive side, the DHS employees' survey results show that the overwhelming majority of its employees believed in the agency's mission with more than 85 per cent believing that the work they do is important.
>
> (Coburn 2015, p. 157)

Another critique focuses on the broad mandate of the new department. FEMA's response (or lack thereof) to Hurricane Katrina in Louisiana was seen as a sign that the management of DHS was not yet up to the task of managing such a vast bureaucracy. In a 2015 report by Senator Tom Coburn (Republican), he made the following assessment of DHS:

> [b]ased upon the available evidence, DHS is not successfully executing any of its five main missions. Many of DHS's programs, in

fact, are ineffective and should be reconsidered. One of the most significant challenges DHS faces is Congress. Parochial politics and overlapping jurisdiction between various congressional committees and subcommittees too often hinder and impede DHS's mission and programs. Reforming DHS, therefore, must begin with changing Congress's approach to homeland security.

(pp. 3–4)

Coburn further pointed out that

[a]dding to DHS's difficulties ensuring border security is the problem of potential corruption within the Department's workforce; which causes additional operational challenges. The issue of potential corruption within CBP is well-documented. For example, GAO issued a report on corruption and misconduct in December 2012, finding that more than 140 current and former CBP employees had been arrested for corruption offenses, such as smuggling, and 125 had been convicted as of late 2012.

(2015, p. 46)

Coburn concluded that

DHS should be forced to meet its responsibility for upholding the rule of law, including removing illegal immigrants—particularly those that threaten public safety and domestic security. DHS's visa programs that have apparent criminal or national security vulnerabilities, including the Student Exchange and Visitor Program and EB-5 visa programs, should be reformed, suspended, or ended to mitigate potential vulnerabilities.

(2015, p. 153)

An important change after 2001 was a renewed focus on tracking foreign students. Several of the 9/11 attackers had entered the U.S. on student visas. Several of them had gone to flight schools, and no red flags were raised when they overstayed their visas. Visa overstayers are a general problem for immigration enforcement, but the government has taken important measures since 9/11 to track and regulate the flow of students.

A controversial piece of legislation which passed after 9/11 was the USA PATRIOT Act (Uniting and Strengthening America by Providing Appropriate Tools Required to Intercept and Obstruct Terrorism). The Department of Justice summarized the main components of the act as allowing law enforcement to use tools that were allowed to investigate organized crime to investigate terrorism, allow and encourage information sharing across agencies (something which hindered detection of the 9/11 plot), updating laws to account for new technology (like cell phones and encryption) and new threats, and increasing penalties for terrorist acts.[4] However, the act also raised major concerns for civil liberties at the time. For example, a Congressional Research Service report stated that "critics have suggested that it may go too far. The authority to monitor e-mail traffic, to share grand jury information with intelligence and immigration officers, to confiscate property, and to impose new book-keeping requirements on financial institutions, are among the features troubling to some" (Doyle 2002, p. iii). The collection of personal data by intelligence agencies has been criticized, and in some cases curtailed by the judiciary.

The terror of attacks on September 11, 2001 were a major turning point for the immigration debate in the United States. Tichenor foresaw the potential impact when he wrote that "...new international crises or threats episodically have served as important catalysts for major immigration reform, altering the incentives and capacities of political actors to break policy stalemates" (2002, p. 9). The post-9/11 era saw a great deal of change in immigration policy, particularly in terms of the institutional structures for enforcing immigration control policies. However, it was also a time of policy stalemate in terms of immigration reform.

After the IIRIRA in 1996, Congress, much as it had been in the post-WWII era, acted mainly as a veto point for immigration reform. As in the 1950s, two patterns emerged: There was an increasing number of migrants and a growing sense that "something" must be done, yet the status quo could not be overcome. The George W. Bush Administration was supportive of immigration reform, but its efforts to promote reform were put on hold after 9/11. Later, even with this supportive president whose party controlled both chambers of Congress in 2005 and 2006, comprehensive immigration reform (CIR) legislation failed to pass both Houses in the 109th and 110th Congresses.

Tom Wong (2017) argued that one of the more important pieces of legislation for mobilizing immigrant communities and undocumented immigrants was H.R. 4437, the Border Protection, Antiterrorism, and Illegal Immigration Control Act of 2005. This legislation was considered a threat by immigrant communities because it "sought to criminalize unlawful *presence* in the United States, which is currently a civil offense" (Wong 2017, p.7). Although the legislation was not voted into law, it triggered mass mobilization in which millions of immigrants and their supporters marched in the streets and played a key role in mobilizing more naturalized citizens to vote. It also added to the level of partisanship and a stalemate around immigration reform that would play a role into Barack Obama's presidency.

The next attempt at immigration reform took place in Barack Obama's second term, with the passing of the "Gang of 8" immigration bill in the Senate on June 27, 2013. This bill, officially S. 744 Border Security,

Economic Opportunity, and Immigration Modernization Act, passed with 14 Republicans and two independents joining 52 Democrats in voting for the bill. As a result of several changes in the political context in 2013, many expected that immigration reform would finally occur. As noted by the press, it seemed that the grassroots momentum was on the expansionary side.[5] For example, whereas talk show radio led and encouraged pushback on CIR bills during the George W. Bush Administration, it seemed no longer to have the same pull or even desire to lead a campaign against the Senate bill.[6] In addition, Republicans seemed primed to support CIR as a way to make inroads into the Hispanic community, which had supported Obama's re-election by 70 per cent (Wanlund 2014). Religious groups had also come out in support of CIR, including evangelical Christians, who formed the Evangelical Immigration Table to push for comprehensive immigration reform.

Even public opinion seemed to align with pro-CIR push. Although overall support for a pathway to legal status had dropped slightly from a high of 73 per cent in February 2014 to 68 per cent in July, Pew polls also found that 61 per cent of the population said that "it was extremely or very important that Congress and the president pass 'significant new immigration legislation.'"[7] Yet, despite this political context, by the summer of 2014, Speaker of the House John Boehner stated that the House would not consider the Senate bill.

This stalling of the bill in the House occurred for several reasons. Though many in the GOP were worried about losing Hispanic voters to the Democratic party as previously mentioned, they were also worried about challenges from within their party, specifically from Tea Party opponents in run-off elections. Emblematic of this fear was the House Minority Leader Eric Cantor's loss to Dave Brat in a primary election. Although Cantor did not support the Gang of 8 Senate bill, he had made comments supportive of immigration reform, which many have argued contributed to his loss.[8]

Also, though public opinion in general was positive on creating a way for undocumented migrants to regularize their status, support by self-identified Republicans had fallen from February to July of that year from 64 per cent to 54 per cent.[9] This decrease in support was even greater in those that leaned towards the Tea Party with support for regularization dropping from 56 per cent to 41 per cent.

It was at this point that supporters of immigration reform found themselves in 2014. Congress proved an unmovable veto point, and as long as the debate was contained in Congress, hopes for policy change were unlikely to be realized. Although the makeup of the anti-CIR coalition had changed, it still had a role to play due to the increasingly important Republican primary system wherein those sympathetic to reform were targeted by challengers on the right.

Australia

Australia is a "classical country of immigration" in that its strategy to become a nation-state was based on European migration (Castles, Vasta, and Ozkul 2014, p. 128). Not unlike the United States, the rise and fall of racialized immigration policy in Australia spanned from the beginning of the 20th century until the 1960s and 1970s. Australia is a former British settler colony that originated as a penal colony in the late 18th century, but free settlement was also encouraged as a result of the potential of its natural resources. Subsequent to the discovery of gold in the 1850s, employers began to see non-white immigration as a means to control wages and stem unionization. As in the U.S., the use of Chinese labor became a source of political tensions in the latter half of the 19th century.

The Immigration Restriction Act of 1901, or the White Australia Policy, was passed in order to limit immigration from non-white countries and to deport "undesirable" migrants who were already present. Favoring migrants from the U.K. over others, this act created the dictation test where immigrants were tested on their writing ability in a language chosen by the immigration officer. As it was not required to administer the test in a language the person spoke, the test was easily adjusted to keep out non-preferred migrants.

Nonetheless, the Australian immigration minister pushed for Australia to "populate or perish" after World War II (Castles et al. 2014, p. 130). Because there were not enough British immigrants to achieve the population growth needed, policies were implemented to allow displaced persons from elsewhere in Europe to migrate. From this time on, immigration policies started to loosen, allowing southern and eastern migrants and even some temporary migration from the Middle East and Asia. In 1957, the Liberal Government relaxed policies toward non-Europeans even more, allowing them to apply for citizenship after 15 years in the country. The Migration Act of 1958 abolished the dictation test and removed references to race, but the White Australia Policy was not officially abolished until the Migration Act of 1966. In 1973, it was officially renounced by the Whitlam government as they ushered in the current policy of multiculturalism.[10]

Today, more than one quarter of Australian residents were born overseas.[11] In addition to multiculturalism, Australia prioritizes skilled migration. Consider the way immigrants have become permanent residents since the mid-1980s. Annually, only about 10,000 to 15,000 do so via humanitarian visas and roughly 50,000 via family visas. By contrast, the number who have become permanent residents from skilled labor visas has grown steadily from about 10,000 in 1984–1985 to 113,725 by 2010. Australia also grants "Subclass 457" (business long-stay) visas, which have shown similar growth, from about 25,000 in 1996–1997 to roughly 100,000 by 2008–2009 (Castles et al. 2014, pp. 131–132).

The Islamic extremist attacks of 9/11 in the U.S. and in Bali, India in 2002 brought immigration politics to center stage in Australia. The Howard government, which held office from 1996 until 2007, was already skeptical of multiculturalism. The attacks led Howard to both participate in the "Coalition of the Willing" (i.e., the beginning of the fight alongside the U.S. in Iraq) and to issue a policy statement, *United in Diversity*, in 2003. *United in Diversity* emphasized unity around Australian values at the expense of diversity and reflected Howard's belief that Australia was still fundamentally a European-heritage country that others were obliged to adapt to. In 2011, the Australian Labor Party, by then back in power, issued a recommitment to multiculturalism (Castles et al. 2014, pp. 144). Controversy over the politics of asylum remains to this day.

Canada

Canada began as French and British territory, with the initial focus of colonial administrators on exploiting resources rather than settlement. Early settlement in the Eastern part of the territory would come from Scottish, German, and Irish settlers, along with French and British colonists. Britain took over sole administration of the colony in 1759–1760, which was complicated after the departure of the French by the presence of a substantial French-speaking population. Canada remains an officially bilingual country.

Many British loyalists moved to Canada after the end of the War of Independence in the United States, fearing retribution for their support of the crown. Colonial administrators provided support to settlers through the provision of land and supplies, but there was no particular organization or process to the movement. For many migrants, Canada was a second-choice destination, when entry to the United States was not possible or restricted.

Immigration has been seen as an important component of nation-building for Canada, up to the present day. The focus was initially on building the original colonial settlements and then shifting focus to the Western territories in the mid- to late 1800s. As with the U.S., by the mid-1800 waves of Irish migrants came with the potato famine and became the basis for the working-class labor force, although their Catholicism was considered an issue, along with social ills that prevailed in many Irish neighborhoods. The Irish remained a separate minority in many cities.

As in the U.S., Canadian authorities became concerned with Chinese migration and passed restrictions on Chinese migrants in 1885. Agriculture became an important component of the economy in the early 1900s with a push for settlers in the Western territories. "Unabashedly colonial, the government defined immigrants who did not originate from the British Isles as foreign; and, unabashedly North American, excluded white, English-speaking immigrants from the U.S. from this category."[12] Canada's immigration policy would have a preference for Northern and Western Europeans, mirroring racist policies in the U.S., particularly against immigrants from Asia and African Americans, particularly with the passage of the 1906 Immigration Act, which would be amended in 1919 to add more restrictions, "The governor-in-council (i.e., federal cabinet) was additionally authorized to prohibit immigrants of any nationality, race, occupation, and class because of their 'peculiar customs, habits, modes of life and methods of holding property.'"[13]

Canada's policies would remain restrictive until after World War II, when policies shifted from a focus on low-skilled to high-skilled, urban immigrants. Canada, with a low birth rate, has maintained a high rate of immigration into the 21st century, using a point system introduced in the late 1960s. Since this time, Canada has also become a more multiracial country, as immigrants have come from more regions of the world, including refugees from various conflict regions, such as Syria.

Canada has been seen as an attractive destination for high-skilled immigrants and has seen, for example, Toronto, the capital of the province of Ontario, become the focal point for a tech boom with companies like Microsoft, Intel, and Samsung developing major projects in the city.[14] As Canada competes with the U.S. for skilled labor, it will have to focus also on immigrant integration and security issues. Canada has also been open to refugees from the Middle East, with restrictions in the U.S. pushing more migrants to declare asylum in Canada, raising issues for politicians at the federal and provincial levels.[15]

Conclusion

Although the U.S., Australia, and Canada consider themselves countries of immigration and have considered immigration an important part of their nation-building processes, the history shows that restrictive immigration policies have been the rule rather than the exception. Politicians in the late 1800s and early 1900s had a clear idea of the type of immigrants whose emigration they wanted to encourage and those whom they hoped to exclude. These policies impacted the demographics of these countries from the mid- to late 1900s. As we explore specific policy areas in the upcoming chapters, it is important to keep in mind the sources of immigration policy and how the history of a country can play a role in the evolution of its policies. In Chapter 4, we examine developments in more recent countries of immigration.

KEY TERMS

Americanization Efforts started in the 1920s to assist in the assimilation of immigrants. "Nativists believed that classes in American history, politics, and culture would enhance the socialization process, instill middle-class values, and wean newcomers away from their immigrant heritage by making them 'one of us.'" See https://ehistory.osu.edu/sites/ehistory.osu.edu/files/mmh/clash/Imm_KKK/Immigration%20Pages/Subnarratives/Americanization.htm.

Chinese Exclusion As noted on the African American Policy Forum website, "The Chinese Exclusion Act was the first immigration law that excluded an entire ethnic group. It also excluded Chinese nationals from eligibility for United States citizenship." See their website for examples of documents and a video about racism toward Chinese immigrants http://aapf.org/chinese-exclusion-act.

Department of Homeland Security (DHS) The DHS was created in the wake of the 9/11 terrorist attacks to better coordinate the activities that were formerly under the INS and added the Federal Emergency Management Agency (FEMA) and the Coast Guard to its portfolio. The cabinet-level department divided the main functions of the former INS into three bureaus: U.S. Customs and Border Protection (including the Border Patrol), U.S. Immigration and Customs Enforcement (ICE), and U.S. Citizenship and Immigration Services.

Dillingham Commission As noted in *Smithsonian Magazine*, "Congress created the Commission in 1907 in an effort to find a compromise between proponents and opponents of immigration...the commission recommended passage of the literacy test, calling it 'the single most feasible' method of exclusion. Restrictionists viewed this as an endorsement of their cause and used the recommendation to secure the test's eventual passage by Congress in 1917. See https://www.smithsonianmag.com/history/1911-report-set-america-on-path-screening-out-undesirable-immigrants.

Employer Sanctions The U.S. Citizenship and Immigration Services (USCIS) website states that employer sanctions are "[a] series of civil fines or criminal penalties for violating regulations that prohibit employers from hiring, recruiting or referring for a fee aliens known to be unauthorized to work in the United States, or continuing to employ foreign nationals knowing they are unauthorized, or hiring an individual without completing Form I-9." See https://www.uscis.gov/tools/glossary.

Eugenicist Eugenicists understood various human and social problems as rooted in the defective "germ-plasm" of individuals or certain racial/ethnic groups. Claiming to base their theories on scientific evidence and methods, eugenics supporters rationalized "scientific racism" in the late 19th and early 20th centuries and helped shape state policies of sterilization, miscegenation prohibition, and immigration restriction. See https://cla.umn.edu/ihrc/news-events/other/eugenics-race-immigration-restriction.

Federation for American Immigration Reform (FAIR) FAIR is an anti-immigration organization founded in 1979 (https://www.fairus.org/).

Their website states, "FAIR seeks to reduce overall immigration to a more normal [sic] level. Reducing legal immigration levels from well over one million presently to 300,000 a year over a sustained period will allow America to manage growth, address environmental concerns, and maintain a high quality of life." An article by *Politifact* takes on the issue of whether FAIR should be considered a hate group. See https://www.politifact.com/florida/article/2017/mar/22/center-immigration-studies-hate-group-southern-pov/.

Gentleman's Agreement   In this agreement with the U.S. in 1907, Japan agreed to limit labor emigration, and the U.S. government agreed to avoid discrimination of Japanese people in the U.S., including exempting Japanese students from segregation in San Francisco, and a prohibition on Japanese entering continental U.S. from Hawaii. The U.S. treated Japanese immigrants more favorably than Chinese because of Japan's military strength.

Immigration Act of 1921   The 1921 Act created quotas based on the 1910 census that limited immigration to three per cent per year of each European nationality already residing in the United States.

Immigration and Customs Enforcement (ICE)   ICE is the part of the Department of Homeland Security that focuses on internal enforcement of immigration law, including enforcement and removal operations. According to their website, "[t]he majority of its immigration enforcement mission takes place in the interior of the country," coordinating with law enforcement and using biometric and biographic information to identify priority aliens who are incarcerated in the U.S." See https://www.ice.gov/overview.

Immigration and Naturalization Service (INS)   The INS was created with Executive Order 6166 of June 10, 1933, uniting the Bureau of Immigration and Bureau of Naturalization into one agency, the Immigration and Naturalization Service. As noted on the U.S. Citizenship and Immigration Services website, "[t]he Immigration and Naturalization Service (INS) has not existed since March 1, 2003. On that date, most INS functions were transferred from the Department of Justice to three new components within the newly formed Department of Homeland Security. USCIS is one of those three components. U.S. Immigration and Customs Enforcement (ICE) and U.S. Customs and Border Protection (CBP) are the other two." See https://www.uscis.gov/archive/blog/2011/04/did-you-know-ins-no-longer-exists.

Labor Unions   Labor unions, organized associations of workers, often in a trade or profession, formed to protect and further workers' rights and interests, developed in the late 1800s in the era of industrialization (e.g., the Federation of Organized Trades and Labor Unions was formed in 1881, and the American Federation of Labor was founded in 1886). See https://www.investopedia.com/financial-edge/0113/the-history-of-unions-in-the-united-states.aspx.

Nativism   Nativism is the promotion of policies protecting the interests of native-born or established inhabitants against those of immigrants.

Reed–Johnson Act of 1924 (i.e., National Origins Quotas)   The 1924 Act limited immigration to two per cent per year of each nationality, based on the 1890 census when there were fewer immigrants coming from Southern and Eastern Europe. The annual ceiling from the 1921 Act of 387,803 was reduced to 186,437 by the 1924 Act.

Select Committee on Immigration and Refugee Policy (SCIRP)   SCIRP was created in 1979 and its report *U.S. Immigration Policy and the National Interest* placed emphasis on civil rights values. The Committee comprised civil rights leaders and like-minded legislators. The report emphasized not only that immigration was a positive force in the national interest, but also that illegal immigration was a serious problem.

United Farm Workers (UFW)   According to their website, the UFW was "[b]egun in 1962 by Cesar Chavez, Dolores Huerta, Gilbert Padilla, and other early organizers. The UFW of America is the nation's first enduring and largest farm workers union. The UFW continues organizing in major agricultural sectors, chiefly in California." See https://ufw.org/about-us/our-vision/.

USA PATRIOT Act   The official title of the USA PATRIOT Act is "Uniting and Strengthening America by Providing Appropriate Tools Required to Intercept and Obstruct Terrorism (USA PATRIOT) Act of 2001." The legislation was passed after the terror attacks of 9/11 and focused on coordinating the efforts of law enforcement agencies that were not effective in stopping the terrorists responsible for crashing planes into the World Trade Center in New York City, The Pentagon, and a thwarted attempt at the U.S. Capitol that crashed in a field in Pennsylvania. The U.S. Treasury website states the purpose of the PATRIOT Act is "to deter and punish terrorist acts in the United States and around the world, to enhance law enforcement investigatory tools, and other purposes." See https://www.fincen.gov/resources/statutes-regulations/usa-patriot-act.

U.S. Customs and Border Protection (USCBP)   The USCBP website states the following: "With more than 60,000 employees, U.S. Customs and Border Protection, CBP, is one of the world's largest law enforcement organizations and is charged with keeping terrorists and their weapons out of the U.S., while facilitating lawful international travel and trade. As the United States' first unified border entity, CBP takes a comprehensive approach to border management and control, combining customs, immigration, border security, and agricultural protection into one coordinated and supportive activity." See https://www.cbp.gov/about.

NOTES

1 See "The Burlingame-Seward Treaty, 1868." U.S. Department of State, Office of the Historian. https://history.state.gov/milestones/1866-1898/burlin game-seward-treaty, accessed 10/12/2019.
2 Ronald Reagan, "Statement on Signing the Immigration Reform and Control Act of 1986," November 6, 1986, https://www.reaganlibrary.gov/research/ speeches/110686b accessed April 15, 2020.
3 See "Critics: Homeland Security Agency Too Big, Too Ineffective." *Orlando Sentinel* published 9/14/2019. http://articles.orlandosentinel.com/2003-09-14/ news/0309130029_1_homeland-dhs-security, accessed 10/12/2019.
4 See "The USA PATRIOT Act: Preserving Life and Liberty." Department of Justice Website (U.S. Government). https://www.justice.gov/archive/ll/high lights.htm, accessed 10/12/2019.
5 See "Showing Grass-Roots Support for Immigration Overhaul." *The New York Times* published 5/2/2013. http://www.nytimes.com/2013/05/02/us/across-the-country-supporters-rally-for-immigration-overhaul.html, accessed 10/12/2019.
6 See "Will Conservative Talkers Take on Immigration Reform?" Pew Research Center. http://www.journalism.org/2013/02/01/will-conservative-talkers-take-immigration-reform/, accessed 10/13/2019.
7 See "Surge of Central American Children Roils U.S. Immigration Debate." Pew Research Center. http://www.people-press.org/2014/07/16/surge-of-cen tral-american-children-roils-u-s-immigration-debate/2, accessed 10/13/2019.
8 See "Make No Mistake: Immigration Reform Hurt Eric Cantor" *The Washington Post* published 6/11/2019. http://www.washingtonpost.com/blogs/the-fix/ wp/2014/06/11/yes-immigration-reform-hurt-eric-cantor/, accessed 10/12/ 2019, and "Eric Cantor Loss Kills Immigration Reform." *POLITICO* published 6/10/2014. http://www.politico.com/story/2014/06/2014-virginia-primary-eric-cantor-loss-immigration-reform-107697.html, accessed 10/12/2019.
9 See "Surge of Central American Children Roils U.S. Immigration Debate." Pew Research Center. http://www.people-press.org/2014/07/16/surge-of-cen tral-american-children-roils-u-s-immigration-debate/2, accessed 10/13/2019.
10 See "White Australia Policy Ends." National Australian Museum. http:// www.nma.gov.au/online_features/defining_moments/featured/end_of_the_whi te_australia_policy, accessed 10/12/2019.
11 See "Australia's Population by Country of Birth." Australian Bureau of Stat-istics. http://www.abs.gov.au/ausstats/abs@.nsf/Previousproducts/3412.0Main %20Features32014-15?opendocument&tabname=Summary&prod no=3412.0&issue=2014-15&num=&view, accessed 10/12/2019.
12 See "Immigration in Canada." *The Canadian Encyclopedia* last revision 9/ 19/2017. https://www.thecanadianencyclopedia.ca/en/article/immigration, accessed 10/12/2019.
13 See "Canadian Immigration Acts and Legislation." Canadian Museum of Immigration. https://pier21.ca/research/immigration-history/canadian-immi gration-acts-and-legislation, accessed 10/12/2019.
14 See "As Silicon Valley Eyes Toronto, Some Worry Tech Boom Could Hurt Canada." *The Washington Post* published 9/25/2018. https://www.washing tonpost.com/world/2018/09/25/silicon-valley-eyes-toronto-some-worry-tech-boom-could-hurt-canada/?utm_term=.f1d325ff7302, accessed 10/12/2019.
15 See "Never a Dull Moment When It Comes to Immigration." *Forbes* published 9/26/2019. https://www.forbes.com/sites/andyjsemotiuk/2018/09/26/never-a-dull-moment-when-it-comes-to-immigration/#2db786d459e4, accessed 10/12/ 2019.

REFERENCES

Anderson, Stuart. 2011. "Answering the Critics of Comprehensive Immigration Reform." *Cato Institute Trade Briefing Paper*, no. 32. https://www.cato.org/publications/trade-briefing-paper/answering-critics-comprehensive-immigration-reform, accessed 10/12/2019.

Australian Bureau of Statistics. 2016. "Australia's Population by Country of Birth." http://www.abs.gov.au/ausstats/abs@.nsf/Previousproducts/3412.0Main%20Features32014-15?opendocument&tabname=Summary&prodno=3412.0&issue=2014-15&num=&view, accessed 10/12/2019.

Castles, Stephen, Ellie Vasta, and Derya Ozkul. 2014. "Australia: A Classical Immigration Country in Transition." In James Hollifield, Philip L. Martin, and Pia Orrenius, Editors, *Controlling Immigration: A Global Perspective* (3rd ed.). Palo Alto, CA: Stanford University Press.

Coburn, Tom. 2015. "A Review of the Department of Homeland Security's Missions and Performance." *A Report by Senator Tom Coburn, Ranking Member, Committee on Homeland Security and Governmental Affairs, U.S. Senate, 113th Congress.* https://www.hsgac.senate.gov/imo/media/doc/Senator%20Coburn%20DHS%20Report%20FINAL.pdf

Department of Home Affairs (Australian Government). 192009–2014. "Abolition of the 'White Australia' Policy." http://www.europarl.europa.eu/meetdocs/2009_2014/documents/danz/dv/0220_13_1/0220_13_1en.pdf accessed 10/12/2019.

Doyle, Charles. 2002. "The USA PATRIOT Act: A Legal Analysis." *Congressional Research Service RL 31377.* Washington, DC: Library of Congress. https://fas.org/irp/crs/RL31377.pdf, accessed 10/12/2019.

Hirota, Hideki. 2016. *Expelling the Poor: Atlantic Seaboard States and the Nineteenth-Century Origins of American Immigration Policy.* New York: Oxford University Press.

Hutchinson, Edward P. 1981. *Legislative History of American Immigration Policy 1798–1965.* Philadelphia: University of Pennsylvania Press.

Lee, Erika. 2019. *America for Americans: A History of Xenophobia in the United States.* New York: Basic Books.

Lytle, Kelly. "Constructing the criminal alien: a historical framework for analyzing border vigilantes at the turn of the 21st century." (2003).

Motomura, Hiroshi. Americans in waiting: The lost story of immigration and citizenship in the United States. Oxford University Press, 2006.

Tichenor, Daniel J. 2002. *Dividing Lines: The Politics of Immigration Control in America.* Princeton: Princeton University Press.

Wanlund, Bill. 2014. "Is Immigration Overhaul Stalled? *CQ Researcher.* https://library.cqpress.com/cqresearcher/document.php?id=cqr_ht_immigration_2014&type=hitlist&num=6, accessed 10/12/2019.

Wong, Tom. 2017. *The Politics of Immigration: Partisanship, Demographic Change, and American National Identity.* New York: Oxford University Press.

Zolberg, Aristide. 2008. *A Nation by Design: Immigration Policy in the Fashioning of America.* Cambridge, MA: Harvard University Press.

4

IMMIGRATION POLITICS
Britain and France

Introduction: From Empire to the End of Colonialism

This chapter examines the history of immigration policymaking in Britain and France, particularly since World War II. These country comparisons shed light on how differences in institutional structures and party politics impact policymaking, particularly for a policy area that arouses feelings of nationalism (i.e., nativism) and fear. Both countries had long histories of empire and colonialism which impacted the flow of immigrants as well as the type of citizenship for which they were eligible.

Since World War II, millions of immigrants from developing countries have settled in Western Europe. Immigration and immigrant integration have become some of the most salient political issues in Europe over the last two decades. During the post-war recovery, many European countries began to import temporary labor. These workers initially came from Southern Europe and later from former colonies and other developing countries like Turkey. With the economic slowdown of the early 1970s, most European countries stopped importing labor. However, many of the temporary workers settled permanently, and because of **family reunification** and asylum policies, large flows of immigrants and asylum seekers continued to enter Europe. The settlement of these populations, many from Muslim backgrounds, has led to the development of a variety of policies related to immigrant integration. Not all policies are specifically designed as integration policies, but policies related to welfare, labor markets, and cultural policies, in combination with citizenship laws, have created at least the appearance of a set of European approaches to immigrant integration (Favell 1998; Ireland 2004; Sainsbury 2012).

Policy scholars often distinguish between **border control**[1] and **immigrant integration policy**.[2] Control policy defines who may be admitted and how many may be admitted, enables certain branches of law enforcement to police the border, and defines policies around deportation. Immigrant integration policy describes what rights immigrants have (e.g., to healthcare or for their children to attend school) as well as any obligations they have (e.g., to have a job, learn the language, and civic engagement). It can be hard to see clear differences between integration and control policy or to infer what one entails versus the other. As Sainsbury (2012) noted, "Australia and Canada are often pointed to as countries with strong multicultural policies, but at the same time both countries employ an elaborate point system that excludes many immigrants, especially the poor and the uneducated" (p. 16). Viewed in these terms, in general, Western European countries have adopted steadily more restrictive control policy since the 1970s. More recently, many countries have adopted more assimilationist integration policy (e.g., language requirements) but, because of policy innovation in the U.K. and the Netherlands that was ultimately adopted by the EU, immigrant rights are also much more formal today than they were in years past (Givens and Evans Case 2014).

In contrast to the years following WWII when Britain and France were quite welcome and opening, today these countries are reluctant to receive immigrants. Furthermore, despite the vastly different histories, national myths, cultures of citizenship, and standard operating procedures (Cornelius 2004), similarities in approaches to immigration control policies in these countries is clearly evident (noted by Freeman as early as the 1970s). Do governments have any real choice in how they respond to migration? How much attention should be paid to post-war political discourses (as opposed to other factors like economics)? Many countries in Europe responded to the oil shocks of the early 1970s by breaking from their relatively liberal immigration regimes. The integration questions of the 1980s, asylum problems of the 1990s, and finally the national security concerns of the 2000s further spurred debate and action. Exogenous factors like these are overwhelming; policymakers must go beyond routine updates and change the nature of their goals (Hall 1993).[3]

Unlike in the United States, where migration largely coincided with nation-building efforts, in Europe it came much later. As Foner (2005) concluded in her book *In a New Land*, in the U.S. there has always existed an immigrant myth, a story retold innumerable times over the last century about how the European immigrants came into the U.S. through Ellis Island and made America with their efforts to assimilate and build a new life. This is not to say that migrants played no role in Europe's development in the 19th century or that there was no immigration prior to World War II. The point rather is to emphasize that European nations largely developed a sense of "nationhood" prior to large scale immigration. Europeans have thus generally not included immigration as a process or migrants as individuals in their idea of nationhood. Where large migrant populations did exist, they were perceived as threats to European nation building, and the groups concerned were either expelled or forcibly assimilated through (often brutal) means (Tilly 1978). As such, it has been difficult to approach immigration as just another issue, especially when France and the U.K. have actively sought to eliminate "immigration" from their governance vocabulary from the very beginning. Whereas U.S. immigration has always been an integral component of nation building, for the European countries under analysis, it has at best been intentionally limited to an issue of economic and demographic concern.

Because of its low birth rates, Europe faces a demographic problem. Coleman wrote that after 2025 Europe will be, to put it bluntly, in trouble. "Europe has substantial reserves of employable manpower which exceed any short-term demographic deficiencies; however, their mobilization will require structural readjustments and the effects of enhanced workforce participation to age 65 cannot extend much beyond 2025" (Coleman 2002, p. 367). Freeman also pointed out that "Europeans, having been artificially promoted to nonmanual jobs, are loath to return to less desirable tasks, and owners cannot operate profitably and pay high enough salaries for the most unpleasant positions to attract Europeans to them" (Freeman 1979, p. 153). Ultimately, the demographic problem can only be fixed with actual improvements in the birth rate itself. However, immigration is absolutely necessary in the short-term.

Within the context of broader economic and demographic pressures, individual countries' experiences with immigration and the subsequent settler populations have varied significantly. In the following section, we begin with the case of Britain, followed by France. Each country has different starting points, as described in Chapter 1, and many of the decisions made on immigration policy were driven by politics and the response of politicians and the populace to the nature of the flows from World War II through the 1990s.

Britain

In 1945, when the passenger ship Empire Windrush arrived with immigrants from the Caribbean, a trend began that would influence British demographics and politics for the foreseeable future. As Freeman reported, from 1951 to 1961 the number of non-white persons per 1,000 went from 1.7 to 7.3 (Freeman 1979, p. 45). As a result of colonial migrations flows, immigrants to Britain come primarily from India, Pakistan, Bangladesh, and the Caribbean. As described in Chapter 2, the British colonial period was marked by a strong paternalism toward the colonized. **Decolonization**, that is, the withdrawal of a colonial power from a country when it gains independence, accelerated after WWII, and the need for labor on the British mainland led to expansive policies toward labor migration from the former colonies, referred to as the **Commonwealth**. However, as Freeman (1979) noted, "[t]he most important aspects of the political landscape on which immigration and race emerged were linked to the colonial heritage" (p. 47).

Britain's colonial past has had an obvious impact on immigration and citizenship policy. What becomes clear in any study is the extent to which Great Britain lacked a coherent citizenship policy until it was forced to decide on one by the influx of Commonwealth immigrants after World War II. Although today Britain is often grouped with countries that have espoused multicultural approaches to immigration (or at least one would assume so by the numerous "Multiculturalism Fails in Britain" headlines following the London terrorist bombings in July 2005), a careful review of immigration policies reveals that often policies were motivated by concern about the racial makeup of Commonwealth immigrants.

Green (2007) pointed out that between the 1950s and 1970s, the Commonwealth nations provided a majority of immigrants to Britain. With the enlargement of the European Union (EU) in 2004 to the Eastern and Central European countries, immigration to Britain has diversified. The wars in the Balkans in the 1990s also brought in a number of asylum seekers. In 2004, the inflow of migrants per 1,000 inhabitants stood at 8.3, up from 3.9 in 1995. Of those immigrants arriving in 2004, 37.8 per cent came because of the family reunification policy or because they were accompanying family members (Organisation for Economic Co-operation and Development 2006).

Joppke (1999) argued that "[t]he logic of British immigration policy is thus determined by the devolution of empire. Immigration policy has essentially been about restricting the entry and settlement of the former subjects of empire... Accordingly, the peculiarity of British immigration policy is that it is directed not against aliens, but against former co-nationals" (p. 100). When outlining the usual pattern in migratory recruitment, Zolberg (2008) noted that "importing" countries first tap into neighboring labor pools, such as the Bretons in France and the Irish in Britain in the 19th century, and only then expand into the more distant pools. The case of British immigration following the WWII is one where the "neighboring" pools were geographically distant lands of the former (or still in some cases constituted a part of) the British Empire and were thus geopolitically convenient. This geopolitical convenience, however, soon became a social problem, as many Commonwealth immigrants were not white.

On the political front, it was clearly the right that was in favor of more control of immigration, whereas it was only under Labour governments that **race relations** legislation was passed. Freeman (1979) argued that the Conservative party went against its own interests in supporting control legislation; however, it is clear that anti-immigrant elements of the party were able to hold sway in the passage of legislation.

As race and color became a part of the public consciousness, immigration increasingly became a subject of public and political debate. As the numbers of ethnic minority immigrants rose, the balance shifted between those who favored an inclusive policy toward members of the Commonwealth and colonies, and those who argued for restrictions (Bleich 2003, p. 39) The electorate began to put more pressure on mainstream politicians to halt the influx of immigrants (Money 1999). Therefore, unlike in France and where the 1970s oil shocks were the main catalyst, the issue of restricting or somehow curbing immigration became part of the political agenda much sooner in Britain, mainly due to race, which is clearly delineated by Freeman (1979).

During this time period, fear of a clampdown generated a surge of ethnic minority immigrants, as individuals from the Commonwealth and colonies rushed to Britain to "beat the ban" announced by the Conservative government in 1961. New Commonwealth immigration rates in 1960 were 57,700 and increased in 1961 to 134,600. During the first six months of 1962 the number was 94,900 (Layton-Henry 1992, p. 13). During the Queen's Speech on October 31, 1961, the Conservative government introduced legislation "to control the immigration to the United Kingdom of British subjects from other parts of the Commonwealth."[5] The Labour Party resisted the Commonwealth Immigrants Act (CIA) saying that the bill was embodying pure race restrictions not only because it came in response to public statements about preserving British "whiteness" but also because it exempted the Irish from immigration control (even though hundreds of thousands of them were entering during the same era) (Bleich 2003, p. 45).

The 1962 Commonwealth Immigrants Act was a response to the serious outbreaks of racial violence, passed by the Conservative government of Harold Macmillan. This law was used to reverse the privilege of Commonwealth subjects to enter Britain and become citizens. A voucher system replaced this privilege with the intent of slowing non-white immigration (Freeman 1979). Joppke argued that it was essentially a labor-market measure, "but one that made no sense in the context of a full employment economy" (Joppke 1999, p. 108). Ultimately, as Joppke concluded, the wording of the bill was definitely not racist, but its effect, most definitely intended, was. Immigration from ethnic minorities into the U.K. dropped dramatically after this. But there was a second influx after initial immigrants settled in Britain and began to bring over their families. This stream of family reunification was not stringently controlled by state policies.

Both Freeman (1979) and Joppke (1999) described the 1968 **Africanization policy** in Kenya as the main development that led to more restrictions on immigration in the late 1960s. Fearing an influx of Asian refugees fleeing Kenya's Africanization, the Labour government rushed a bill through Parliament in just three days withholding the entry rights of all emigrants who had personal connections to the United Kingdom either by birthplace, parents, or grandparents. Even though Labour had argued forcefully against the 1962 Act, it went even further with blatant racialization of immigration policy. It allowed the country to refuse to accept 200,000 of its own East Asian citizens. The new immigration controls, based on parentage, were argued to be, according to Home Secretary Callaghan, "geographical, not racial" (Joppke 1999, p. 109). However, as Joppke argued, "racial disharmony" was most definitely the cause of the 1968 Act.

On April 20, 1968, Enoch Powell (a member of the Conservative shadow cabinet) pronounced his famous "rivers of blood" speech in Birmingham in which he articulated in inflammatory rhetoric a doomsday scenario for Britain's multiracial future. He believed that the Commonwealth immigrants would not integrate into British society and that the Race Relations Bill would entrench this problem (Bleich 2003, p. 74). Despite the positive response Powell's speech received in some quarters, the Labour government continued to pursue measures to help immigrant communities. In 1969 the Local Government Grants (Social Need) Act was passed. This measure was designed to fulfill Prime Minister Harold Wilson's promise to aid communities with ethnic minority immigrants (Young 1983).

The election of 1970 saw the Labour Party lose control of government. The Conservative government of Edward Heath was elected in some part due to its promise to bolster controls on Commonwealth immigration. The result was the **Immigration Act of 1971**, with a new category of "patrials" (i.e., persons allowed free entry into the U.K. whose parent or one grandparent was born in the United Kingdom), thus restricting the entry of persons from the "new" Commonwealth. The Labour Party opposed the act and reaffirmed that while controlling immigration on the basis of labor demand was sound, doing so on the basis of race was unacceptable. Joppke (1999) argued that the act was crucial in that it

> was the first immigration act to deal jointly with aliens and Commonwealth citizens, and it thus completed the development of assimilating Commonwealth citizens to aliens, already the rationale of previous legislation. This included the replacement of employment vouchers by the more rigid work-permit requirement already in place for aliens, greater deportation powers of the state, and a rockier transition path from temporary to permanent settlement.
>
> (p. 111)

He went on to state that the principle of patriality[4] was introduced and built on the 1968 concept of substantive connection, which had been introduced by Labour. The Act still clung to the colonial idea of citizens "with and without the right to enter, rather than drawing this line between aliens and citizens as is 'normally' the case" (Joppke 1999, p. 111). This was a ludicrous conception to be hanging on to, since a citizen of a country, by definition, has the right to enter his or her own state.

Freeman argued that the Labour Party was caught between a rock and a hard place, "between the dictates of its conscience, ideology, and militants, and the imperatives of a winning electoral strategy" (Freeman 1979, p. 158). Being a working-class party, it could not ignore the xeno-phobic and racist inclinations of its constituents if it were to win elections, while at the same time its roots were in the workers' movement grounded in theories of worldwide solidarity. Freeman concludes that it is unclear whether acquiescence in a racially restrictive immigration regime helped it any at the polling stations, after all they did lose the 1971 election to the Conservatives, but what is clear is that this acquiescence "seriously dam-aged the leadership's standing among the 'Labor Left'" (Freeman 1979, p. 158). Joppke similarly argued that in Britain, the Labour Party quite often fell under the sway of illiberal opinion.

Following the Act of 1971, which essentially barred groups from entering Britain altogether, Britain was faced with the issue of family reunions. Unlike France, however, the system of "entry clearance allowed the drama of denied family reunion to be conveniently displaced overseas… far away from the controlling sight of liberal opinion." (Joppke 1999, p. 114) Therefore, Britain was much harsher towards family reunions than either of the other two countries. It became notoriously difficult, for example, for husbands and fiancés to enter. In 1974 the Labour government did allow a concession to the husbands, only to revoke it in 1977 and to see the Conservatives, under Thatcher, campaign on the very issue (Joppke 1999, p. 120).

The Labour government of James Callaghan proposed creating new sub-sets of citizenship in a 1977 Green Paper, an idea that was ultimately adopted by the Tories as the **British Nationality Act (BNA) of 1981**. This act created new sub-sets of citizenship: British Citizenship, the British Dependent Territories Citizenship, and British Overseas Citizenship. Fur-thermore, both *jus soli* (birthright citizenship) and British Citizenship based on Commonwealth patrials was phased out. Joppke (1999) argued that the abolition of *jus soli* was primarily done because parents whose child was a British citizen would be more difficult to deport.

The new Conservative government essentially barred foreign husbands and fiancés from settlement in Britain with a 1980 law (a law that was both racist and sexist, since it assumed that the proper place of residence for a woman was with the husband, not the other way around), but also created a loophole for women born or with a grandparent or parent born in the U.K. (to prevent white Anglo women from having their foreign husbands not allowed into the U.K.) (Joppke 1999, p. 121).

Such a strict rule was soon brought before the European Commission on Human Rights and in a White Paper of October 1982 the government decided that all British citizens would be allowed to join their spouses. The Court found in 1985 that the 1980 law was discriminatory on the ground of sex. However, the Court did allow Britain to protect the inflow of immigrants, just not based on sex. The British government then turned the ruling into its favor, by making both reuniting the husbands and wives with their spouses in Britain more difficult, essentially using the European Court ruling to create an even tougher standard that was still racist in intent (since the European Court did not deem that part of the law illegal).

The Conservative government passed the Immigration Act of 1988 that removed Section 1(5) in order to incorporate full sex equality. This change was in large part motivated by the European Court ruling of 1985 mentioned above. The Section 1(5) had enshrined the family rights of settled immigrant men. They now had to prove that they could maintain and accommodate their families. However, the new act had a strange effect of making it more difficult for a British man to bring his American wife into Britain than a Frenchman to bring his. The 1988 Immigration Act had the effect of making it much easier to reject applications on the basis of primary purpose; that is, essentially, the primary purpose of the marriage was indeed to emigrate, giving immigration officers incredible power to measure the intent of one's application. "The primary-purpose rule puts applicants into a catch-22 situation because the very application can be taken as evidence that the principal reason of the marriage is immigration to Britain" (Joppke 1999, p. 126). British law on family reunion was thus in the early 1990s quite sub-par in terms of normative liberal standards when compared with the rest of the EU. A British citizen had more protections under the EU cannon than under British law.

Ultimately, British immigration policy can be elucidated as racially motivated for the longest period of the post-World War II era, at least until the 1997 Labour Party win. On one hand, a number of anti-discrimination acts were pushed through, under the category of "race relations," but on the other, immigration policy was expressly designed to curb non-white migration. A possible explanation for such outward and blatant racist policy could be the lack of any real negative race issue during WWII. Unlike Germany and (Vichy) France, the U.K. was not involved in mass expulsions of Jews to concentration camps. Both in Germany and in France, the experiences of anti-Semitic governments have left a powerful impact on how foreigners and migrants are treated. Furthermore, more of Britain's post-WWII immigrants were non-white due to the racial composition of the colonies. These two factors combined to create what was the most outwardly racist immigration policy of our three cases. The British government attempted to allay its racist immigration policy by being proactive on the side of improving "race relations" within the U.K. In fact, limiting the number of non-white people who entered the U.K. became a crucial element in improving these "race relations."

French Immigration Policy after World War II

France is a country that has had a long history of immigration, both from its colonies and other parts of Europe. During the period of industrialization in the late 1800s and early 1900s, France not only had to rely on workers from rural areas, but also foreign labor. For example, Clifford Rosenberg (2006) pointed out that "France, however, was the only country – indeed it was the first in the world – to create substantial assistance programs and, at the same time, to resort to massive foreign immigration to satisfy its labor needs" (p. 4). Rosenberg goes on to argue that it was the need to differentiate nationals who were eligible for assistance, from non-nationals who were not, that led to many of the policies during the inter-war period. The record keeping that was developed fed into the Nazi extermination of Jews in France. It is partially this history that led post-war France to reject categorization of immigrants, while ignoring discrimination.

During the French *Trente Annees Glorieuses* (**Thirty Glorious Years**) France needed migrant labor to fuel its growing industry. The *Office National de l'Immigration* (ONI – **National Immigration Office**) was created to recruit foreign labor. As Dominique Schnapper, Pascale Krief, and Emmanuel Peignard argued, immigration policy was considerably liberal: "any foreigner, whether he had a legal or illegal status, or even if he had entered the country with no more than a tourist visa, was to be accepted and regularized by the government if a company would employ him" (Schnapper et al. 2003, p. 19). In 1968 only 18 per cent of employed foreigners had applied with the National Immigration Office branch in their own country.

Freeman argued that immigration policy was largely a failure in meeting the needs of the labor market and that by 1968 the government had to allow illegal immigration in order to satisfy labor demands. This led to a public backlash, and in 1972 efforts were made to restrict non-European immigration and to deal with illegal population. These efforts ultimately concluded with serious resistance on the part of foreign workers, unions and opposition parties. "In September [1972] a serious outbreak of racial violence in France led the Algerian government to suspend any further emigration of its citizens to France for the remainder of the year" (Freeman 1979, p. 156).

French governments of the 1960s and early 1970s were "unable or unwilling to resist the pressures from labor-hungry employers and governments of developing countries to keep the migratory taps flowing" (Blatt 1996, p. 77). During the *Trente Annees Glorieuses*, the foreign population steadily increased from 1.75 million to 3.4 million. Most of the migrants came at first from rural areas of Spain and Algeria and were predominantly male. From the mid-1960s onward there was also a high number of Portuguese immigrants compared with those from other countries, even larger than the number of workers from Spain and Algeria. "In 1975, there were 498,000 Spanish, 710,690 Algerian and 759,000 Portuguese persons in France" (Schnapper et al. 2003, p. 20). After the oil shocks of the early 1970s, French immigration policy has subsequently dealt mainly with family reunifications and asylum seekers, finally culminating in concerns about integration and security post 9/11.

This reassertion of government control over immigration began with the center-right government of Valery Giscard d'Estaing, who created a cabinet-level Secretary of State for Immigration and in July 1974, "temporarily" suspended all immigration to the country until matters could be brought under control. Paul Dijoud was the first of Secretary of State (or Vice Minister) for foreign workers in France. Dijoud focused on the following two aims: "stopping all new immigration, even family immigration, and improving the social situation of the established immigrant population" (Verbunt 1985, p. 137). Giscard also issued a 25-point plan in October 1975 on how to improve living conditions of foreigners. This was followed by a voluntary repatriation plan as the economy remained in recession.

Hargreaves (1995), however, argued that by the late 1960s the government was already becoming worried about the "ethnic composition" of the migrant population and that the roots of the 1970s reassertion of control therefore were not purely economic. Hargreaves also pointed out that with a legal challenge before the *Conseil d'Etat* in the mid-1970s, the executive's ability to regulate immigration with executive orders was challenged and declared to be illegal, "forcing the government to amend the measures and/or submit them to Parliament in the form of draft legislation open to analysis and argument from all sides of the political spectrum" (Hargreaves 1995, p. 180). Hargreaves offered many examples from the early 1980s where the politicization of immigration often descended into a competition over who could be "tougher" on immigrants, regardless of party lines (Hargreaves 1995, p. 182).

Hargreaves argued that the mainstream parties agreed on three points: that immigration should be forcefully curtailed, that immigrants should be encouraged and supported to return, and that the immigrants already in France should be assisted in their efforts to assimilate into French society. The truce was accomplished as the Right withdrew its policy of mass repatriation while the left wing dropped its "flirtation with multiculturalism" (Hargreaves 1995, p. 188).

Miller, however, largely offers a different view, arguing that the left wing in France, and especially its civil society branches, was much more pro-immigrant, therefore indicating a higher level of contestation between political parties. Miller asserted that the government wanted to regain control over immigration from the employers already in the mid-1960s under Prime Minister Pompidou during the de Gaulle Presidency. In 1966 the Directory for Population and Migrations was created within a new ministry that combined those of labor, public health, and population. Miller argued that "the guiding idea behind immigration policy modifications at this juncture was to assert governmental control through compliance with the law instead of further acquiescence to a de facto reversion to employer monopoly over foreign worker recruitment" (Miller 1981, p. 14). Miller found that one of the main reasons behind this effort was government desire to curb legalizations of workers. Therefore, prior to 1968, a watershed year for so many policies in France, government employed a laissez-faire approach towards immigration, due to the needs of business.

The soaring social costs of so much illegal immigration was one of the reasons for restricting legalization (Miller 1981). The government wanted to shift the burden of social costs on the employer. Therefore, as early as 1967, the French government was looking for ways to curb immigration, while at the same time improving the living conditions for the immigrants already in France (Miller 1981). Miller, unlike Hargreaves, does not refer to the ethnic composition of migrants as a reason for curbing migration.

Miller argued that the first important development for controlling immigration was the so-called Fontanet Directive – initiated by the then Minister of Labor Joseph Fontanet, under Prime Minister Pompidou and President de Gaulle.

> On February 23, 1972, the French government further restricted access to legalization. A governmental directive known as the *circulaire Fontanet* closed legalization to all but skilled laborers. Furthermore, in order to provide social protection for immigrants as well as to restore governmental control, the *circulaire Fontanet* made the legislation procedure far more complex than had heretofore been the case.
>
> (Miller 1981, pp. 14–15)

The Employment Agency was required to try to find a French worker within a three-week period before a foreigner could be recruited for the employer.

Fontanet's successor was Georges Gorse. During his tenure as the Minister of Labor, in 1974, under the Presidency of Pompidou and the right wing Prime Ministership of Pierre Messmer and Jacques Chirac, the recruitment of all non-seasonal foreign workers stopped. However, in the mid-1970s numbers of refugees and asylum seekers began to swell. "Indeed, refugees accounted for 45, 58, and 69 per cent, respectively, of all aliens admitted through the legalization procedure in 1976, 1977, and 1978" (Miller 1981, p. 17). Refugees from the civil war in Lebanon were particularly numerous because most shared linguistic affinity with France.

Regarding the position towards immigrants of the non-governmental sector, Freeman points out how both the Communist party dominated CGT and the socialist dominated CFDT alternated in their views towards immigration, from initial support for controls to an approach favoring ameliorating the situation of immigrants already in France. The two federations have often worked together to address the issue of immigration, signing joint accords and communiqués in 1966 and 1971. Freeman noted how the unions have adopted typical class arguments in dealing with the issue of immigration. He continues to explain their position in the late 1970s:

> The basic premise of the unions with regard to immigration regulation is that a failure of planning and adequate controls has caused present French policy to be extremely exploitative. Only a carefully planned policy which guarantees each worker a job, adequate housing, and equal working conditions can ensure that migrants will not be used to weaken the position of indigenous workers. Toward that end, both confederations endorse the principle of restoring the National Immigration Office to its monopoly over-all immigration into France (Freeman 1979, p. 160).

Of particular importance to the immigration policy of France was the 1980s garment workers crisis. In 1980, the presidential election of 1981 was on everyone's mind. By the 1980s the repatriation scheme initiated by the government in 1975 had clearly failed. On February 8, 1980 a television program aired a documentary titled "French Confection" and shed light on the horrible working conditions of tens of thousands of illegally employed aliens, predominantly Yugoslav and Turkish. Hunger strikes by the employees of the garment industry were followed by support from the Catholic Church and the Unions (in particular the CFDT). Even the Turkish ambassador to France got involved. Miller argued that the "disagreements over immigration policy [within the neo-Gaullist wing of the governing coalition] contributed to the disharmony within the majority that enabled the French left to win the presidential election and subsequent legislative elections of 1981" (Miller 1981, p. 19). Francois Mitterrand used the immigration issue in his campaigns, especially focusing on the horrible conditions under which illegal aliens lived and worked. The Socialist government voted in after Mitterrand was elected President placed an immediate stop on all deportations, save for those that had to deal with threats to national security. The government also convened an Immigrants National Commission that endorsed a legalization policy in May of 1981. The newly created Ministry of Social Affairs and National Solidarity took over the responsibility for implementation of policy toward immigrants. Miller (2002) recounted as follows:

> A government *circulaire* of July 6, 1981, formally ordered the cessation of deportations... An interministry *circulaire* of August 11, 1981, laid out the criteria for legalization. To be eligible, an alien had to have arrived in France before January 1, 1981 and have stable employment. Proof of residency prior to the cutoff date could be based on entry stamps on valid passports; social security documents;

rent, gas or electricity receipts; wage slips or correspondence. Proof of
stable employment included possession of a work contract valid for
a minimum of one year or its equivalent. (p. 23)

These conditions were further loosened on October 22, 1981, permitting
even aliens with false papers to apply.

Family reunion also became a crucial factor in French immigration
policy. A *circulaire* by the Ministry of the Interior offered a window
between February 1, 1989 and February 1, 1990 for the spouses of French
citizens to legalize their status. They had to have been married for longer
than a year. Parents of French citizens were also allowed to legalize their
status, if they could prove that they still contributed to the support of their
children and could establish residency of over one year in France. The law
of August 24, 1993 introduced the right to family reunion (*regroupement
familial*). Between 1982 and 1990, "approximately 100,000 immigrants
continued to arrive" despite the supposed stop on immigration. "This was
mainly due to family reunion from Morocco and Tunisia, as well as both
family reunion and the arrival of refugees from Africa and South-East Asia.
According to the INSEE census (National Institute of Statistics) carried out
in 1999, 4,310,000 people living in France (7.4 per cent of the population)
were immigrants and 3,260,000 (5.6 per cent of the population) were foreigners" (Schnapper et al. 2003, p. 20).

Civil society played an important role in France in liberalizing immigration
policy. In the 1990s, for example, there were repeated calls for legalization of
asylum seekers. Schnapper et al. (2003) highlight the role that the civil society
plays in legalizations arguing that the illegal immigrants "can appeal to
a French sense of justice and fairness, a humanitarian tradition and class or
religiously inspired solidarity" (p. 31). Therefore, "[e]very child has the right
to an education, even if his/her parents are illegal immigrants (according to
laws passed on July 11, 1975, July 10, 1989, as well as ordinance of the *Conseil d'Etat* issued on November 11, 1989)" (Schnapper et al. 2003, p. 24).
The French model of integration does have quantifiable effects on society.
Schnapper et al. go on to state that, "school results achieved by children of
immigrants and autochthonous pupils from the same socio-economic backgrounds are similar" (Schnapper et al. 2003, p. 24).

After the 1993 elections in France, the Rally for the Republic (RPR) and
French Democratic Union (UDF) coalition was swift to implement policy
change. Prime Minister Balladur's government's first legislation introduced
to the Parliament was the reform of citizenship law, as well as two other
pieces of legislation "providing for tougher immigration controls and more
wide-spread identity checks by police" (Hargreaves 1995, p. 173). This legislation was similar to legislation proposed by the Chirac government in 1986.
Because of opposition from a variety of groups, the 1986 bill was tabled,
however Chirac called for a special commission of *sages* (i.e., wise men) to

review the *Code de la Nationalité Francaise* (CNF – French Code of Nationality). The recommendations of this commission would form the core of the legislation introduced by the Right when they returned to power in 1993. The legislation introduced by the Balladur government made it no longer automatic for children of parents born in France to become citizens. As described above, citizenship would have to be requested between the ages of 16 and 21. This process required that the youth go in front of a judge or administrative authority to request citizenship and prove that she has resided in France for the preceding five years. Other provisions added criminal offenses that could cause the denial of citizenship. Although this could be considered a mere symbolic change, it does add another step to a process that had been automatic.

Immigration politics were impacted in the 1980s by the rise of the radical right *Front National* (FN) led by Jean-Marie Le Pen. The FN had an electoral breakthrough in 1983 elections in the town of Dreux, which was followed by success in European Parliament elections. At the legislative level, the FN has won as much as 15 per cent of the vote in the 1997 election but was only able to win one seat in the French Assembly. As Givens (2005) has argued, the unwillingness of the French mainstream right to coordinate with the FN made it difficult for the party to win seats. However, this did not mean that the mainstream right ignored the issues raised by the FN.

When the French right was campaigning for both the 1986 and 1993 elections, they took on an anti-immigrant stance to take away the issue from the extreme-right FN. The center right in France not only incorporated the rhetoric of the FN, but in relation to citizenship policy they also pursued legislation to make naturalization less automatic (one of the FN's demands). In his analysis of immigration policy in France, Hargreaves (1995) argued that the change in French citizenship law in 1993

> was designed to appeal to the sizeable minority among the electorate which was tempted by the more exclusionary arguments of the FN. Had it not been for the rise of the FN in the mid-1980s and the threat this posed to the electoral base of the RPR and UDF, it is doubtful whether the traditional centre-right parties would have implemented or even proposed the changes which have now been made in the CNF [Code de la Nationalité Française].
>
> (Hargreaves 1995, p. 176)

However, the FN also played a role when the RPR/UDF government was unable to change policy:

> Anxious to staunch the loss of their supporters to the FN, the traditional centre-right parties hardened their policy platform on immigration and related issues. After gaining a narrow election victory

> in March 1986, they formed a government ... who announced
> that the government would introduce legislation ending the auto-
> matic acquisition of French nationality by people of foreign origin
> (Hargreaves 1995, p. 169).

Hargreaves also noted that "Wayland (1993) has underlined the important differences in the political opportunity structure prevailing at the
time of the Chirac and Balladur governments as well as differences in
resource mobilization by those opposed to the reform" (Hargreaves 1995,
p. 175). In 1986, Chirac had to pull back his reform, since his government only had a slim majority in Parliament and opposition to the change
was fierce. In 1993, Balladur had a landslide majority and the anti-racist
movement was on the decline. Thus, the political opportunity structure
was such that policy change was possible in 1993.

The role of the extreme right parties should not be underestimated, as compared with public opinion. Hargreaves reported that the French public, while
"feeling that 'something needs to be done' about immigration" (Hargreaves
1995, p. 175), did not show strong support for tougher naturalization laws.
He noted that "when asked specifically if children born to immigrants should
automatically acquire French citizenship on reaching the age of majority,
those in favour of retaining this provision have generally outnumbered those
against by two to one" (Hargreaves 1995, p. 174). It appears that in the case
of French policy, the presence of the extreme right played a greater role than
public opinion did in the government's decision to change policy.

French policy into the 21st century focused more on issues related to
Muslim immigrants and terrorism. Debates around what it meant to be
French came to the fore under the presidency of Nicolas Sarkozy. Violent
protests in the suburbs, in response to police brutality and the deaths of
young men of migrant background, also impacted political debates.
Nationalism collided with terrorism by Muslim extremists in 2015, with
a devastating attack in Paris in November of 2015 that resulted in the
deaths of 130 people. As noted by historian Peter Gatrell, "[i]t came
hard on the heels of January 2015 when terrorists stormed the Paris
offices of the French satirical magazine *Charlie Hebdo*, killing twelve
people, many of them cartoonists, and injuring eleven others" (Gatrell
2019, p. 363). These attacks would lead to even more resistance to
admitting asylum seekers from Muslim countries, and more support for
radical right politicians, like Marine Le Pen, as we discuss in Chapter 6.

Conclusion

French immigration control policy has been largely driven by political
concerns, including the rise of the extreme right and anti-immigrant sentiment. Immigration flowed fairly freely until the 1970s labor importation

stop, and afterward policies became more restrictive, in terms of both immigration control and citizenship. Much of this was a response to the rise of the National Front and the racist rhetoric utilized by their leader, Le Pen, but little of this discourse was utilized by the mainstream parties. In the 21st century, both France and Britain had to face concerns about Muslim "home grown" terrorists that were not necessarily related to immigration but led to calls for more immigration control.

In Britain, political elites would become more focused on their place in the EU and the impact of intra-EU migration, particularly from Eastern Europe. Internal and external migration would remain high on the agenda as parties competed to be tough on immigration, with support for nationalist parties increasing in European Parliament elections. We discuss these developments in British and French immigration politics in Chapter 6.

KEY TERMS

Africanization Policy In 1964, the government of Kenya adopted an "Africanization" or "Kenyanization," plan to replace non-citizens, particularly Asians, with citizens in key areas of the economy. Many of those who lost their jobs sought to gain entry to Britain. As noted in an article from the *New York Times*, "[w]hen Kenya became independent of Britain in 1963, the Asians chose British citizenship in the belief that they would always find a haven in Britain. In the meantime, Kenya's Africanization policy, aimed at giving Africans priority in jobs, has resulted in mass unemployment for Asians." See https://www.nytimes.com/1971/04/11/archives/britain-is-target-of-kenyan-asians-immigration-restriction-on.html.

Border Control Policy Control policy defines who may be admitted and how many may be admitted, enables certain branches of law enforcement to police the border, and defines policies around deportation.

British Immigration Act of 1971 and Patrials The Immigration Act of 1971 created a new category of "patrials" (i.e., persons allowed free entry into the U.K. whose parent or one grandparent was born in the United Kingdom), thus restricting the entry of persons from former colonies of the "New" Commonwealth.

British Nationality Act (BNA) of 1981 This Act created new sub-sets of citizenship: British Citizenship, the British Dependent Territories Citizenship (BDTC), and British Overseas Citizenship (BOC). Furthermore, both *jus soli* (birthright citizenship) and British Citizenship based on Commonwealth patrials were phased out.

Circulaire Fontanet In the early 1970s, France sought to limit illegal and unskilled immigration. The *circulaire Fontanet* closed legalization to all but skilled laborers. The legislation also made the legalization procedure far more complex.

Code de la Nationalité Francaise **(CNF – French Code of Nationality)** This refers to the French citizenship laws. These laws have changed regularly over time in response to immigration flows from former colonies and other countries.

Commonwealth "The Commonwealth" website states that "[t]he Commonwealth is one of the world's oldest political association of states. Its roots go back to the British Empire when some countries were ruled directly or indirectly by Britain. Some of these countries became self-governing while retaining Britain's monarch as head of state. They formed the British Commonwealth of Nations. See http://the commonwealth.org/our-history.

1962 Commonwealth Immigrants Act This law was used to reverse the privilege of Commonwealth subjects to enter Britain and become citizens. A voucher system replaced this privilege with the intent of slowing non-white immigration. See http://www.nationalarchives.gov.uk/cabinet papers/themes/commonwealth-immigration-control-legislation.htm.

Decolonization Colonialism is a process whereby a nation establishes and maintains governance over overseas territories. Decolonization is the process by which those colonies gain independence, either through peaceful means or via native rebellion. See "The Map as History," https://www.the-map-as-history.com/Decolonization-after-1945.

Family Reunification A series of judicial rulings allowed immigrants to bring their families to join them in the countries where they had settled. This meant that the flow of migrants continued even after countries in Europe stopped the importation of labor in the early 1970s.

Immigrant Integration Policy Immigrant integration policy describes what rights immigrants have (e.g., to healthcare or for their children to attend school) and any obligations they have (e.g., to have a job, learn the language, and civic engagement).

National Immigration Office Known by the acronym ONI in France, this office was created to manage the importation of migrant workers after World War II.

Race Relations Race relations policy in Britain began with the 1965 Race Relations Act. "The Race Relations Act of 1965 aimed to prevent racial discrimination. However, it was a weak piece of legislation and only spoke of discrimination in specified 'places of public resort,' such as hotels and restaurants, as being illegal... The Race Relations Act 1968 was intended as a counterpart to the Immigration Act of the same year. While the Immigration Act sought to limit immigration, the Race Relations Act was aimed at enabling the more effective 'integration' of immigrant communities. Provisions were extended to cover housing and employment; the Race Relations Board was expanded and the Community Relations Committee was created to combat discrimination and prejudice through education." See http://

www.nationalarchives.gov.uk/cabinetpapers/themes/discrimination-race-relations-policy.htm.

Trente Annees Glorieuses **(Thirty Glorious Years)** This refers to the 30 years of strong economic growth in France after World War II. The period lasted from 1945 to 1975. Much of the growth was driven by industrialization and the importation of migrant labor.

NOTES

1 "Border control" policy is often just called "control" for short. It is also sometimes known simply as "immigration policy."
2 Sometimes called "immigrant policy."
3 That is, policymakers must adopt what Peter Hall has called the "third order of change" (Hall 1993, p. 280).
4 In Britain (formerly) a person with a right by statute to live in the United Kingdom, who is not subject to immigration control.
5 See "The Queen's Speech." *Hansard* published October 31, 1961. https://api. parliament.uk/historic-hansard/lords/1961/oct/31/the-queens-speech, accessed 10/12/2019.

REFERENCES

References marked with an asterisk are sources that can be used for further research and information

Blatt, David Stuart. 1996. "Immigration Politics and Immigrant Collective Action in France, 1968-1993." PhD Dissertation, Government Department, Cornell University, Ithaca, New York.

Bleich, Eric. 2003. *Race Politics in Britain and France: Ideas and Policymaking Since the 1960s.* Cambridge, UK: Cambridge University Press.

Calavita, Kitty. 1998. "Immigration, Law, and Marginalization in a Global Economy: Notes from Spain." *Law & Society Review* 32(3): 529.

Coleman, David A. 2002. "Populations of the Industrial World – A Convergent Demographic Community?" *Population, Space and Place* 8(5): 319–344.

Cornelius, Wayne A. 2004. "Spain: The Uneasy Transition from Labor Exporter to Labor Importer." In Wayne A. Cornelius, Takeyuki Tsuda, Philip L. Martin, and James F. Hollifield, Editors, *Controlling Immigration: A Global Perspective* (2nd ed.). Palo Alto, CA: Stanford University Press.

Favell, Adrian. 1998. *Philosophies of Integration.* London: MacMillan.

Foner, Nancy. 2005. *In a New Land.* New York: NYU Press.

Freeman, Gary P. 1979. *Immigrant Labor and Racial Conflict in Industrial Societies: The French and British Experience, 1945–1975.* Princeton, NJ: Princeton University Press.

Gatrell, Peter. 2019. *The Unsettling of Europe: How Immigration Reshaped a Continent.* New York: Basic Books.

Givens, Terri. 2005. *Voting Radical Right in Western Europe.* New York: Cambridge University Press.

Givens, Terri and Rhonda Evans Case. 2014. *Legislating Equality: The Politics of Antidiscrimination Policy in Europe*. London: Oxford University Press.

Hall, Peter. 1993. "Policy Paradigms, Social Learning, and the State: The Case of Economic Policymaking in Britain." *Comparative Politics* 25(3): 275–296.

Hargreaves, Alec G. 1995. *Immigration, 'Race' and Ethnicity in Contemporary France*. London: Routledge.

Hollifield, James F., Philip L. Martin, and Pia M. Orrenius, Editors. 2014. *Controlling Immigration: A Global Perspective* (3rd ed.). Palo Alto, CA: Stanford University Press.

Ireland, Patrick. 2004. *Becoming Europe: Immigration, Integration, and the Welfare State*. Pittsburgh: University of Pittsburgh Press.

Joppke, Christian. 1999. *Immigration and the Nation-State*. New York: Oxford University Press.

Layton-Henry, Zig. 1992. *The Politics of Immigration: Race and Race Relations in Postwar Britain*. London: Wiley-Blackwell.

Levinson, Amanda. 2005. *The Regularisation of Unauthorized Migrants: Literature Survey and Case Studies*. Oxford, UK: University of Oxford, Centre on Migration, Policy and Society.

Miller, Mark J. 1981. *Foreign Workers in Western Europe: An Emerging Political Force*. Santa Barbara, CA: Praeger.

Miller, Mark J. 2002. "Continuity and Change in Postwar French Legalization Policy." In Anthony M. Messina, Editor, *West European Immigration and Immigrant Policy in the New Century*. Santa Barbara, CA: Praeger.

Money, Jeannette. 1999. "Defining Immigration Policy: Inventory, Quantitative Referents, and Empirical Regularities." Paper presented at the Annual Meeting of the American Political Science Association, Atlanta, GA, September 2–5.

Organisation for Economic Co-operation and Development. 2006. *International Migration Outlook*. Paris: SOPEMI.

Perlmutter, Ted. 2014. "Italy." In James F. Hollifield, Philip L. Martin, and Pia M. Orrenius, Editors, *Controlling Immigration: A Global Perspective*. Palo Alto, CA: Stanford University Press.

Sainsbury, Diane. 2012. *Welfare States and Immigrant Rights: The Politics of Inclusion and Exclusion*. New York: Oxford University Press.

Schnapper, Dominique, Pascale Krief, and Emmanuel Peignard. 2003. "French Immigration and Integration Policy. A Complex Combination." In Friedrich Heckman and Dominique Schnapper, Editors, *The Integration of Immigrants in European Societies*. Stuttgart, Germany: Lucius and Lucius.

Tilly, Charles. 1978. *From Mobilization to Revolution*. New York: Longman Higher Education.

Verbunt, Gilles. 1985. *European Immigration Policy: A Comparative Study*. Cambridge, UK: Cambridge University Press.

Young, C. 1983. "The Temple of Ethnicity." *World Politics* 35(4): 652–662.

5

IMMIGRATION POLITICS
Germany and Newer Countries of Immigration

Introduction

As noted in Chapter 4, the aftermath of World War II led to immigration from former colonies to France and Britain. For other countries that did not have the same kind of colonial ties, the first flows after the war came from other parts of Europe, but as countries like Germany began to recover from the war, they reached out to other countries like Turkey for the workers they needed to rebuild. These "newer" countries of immigration initially focused on labor flows, particularly during the 1950s and 1960s. It wasn't until the 1970s and 1980s that they began to grapple with the fact that communities had developed, and the laborers had become settlers.

Germany

After World War II, Germany struggled to recover from the devastation wrought by the war. Since World War II, Germany has received over 20 million immigrants, refugees, and expellees (Muenz and Ulrich 1998). However, as this section shows, most of these immigrants were never perceived as foreigners because they were ethno-cultural Germans. By contrast, at the peak of labor migration in 1973, the 2.6 million *Gastarbeiter* (**guest workers**), many of whom eventually became permanent settlers, were perceived as foreigners. In recent years, Germany's self-understanding has come under increasing assault. German governments have grappled with reconciling the traditional conception of citizenship with modern demands of the economy for highly skilled workers and the integration of non-ethnic Germans.

Two relatively recent historical reviews of German immigration policy development come from Joppke (1999) in *Migration and the Nation-State* and Rita Chin (2006) in *The Guest Worker Question in Postwar Germany*. Chin and Joppke have both addressed the issues of immigration policy in Germany, with Joppke taking a comparative approach with the British and U.S. cases. The two authors provided similar descriptions of the development of immigration policy after World War II. Joppke's focus is on the challenge that immigration poses to the nation-state, and the resilience of the nation-state in the face of the influx of immigrants, most of whom are coming from developing countries. For this section, we draw on Joppke's analysis and description of the development of German immigration policy.

We combine Joppke's emphasis on political developments with Rita Chin's more detailed focus on guest workers, particularly Turkish workers, and their impact on the development of German society. Chin describes the recruitment of migrants, which began as a response to two problems: lack of able-bodied German males as a result of the devastating war and the economic industrial boom of the 1950s and 1960s which coincided with a Europe-wide economic resurgence. The labor shortage was at first ameliorated by an influx of Eastern returnees, a pool of labor that France and Britain could not count on. Millions of Germans were expelled from Poland, Czechoslovakia, Hungary, Romania, and Yugoslavia in what were essentially United Nations and Western powers' sanctioned ethnic cleansing operations (Chin 2006).

The migration patterns of these *Aussiedler* (i.e., ethnic Germans from Eastern Europe) played a very important role in German immigration discourses, and it is useful here to go into their story in some depth. According to Oezcan (2004), between 1945 and 1949 almost 12 million German refugees and expellees arrived in Germany. Their assimilation went rather smoothly, both because of the economic boom underway and because of their ethnic origin. Also, between 1945 and the construction of the Berlin Wall in 1961, somewhere around 3.8 million Germans fled from Eastern to Western Germany. Even after the construction of the Berlin Wall, around 400,000 Germans moved from the GDR (i.e., German Democratic Republic) to the FRG (i.e., Federal Republic of Germany). After the initial flight of the *Aussiedler* in the 1940s, almost 1.4 million more moved to West Germany between 1950 and 1987. Following the fall of the Iron Curtain a further three million ethnic Germans returned between 1988 and 2003, 2.2 million from the former Soviet Union, 575,000 from Poland and another 220,000 from Romania.

Ultimately, however, ethnic German migration was not enough to feed the *Wirtschaftwunder* (economic miracle) in the 1950s. In response to ever increasing labor shortages, and as a way to shore up close ties with its neighbor Italy, the Adenauer government decided to conclude a labor recruitment agreement with Italy on December 22, 1955. However, this was only a stopgap measure as in August 1961 the Berlin Wall went up, cutting off a ready supply of Eastern German labor as we have already indicated. Furthermore, new welfare state laws reduced work hours and set a lower pension age, leading to even more shortages. Germany responded by signing a treaty with Spain on March 29, 1960, with Greece the following day, with Turkey on October 30, 1961, with Portugal on March 17, 1964, and with Yugoslavia on October 12, 1968 following Marshall Tito's decision to open his country completely to Western tourism, trade, and migration.

It was essentially the conservative, pro-business, **Christian Democratic Union** party (CDU) that concluded all these recruitment agreements, except the one with Yugoslavia that was concluded under the Grand Coalition. The **Social Democratic Party** (SPD) and the trade unions remained skeptical, mainly because of the obvious labor competition the migrants would pose to the German worker, but their fears were allayed when the government expanded the welfare state arrangements and guaranteed wage levels and preference in hiring for German workers. The influx of unskilled labor allowed about 3 million Germans to become white-collar workers between 1961 and 1973 (Chin 2006, p. 49).

Why would the same people who lived under the racist Nazi regime be so willing to open their borders to non-Germans? Chin argued that, in part, this was because after the Holocaust, the German government officially wanted to appear as being open to non-Germans. In fact, this discourse was made the focal point of Labor Minister Blank's comments in 1964 that the labor program made a reality "the merging together of Europe and the rapprochement between persons of highly diverse backgrounds and cultures in the spirit of friendship" (Chin 2006, p. 58). Therefore, the official line was that labor migration promoted West German industry while also strengthening European integration and offering to the world a new image of Germans and Germany.

Although Germany wanted to appear open to non-Germans, they did not consider non-European workers potential settlers. In the treaty signed with Turkey, there was in fact a clause stipulating rotation of laborers (no work visas would be issued for longer than two years). This clause was negotiated only with Turkey and never appeared in the Italian, Spanish, and Greek treaties. The idea of rotation quickly fell out of favor with industry, which would have had to pay for the return of laborers and the importation and re-training of new ones. Therefore, the German government, in a similar situation to that in France with the ONI, approved migration as being a small part of the overall inflow and allowed the imported workers to stay indefinitely. Thus, a large pool of foreign labor was available to maximize the profits of industry.

Despite this change in policy, government officials and policymakers continued to stress that the migration was temporary. The non-European laborers were allowed to come to Germany, but only if their presence did "not adversely affect the interests of the Federal Republic of Germany" (Chin 2006, p. 62). The wording was quite vague so that the German administration would have great latitude in how it dealt with the immigrant labor. The 1938 *Ausländerpolizeiverordnung* (Foreigner Police Regulation) written by the Nazis governed the first 10 years of the labor migration regime. Joppke (1999) wrote that "the introduction of a new Foreigner Law in 1965 was praised at the time as part of a 'liberal and cosmopolitan foreigner policy facilitating the conditions of entry and stay...'" (p. 66). The new law, Joppke argued, increased the sovereignty of the State in determining who received residence permits and was therefore, in fact, even more restrictive than the 1938 Foreigner Police Regulation. Furthermore, the law did not establish any positive residency, it was only in 1978 that Germany introduce a "permanence regulation" (*Verfestigungsregelung*), which made continuous residence a positive step in gaining permanent residency. Prior to 1978, per the no-immigration policy, a local administrator in charge of issuing permits could take continuous residence as a sign that the foreigner had overstayed their welcome. There was some negative reception of the 1965 law, particularly from the government of the state of Hesse, however there was almost no debate when the *Bundestag* voted on the law (*Ausländergesetz*, Foreigner Law) in 1965.

Criticism of immigration increased due to the economic slowdown in 1966, foreshadowing the effect of the oil crisis of 1973. The number of unemployed went from 105,743 in August of 1966, peaking at 673,572 by February of 1967. As a result of the recession and of "ideological consolidation" between the SPD and the CDU under a grand coalition government, a new party, the National Democratic Party (NPD), made surprising gains in state elections in Hesse and Bavaria, and nearly overcame the 5 per cent electoral threshold in the 1968 parliamentary elections with 4.8 per cent of the vote. One of their main positions in the campaign was that German labor should have priority over migrants. The NPD was one of the first post-war European parties to capitalize on anti-immigrant sentiment (Givens 2005).

The 1970s were, however, when Turks officially became the single largest immigrant group. Their numbers grew rapidly, as Chin described, "In 1970, there were 469,200 Turks in Germany, compared to 573,600 Italians and 514,500 Yugoslavians. By 1971, the Turkish population had risen to 652,800, while the number of Italians and Yugoslavians remained relatively constant" (Chin 2006, p. 77). The multinational nature of foreign labor soon disappeared and "guest worker" became synonymous for Turkish migration. In 1973, the recession hit the

German export driven economy hard. Half a million unemployed was a figure that looked notably complicated for government officials alongside the figure of two and a half million foreign laborers. Finally the government had to give in to sustained criticism and on November 23, 1973 halted all foreign labor recruitment, "the so-called *Anwerbestopp*" (Chin 2006, p. 80).

Many saw the *Anwerbestopp* as a direct response to the Arab oil embargo of 1973, but in fact industry leaders and government officials had realized that the guest worker program was not cost effective by the late 1960s. Chin summarized this as follows:

> At the end of 1971, there were nearly 1.8 million labor migrants from Italy, Spain, Greece, Turkey, and Yugoslavia, with the highest concentrations in the states of North Rhine-Westphalia, Baden-Württemberg, and Bavaria. According to one survey, 28 percent of those interviewed had been in the Federal Republic for at least seven years. The percentages of respondents who lived with a spouse were 59 (male respondents) and 90 (female respondents). Of the 63 percent who had children, 46 percent had brought them to Germany. These developments strained German social infrastructure such as housing and schools and created tensions in neighborhoods favored by foreigners (Chin 2006, 110).

Aside from halting recruitment of foreign labor, between 1973 and 1975 there were further steps taken to shrink the number of aliens working and residing in Germany, such as ceasing to grant work permits to foreigners already in Germany, suspension of automatic renewal of work permits, and deportation of illegal workers and foreigners collecting unemployment or social welfare. The increase in unemployment of foreign labor (1.37 million in 1973) became a major concern (Chin 2006, p. 111).

Another policy of the mid-70s designed to curtail the number of immigrants was the Ministry of Labor *Stichtag* (deadline) of November 13, 1974, which made children of foreigners entering Germany after that date ineligible for work permits once they came of age. The Labor Ministry decreed that from January 1, 1975 childcare compensation would be decreased for foreigners. The ministry also designated neighborhoods in cities with a high percentage of foreigners as "off-limits" to any future non-German inhabitants. Chin (2006) noted that all of these policies were undertaken under the heading of "Labor Policy" since West Germany did not see itself as an immigration country and therefore did not have an immigration policy.

However, these policies did not have the effect they intended, especially because the Ministry of Labor continued to ignore the social effects of its "labor" policy. The *Anwerbestropp* increased family reunions as immigrants feared further laws preventing immigration. The same was the case with the *Stichtag* and the decrease in childcare provisions. Due to the ineffectiveness of this "labor" approach, "integration" became the main strategy of the government by the late 1970s. However, as Chin pointed out, this required a considerable ideological shift in orientation from a labor policy to a more social one. The government began to fuel social science research in the realm of "guest workers" to come to terms with social aspects of the program. All the information it had up to that point was focused on the economic aspects of the guest worker program, not the people.

Interestingly, all major parties began to favor integration in the mid-1970s, but with considerably different meanings. Ironically, the CDU was in favor of an integrationist policy which allowed the workers to maintain and preserve their cultural identity but with the ultimate goal of sending the migrants back to their countries of origin, "the Christian Democratic party, in other words, emphasized a program of provisional integration that sought to ensure a conflict-free society, but clung to the possibility that foreigners would ultimately leave" (Chin 2006, p. 121). The key word of CDU's program was "coexistence" with the ultimate goal of repatriation. The FDP advocated a classical liberal approach of equal rights and protections.

Meanwhile, the SPD, as the most dominant party from 1969 to 1982, had the greatest impact on immigration policy. "In the 1975 platform, the party posited integration as a dual process: on the one hand, foreigners needed to become familiar with and accept the customs of Germans; on the other hand, Germans had to adjust to the permanent presence of foreigners and find out more about them" (Chin 2006, p. 122). Therefore, FDP stressed the need for foreigners to accept the German liberal democracy, whereas SDP "understood it as a give-and-take process that involved change not only on the part of guest workers..." (Chin 2006, p. 122) In 1978, under the leadership of the SDP Chancellor Helmut Schmidt, the *Bundestag* passed the *Verfestigungsregel* (Stabilization Statute), which allowed for unrestricted residence permits. A new government position was created, the ***Ausländerbeauftrager*** (**Commissioner for Foreigners' Affairs**), to be in charge of migrant interests and to oversee integration efforts, later to be expanded to also protect the migrants from discrimination

However, these changes were largely administrative and did not undergo a legislative examination. Joppke notes that it was only in 1990 that Germany finally passed a new law related to foreigners at the federal level. Another problem with the legal void was that most of the administrative rules were in fact subject to federal jurisdiction of the *Länder* (i.e., states) and therefore varied according to the political entity in power. As Joppke (1999) illustrated, "the CDU/CSU [**Christian Social Union**] governed southern states of Bavaria and Baden-Wurttemberg have pursued a restrictionist line, for instance, imposing tougher family reunification rules than recommended by the federal government, while SPD-ruled Hesse and Bremen have followed a liberal line, allowing more foreign family members to join their relatives in Germany than recommended by the federal government" (p. 68). The void left over by the state was largely filled by activist groups and the civil society, as well as the courts that have over time defended the individual rights of immigrants over those of the state (see, in particular, Isensee 1974 and Schwerdtfeger 1980).

The courts have continually restricted the ability of the state to pursue the supposed primacy of state interest enshrined in the 1965 Foreigner Law. In the "Arab" case of 1973 the Constitutional Court declared that two Palestinian students with supposed links to terrorists could not be deported because such an order would violate "the plaintiffs' constitutional liberty rights according to Article 2(1) and the principle of legal stateness, guaranteed by Article 19(4) of the Basic Law" (Joppke 1999, p. 72). Aside from staying their deportation and thus thwarting the supposed primacy of state interest, the Court also affirmed the application of constitutional guarantees to foreigners, which in Germany was a precedent-setting case.

The second case of import was the "Indian Case" of September 1978 regarding the renewal of residence permits. The case of an Indian resident who initially entered Germany for vocational training was crucial in that it denied his deportation on the grounds that his continuous residence had created "a constitutionally protected 'reliance interest'" (Joppke 1999, p. 73). Thus his residence had "positive" effects. Furthermore, the Court argued that his permit rejection could not be simply explained by the no-immigration maxim of the Federal government, thus again challenging the 1965 law that explicitly reiterated such maxim.

Chin argued that the creation of the Federal Immigration Czar in 1978 shifted the focus on migration from one of pure economics to one that emphasized integration, however, it also made the "guest worker" question one of general domestic politics, and therefore one that could be assailed by the opposition. This is exactly what Kohl did in the 1982–1983 campaign as he pushed the "foreigner problem" (Chin 2006, p. 180) taking advantage of a consensus that began to emerge between 1978 and 1982. Joppke argued that the backlash against the guest workers and foreigners started in the early 1980s when the two million unemployed Germans equaled the two million employed foreigners. Also, the 1980s saw a steady rise of asylum seekers. Finally, the ethnicity, primarily Turkish, of the foreigners became a salient issue.

After the election of the CDU/FDP coalition with Dr. Helmut Kohl at its head, the Federal Government began the drafting of a new foreigner law immediately. The first draft of the Foreigner Law of September 1983 proposed that children could only come to reside in Germany if they were under 6 years old and that no second-generation foreigners could bring foreign spouses to Germany whatsoever. The CDU–FDP also proposed its first concrete policy in 1983 with the voluntary repatriation program, which offered 10,500DM (about $8,000 USD in today's currency) to each eligible returnee. Overall, these proposals created a rift between the Foreign minister Genscher's liberal FDP and the conservative faction of the CSU, which ultimately Chancellor Kohl decided to alleviate by suspending any further reform.

A reform proposal in February 1988 also had a restrictive approach. This law denied any form of permanent residence to all non-EU foreigners who had come after labor recruitment. It proposed a rotation system with a maximum stay of eight years in Germany. The law did provide for very generous integrative proposals, but only because it treated the labor migrations as a singular non-recurring event of German history. The leaking of the 1988 draft led to the development of a coalition of both political and social actors against the legislation. Particularly notable, according to Joppke, was also the role of Catholic Bishops. Ultimately the Interior Minister Zimmermann was replaced by the CDU's own moderate Wolfang Schauble. Schauble, Joppke argues, took the threat of an anti-immigrant party, the *Republikaner*, seriously and decided to depoliticize the foreigner question by organizing support from the Churches and the FDP to push his new law quickly from first draft in September 1989 to final legislation in April 1990.

The result of Schauble's efforts was the 1990 Foreigner Law. The law completely ignores the "not a country of immigration" maxim. There is no encouragement of return of foreigners. The law basically ratified and put into law the Constitutional Court decisions on the rights of immigrants already elucidated in the Arab, Indian, and Turkish-Yugoslav cases above. Family reunification for second-generation marriages no longer included the one-year waiting period. Spouses and children received their own residency rights. Second and third generation foreigners who had temporarily left Germany had the right of return. It also established the relationship between foreigners and Germans as one of a "partnership." The policy did not extend as far as accepting foreigners as potential Germans.

The fall of the Berlin Wall led to a new influx of workers from the East. Germany began new guest worker schemes designed to assist the developing democracies in the East, particularly focusing on seasonal Polish workers. With reunification, the country had to focus on the re-integration of the Eastern *Länder*, at great cost to the budgets of the

Western *Länder*. Germany also made efforts to moderate the influx of *Aussiedler* in the early 1990s. Oezcan (2004) listed aiding ethnic German communities in countries of origin as one of the methods that the German government attempted to curb the inflows of migrants. Finally, the German government enacted a quota system that set the number of returnees at 225,000 people per year between 1993 and 1999, reducing it to 103,000 in 2000. Ever since then, a steady decrease in ethnic German migrants has continued, with 73,000 in 2003. Furthermore, in another effort to curb this migration, from 1993 onwards all ethnic Germans from countries of Eastern Europe not part of the former Soviet Union have had to prove that they face discrimination because of their origin in order to return to Germany.

One of the most important changes in immigration policy in Germany occurred with the election of an SPD-Green coalition government in 1998. The Kohl government, fearing a resurgence of radical right parties like the *Republikaner* had hung onto the concept that Germany was not a country of immigration. However, the new government, led by Gerhard Schröder, would end this discourse. The Green party was in favor of more inclusive policies for foreigners. The change in discourse led almost immediately to a change in policy, both in terms of citizenship, and a more multicultural approach to immigrant integration.

In 2000 Germany passed a new citizenship law, the first such measure in almost 90 years. For the first time ever, a *jus soli* principle was applied, giving children born to foreigners in Germany citizenship, provided that one parent had residency for at least eight years. Dual citizenship for these children is available until they reach the age of 23, when they need to make a decision on which one to adopt as permanent, a provision made necessary by the staunch opposition from the conservatives. Figures do indicate, however, that a substantial minority retain their original nationality, 43 per cent of those naturalized in 2002 and 48 per cent of those naturalized in 2001.

In the same year Germany introduced a "Green Card" system to satisfy its high-tech information technology (IT) demand, limiting residency to five years. Through December 2002, about 9,614 IT experts entered Germany. The policy had mixed reviews, given that Germany had trouble competing with countries like France and the U.S. that offered permanent residency and eventually citizenship to highly skilled immigrants.

In mid-2000, following consultations with Chancellor Gerhard Schröder, Minister of the Interior Otto Schily created the Independent Commission on Migration to Germany to develop recommendations for future immigration policy, and develop a new approach to immigrant integration. Prominent CDU opposition politician Rita Süssmuth was named chair of the commission. High-level representatives of employers' associations, trade unions, churches, local governments, and political parties were appointed as additional commissioners, bringing their organizations into the consensus-building process.

The Süssmuth Commission published its report in the summer of 2001, and as noted by the European researchers Schneider and Scholten (2015), it acknowledged a new reality: "'Germany needs immigrants' was not only the first stark sentence of the commission's report, but also the most explicit message conveying to the public what was deemed a consensus among key political and societal actors" (p. 84).

Three important recommendations were meant to guide future policy-making: the active selection of qualified immigrants, following the example of the classic immigration countries; the active promotion of integration by way of language and cultural awareness courses for immigrants; and an overhaul of asylum rules. Of these, the proactive selection of immigrants via a skills-based point system was the primary element intended to give Germany a decisive edge in the international competition for economically attractive migrants. The positive experiences of Canada and Australia with the point system functioned as models for the commission.

In November 2001, the SPD and Green coalition introduced a bill for highly qualified migration and integration. Immigration of business entrepreneurs was also encouraged. This bill intended to make Germany a "selective migration" country. Despite opposition from the conservatives, the bill passed both chambers only to be successfully challenged on procedural grounds by the opposition. The bill was reintroduced in January 2003 unchanged, since the original challenge was overturned. In May 2003, the bill passed once more in the lower house, but the opposition Conservatives, who were by then in the majority in the upper house, defeated the measure. In June 2004 the negotiations between the government and the conservative opposition finally yielded a compromise. The compromise included scraping the "core of the law," the point-based system for selecting immigrants based on the Canadian model. This law, taking effect in January 2005 and passed in the twilight of Schroeder's government, is almost a carbon copy of those passed in France and Britain. The attraction of skilled immigrant labor for economic purposes is the main focus, while curbing asylum applications and integrating immigrants already in Germany round out the main policies. Oezcan (2004) of the Migration Policy Institute summarized the new bill:

> The law will allow highly qualified non-EU-workers such as scientists or top-level managers to obtain a residence permit of unlimited duration at the outset. However, companies can only hire non-EU workers if there are no Germans (or foreigners such as EU nationals, who are legally treated as Germans) available for the job. In addition, the immigration of those who plan to establish a business will

also be welcomed. There will be no cap on the numbers of such entrepreneurs, but they will be required to invest at least a million euros in their project and add at least 10 new jobs.

The Bavarian Christian Social Union (CSU) was against an active immigration policy as a matter of principle, and the Christian conservative parties' opposition to any proactive migration policy had public support. The reform project was further burdened by the September 11, 2001 terrorist attacks in the U.S., which increased general fears that foreigners pose a security threat, and ever-climbing unemployment figures. This opposition led to the final version of the law was not what was originally envisioned. The core piece of the original immigration law was lost on the chopping block during the mediation process between the two houses of parliament. There will be no selection of economically attractive migrants according to a point system. Instead, the recruitment ban that was passed in 1973 will remain in effect (this legally binding decree bars active recruitment of foreign labor; exceptions for nurses, IT specialists, and seasonal agricultural workers are legally defined by another decree). Ambitious young people from other non-EU countries still find it difficult to gain permanent residence in Germany.

The law does allow foreign students to remain in Germany for a year after the completion of their studies. However, the CDU managed to negotiate provisions for simplified deportation procedures for reasons of national security, including deporting "religious extremists" (Oezcan 2004). Despite these setbacks, what initially started as a "labor-market policy" (characterized as such by both Joppke and Chin) has become a genuine immigration policy. The current German immigration law essentially converges its migration policy with those of France and Britain. Highly skilled migrants are encouraged, and asylum rights are curtailed.

A new challenge would face European politicians after the 2007–2008 fiscal crisis and Germany's Chancellor Angela Merkel had to take the lead in dealing with the crisis.[1] The economic crisis and the subsequent bailouts needed by countries like Greece and Portugal led to a broad fiscal downturn and concerns about immigration that were also impacted by security concerns after several high-profile terror attacks. In October 2010, German Chancellor Angela Merkel would declare that "multiculturalism had failed utterly" in Germany, blaming social unrest on immigrants who were unable to assimilate into German society. It was not clear what she meant by multiculturalism in this context, given that Germany had few policies one could consider "multicultural." In a seemingly coordinated effort, Merkel's fellow conservative allies, Nicolas Sarkozy in France and David Cameron in Britain, would follow in her footsteps in February of 2010 and 2011, also declaring multiculturalism a failure.

These statements led to a renewed focus on immigrant integration. For example, a 2012 article notes that, "Multiculturalism has been a fiercely controversial topic in Germany in recent years, engendering vigorous debate over the integration of immigrants, many of whom moved to the country in the 1960s as guest workers from Turkey. There are now 16 million people with an immigrant background living in Germany – 19.5 per cent of the country's population."[2] Little was happening, however, in terms of policy at the federal level, with the exception of a law passed in 2012 which improves the opportunities for immigrants to have their foreign university and apprenticeship degrees recognized in Germany.

Conflict in Syria and other parts of the Middle East and Africa would lead to large flows of refugees to Europe, with most heading to Germany (Crawley et al. 2018). Despite her position on multiculturalism, Chancellor Merkel became a champion for fleeing refugees, even in the face of anti-immigrant protests in the country, "Chancellor Angela Merkel urged Germans to turn their backs on a growing grass-roots movement of anti-Muslim protesters, calling them racists full of hatred, and said Europe's biggest economy must welcome people fleeing conflict and war."[3]

Germany has taken in the largest numbers of refugees in Europe going back to the conflicts in the Balkans in the mid-1990s. This has led to large settlements of Muslim immigrants and as the issue of immigration has become more salient across Europe, Germany has seen the rise of an anti-immigrant populist party, the Alternative for Germany (Alternative für Deutschland) that has taken advantage of the issue. There were a few attacks in Germany between 2015–2017, including knife, axe, and truck attacks by individuals linked to Islamic terror groups. A negative campaign against the Muslim community was launched after a series of sexual assaults occurred during the 2015–2016 New Year celebrations in Cologne.[4] The AfD is both a source and outcome of the anti-Islam phenomenon in Germany. The AfD would go on to win 11 per cent of the vote in the September 2016 Bundestag election – the highest percentage for a far-right party since World War II.

In the summer of 2018, the CSU in Bavaria created a crisis as a member of Angela Merkel's government by insisting on harsher control measures on the border, including placing refugees and asylum seekers into detention centers when they cross the border. After striking an initial deal, the crisis returned after the party faced losses in regional elections, leading Merkel to step down as party leader and stating that her current term as chancellor would be her last. Immigration played a role throughout her time in office, and as a headline in the *New York Times* stated, "Already an Exception: Merkel's Legacy Is Shaped by Migration and Austerity."[5]

Spain and Italy

With the establishment of a democratic government and the accession of the country into the EU, Spain became a destination country for immigrants. Unlike the U.S., Spain created its first immigration policy regime in 1985, mainly in response to requirements set by the European Community rather than in response to migration flows. These laws were created with the assumption that the low level of migration into the country would continue as Spain had traditionally been a country of emigration; large-scale immigration only started at the end of the last century and continuing until the present (Cornelius 2004). In 1993, a quota system was created, which called for the government to establish quotas based on employment needs. However, this system faced problems with both regional governments and employers routinely underestimating the number of workers needed. Since establishing their immigration policy regime, there have been six regularization programs: 1986, 1991, 1996, 2000, 2001, and 2005. Many of the first regularization programs were criticized as those they regularized often fell back into illegality due to the complicated nature of Spain's work permit system and culture of short-term labor contracts (Calavita 1998; Cornelius 2004; Levinson 2005).

From 2002 to 2008, Spain's foreign-born population went from 2.3 million to 6 million, making Spain one of the largest immigrant receiving countries in the world. However, between 2008 and 2015, about 3.2 million people left the country. Combined with decreasing numbers of immigrants into the country, this led to a negative migratory balance from 2010 to 2015. Yet this negative balance has been reduced in 2014 and 2015, suggesting that predictions of Spain returning to its former status as a country of emigration may be premature.

Italy, like Spain, had been a country of emigration, with large waves of Italians immigrating to North and South America in the 19th and 20th centuries. It also experienced periods of internal migration from the North to South in the post-War era. In the early 1980s, this flow began to change due to the country's geographic location its need for new workers to fill vacancies left by its declining birth rate. The first substantial attempt at immigration policy was in 1986, when the law n.943/1986 was passed, with the aim of regulating entry and regularizing immigrants who could show they held a job. In order to bring Italian immigration law into accord with the Schengen Agreement, further laws were passed, starting with the Legge Martelli (law n. 39/90) in 1990. Unlike many European countries, Italy's immigration laws have always accepted that due to its declining population, Italy would need to recruit foreign labor (Perlmutter 2014). However, most of the country's immigration legislation has been restrictive, and has not been very effective at importing labor to meet demands. Although most of the mainstream parties are opposed to immigrant regularizations, this has been the country's preferred way of dealing with unauthorized immigrants and meet labor demands. Between 1986 and 2009, Italy had regularized over two million migrants, with the last regularization being held in 2012. Between 2002 and 2011, more than 3.5 million people immigrated to Italy, while 175,000 emigrants left. Immigration peaked in 2007; since then, the number of emigrations has been rising, yet the balance of net migration has remained positive.

EU Immigration Policy

The development and deeper integration of European countries within the EU has led to more policymaking on immigration that impacts most of the member states (countries like the United Kingdom and Denmark have maintained opt-outs on some aspects of EU immigration policy). The creation of a single market in 1985 presented new fears concerning immigration as well as new opportunities to restrict it (Guiraudon 2001, p. 177). As a separate pillar under the 1992 Maastricht Treaty, migration policy remained isolated from the Commission, the Parliament, and European Court of Justice (Guiraudon 2001, p. 177). During the 1990s, member state governments used European institutions as a means of controlling migration. Early European cooperation in this area developed "initially as a network of ad-hoc interior ministry networks" that offered "no new openings to new actors" (Favell 1998, p. 8). Two important examples include the Schengen Group, which was established outside existing European Community institutions, and the Ad Hoc Group on Immigration, the operation of which was coordinated by the EC Commission. Created in 1985, the Schengen Group originally included ministers and state secretaries of Belgium, The Netherlands, Luxembourg, France, and Germany. The Ad Hoc Group on Immigration was established six years later and consisted of interior and justice ministers and senior civil servants from all member states. Both groups were intended "to pave the way for the harmonization of migration policies between participating governments through intergovernmental consultations and to achieve formal harmonization through agreements and conventions" (Leitner 1997, p. 129).

As Givens and Luedtke (2004) noted, immigration policy has mainly focused on immigration control at the EU level. A characteristic feature of the "harmonization" of migration policies emerging from these conventions is that they are primarily based on intergovernmental cooperation and coordination, rather than on transferring immigration matters into Community competence (Leitner 1997, p. 130). The supranational migration framework currently in the making is characterized by the development of common standards which aim first at restricting geographic admission and legal protection of non-European nationals, creating what has been referred to as "Fortress Europe" (Leitner 1997, p. 133).

Deeper European integration in the 1990s and early 2000s led to a push for more harmonization in the areas of immigration and social policies that affect immigrants. Policy proposals have come in many areas, including asylum policy, illegal immigration, visas and border control, labor recruitment, and anti-discrimination policy. Coupled with the unanimity voting requirement on the Council until the passage of the Lisbon treaty in 2009, the lack of sole right of initiative for the Commission meant that it was easier for countries to either block harmonization of controversial immigration issues, or to propose restrictive harmonization of controversial immigration issues, since the Commission normally proposes extensive and relatively expansive harmonization of immigration policies (Geddes 2000). Also, the United Kingdom, Ireland, and Denmark have opt-outs from most EU immigration laws, leaving them free to implement restrictive policies if they so choose (Green 2007).

As mentioned above, it is widely agreed that immigration harmonization has lagged behind other EU policy areas (Geddes 2000; Guiraudon 2000; Lahav 2004). In their analysis, Givens and Luedtke pointed out that "The economic and institutional imperatives of European integration have led to two contradictory political developments: (1) a push by EU institutions ... to develop a common, "harmonised" EU immigration policy that includes Third Country Nationals and (2) a resistance on the part of some member states to this development" (2004, p. 146). The European Council was been selective in its adoption of legislation. With the exception of anti-discrimination policy, very few of the policies that had been adopted by the Council by the early 2000s were considered expansive. These were the directives on the admission of students and researchers, who obviously trigger less public alarm than other categories of immigrants. These directives are similar to the policies related to skilled immigration being adopted in Britain, France, and Germany.

In terms of theoretical explanations for immigration's "lag" as an integrated policy area, Givens and Luedtke analyzed immigration policy at the EU level, showing that "restrictionist national executives protect de facto national sovereignty over immigration (to maximise political capital), either by blocking supranational harmonisation of immigration policy, or making sure that the harmonization that does occur is weighted in favour of law-and-order and security, and is not subject to the scrutiny of supranational institutions and courts" (p. 150). Overall, in terms of immigration policy, the longstanding unanimity voting requirement meant, and for legal migration continues to mean, that a single member state can block harmonization, which in turn often led to no harmonization or to a race to the bottom (Lavenex 2006, p. 1285). Another key difference between immigration policy and most other areas of EU policy was that until 2004 the European Commission did not have the sole right of initiative to propose a policy (which it does in other policy areas), meaning that until 2005 harmonization proceeded in a more bottom-up manner, in line with national interests of maintaining sovereignty in this issue area (Geddes 2000).

Another area where the EU has taken steps is in policy towards TCNs who are long-term residents. In November 2003, the European Council adopted the Directive on the status of third-country nationals who are long-term residents. This directive, with required transposition into national law by 2006, allows TCNs with five years of residence to have a special secure residence status, equal treatment as nationals in areas of employment and welfare benefits, and perhaps most importantly, the freedom to work and live in other EU member states. However, as Groenendijk noted, "[i]t is a status with rights comparable but not equal to those of Union citizens" (2004, p. 121). The directive contains many caveats and national exceptions that restrict TCN rights in practice. At the EU level, both immigration and anti-discrimination policy are determined through largely the same institutional structures, namely the European Council; yet, we see divergent policy outcomes – generally restrictive immigration policy and liberal anti-discrimination policy.

In the area of legal migration, the Commission has provided numerous proposals. There were a series of proposals from EU Justice Commissioner Franco Frattini in the mid-2000s that focused on economic migrants. The central component was the "blue card" that would allow skilled workers to work in an EU member state for an initial two-year period and then be allowed free movement has not resulted in the desired flow of skilled workers, and updates to the system are being contemplated. Other areas that have been an ongoing issue for the EU include developing common policies on immigration and immigrant integration. The following areas of focus have been identified by the European Commission for further development:

- Reducing incentives for irregular immigration
- Border management – saving lives and securing external borders
- Developing a stronger common asylum policy
- Establishing a new policy on regular immigration, modernizing and revising the "blue card" system, setting fresh priorities for integration policies and optimizing the benefits of migration policy for the individuals concerned and for countries of origin (Schmid-Drüner 2018).

The fiscal crisis in 2007 to 2009 led to resentment across Europe, including from countries like Greece, Portugal, and Ireland that needed bailouts to maintain their economies and countries like Germany and France that had to provide support for the struggling countries. The austerity measures imposed as well as the influx of refugees from 2014 to 2016 put a strain on support for the EU. That strain led to increased support for populist parties and leaders across Europe and impacted the **Schengen agreement** that had removed border checks between its signatories.

> The refugee crisis has led to a de facto suspension of those rules that are part of the Area of Freedom, Security and Justice (AFSJ) regulating the handling of asylum claims and the control of the EU's borders. As a result, the Dublin system, the main pillar of the Common European Asylum System (CEAS), was no longer enforced and border controls within the Schengen area were (temporarily) reinstated, effectively suspending the Schengen acquis. (Biermann, Guérin, Jagdhuber, Rittberger, and Weiss 2019, p. 246)

Immigration will continue to be a difficult area for the development of policy at the EU level, given the impact of electoral politics and different positions that member states have taken on immigration and asylum policy. However, coordination of efforts will be critical if new crises develop that impact immigration flows.

Conclusion

Historical developments on immigration policy for newer countries of immigration have been impacted by economics and cultural factors that have led to major policy shifts over the years. The need for labor after WWII led to the importation of guest workers, many of whom would ultimately become settlers. This led eventually to the need to recognize the fact that these populations would become a permanent fixture in society, although this recognition didn't come until the 1990s for some countries. As we describe later in the book, the approach to policies like citizenship and integration policy would be greatly impacted by the nature of immigration flows and how these countries dealt with them over time.

KEY TERMS

Alternative for Germany (AfD)   The AfD is an anti-immigrant party that entered the German Bundestag for the first time in 2016. The party started out focusing on taking Germany out of the Euro zone but shifted to an anti-immigrant message in order to attract voters who were concerned about the influx of immigrant in the early 2010s.

Ausländerbeauftragter **(Commissioner for Foreigners' Affairs)** The federal commissioner for foreigner affairs position was created to oversee policy related to migrant interests and to oversee integration efforts, later to be expanded to also protect the migrants from discrimination.

Ausländerpolizeiverordnung **(Foreigner Police Regulation) of 1938** All residents of Germany were required to register with the police, with all personal details kept with the local police. Foreigners were also asked about their native language, date of entry into Germany, visa status, work permit, etc.

Aussiedler Ethnic Germans in Eastern Europe and the Soviet Union who could prove their German ancestry were given the right to settle in Germany and given citizenship, along with housing assistance.

Christian Democratic Union (CDU) The main conservative party in Germany, generally considered to be a moderate party.

Christian Socialist Union (CSU) The sister party to the CDU, based in Bavaria. Often considered more conservative, particularly on social issues, than the CDU.

Gastarbeiter **(guest workers)** After World War II, Germany was in need of workers and developed agreements for workers to come from countries in Southern Europe and Turkey. The workers were expected to come on a temporary basis.

Green Party A party that began with a focus on the environment but has branched out to other socially progressive issues. Germany has had one of the strongest Green parties in Europe.

Schengen Agreement The Schengen agreement was signed in the mid-1990s by a subset of EU countries that agreed to open their borders and remove customs checks. The agreement has faced many challenges in the face of flows of migrants from Eastern Europe and refugees from the Middle East.

Social Democratic Party (SPD) The Social Democrats are the main party on the left in Germany. They have been more progressive on issues related to immigrant integration, in particular.

Wirtschaftwunder **(economic miracle)** With help from the guest workers, Germany was able to recover from the devastation of World War II relatively quickly. The economy was built on manufacturing and continues to be an economic engine for Europe.

NOTES

1 See "Angela Merkel's Boring Brilliance." *The American Prospect* published 9/26/2013. https://prospect.org/article/angela-merkels-boring-brilliance, accessed 8/14/2019.

2 See "Germany's 'Failed' Multiculturalism Carries on Regardless." *The Guardian* published 9/19/201. https://www.theguardian.com/world/2012/sep/19/germany-multiculturalism-immigration, accessed 8/14/2019.

3 See "Welcome Refugees and Reject Racism, Merkel Says After Rallies." *Reuters* published 12/31/2014. https://www.reuters.com/article/us-germany-merkel/wel come-refugees-and-reject-racism-merkel-says-after-rallies-idUSKBN0K90GL 20141231, accessed 8/14/2019.

4 See "Report: Over 1,200 Women Assaulted in Germany on New Year's Eve." *Deutsche Welle* published 10/7/2017. https://www.dw.com/en/report-over-1200-women-assaulted-in-germany-on-new-years-eve/a-19391708, accessed 10/12/2019.

5 See "'Already an Exception': Merkel's Legacy Is Shaped by Migration and Austerity." *New York Times* published 12/5/2018. https://www.nytimes.com/2018/12/05/world/europe/merkel-legacy-germany.html#, accessed 10/12/2019.

REFERENCES

Biermann, Felix, Nina Guérin, Stefan Jagdhuber, Berthold Rittberger, and Moritz Weiss. 2019. "Political (Non-)Reform in the Euro Crisis and the Refugee Crisis: A Liberal Intergovernmentalist Explanation." *Journal of European Public Policy* 26(2): 246–266.

Calavita, Kitty. 1998. "Immigration, Law, and Marginalization in a Global Economy: Notes from Spain." *Law & Society Review* 32(3): 529–566.

Chin, Rita. 2006. *The Guest Worker Question in Postwar Germany*. New York: Cambridge University Press.

Cornelius, Wayne A. 2004. "Spain: The Uneasy Transition from Labor Exporter to Labor Importer." In Wayne A. Cornelius, Takeyuki Tsuda, Philip L. Martin, and James F. Hollifield, Editors, *Controlling Immigration: A Global Perspective* (2nd ed.). Palo Alto, CA: Stanford University Press.

Crawley, Heaven, Franck Duvell, Katharine Jones, Simon McMahon, and Nando Sigona. 2018. *Unravelling Europe's 'Migration Crisis': Journeys over Land and Sea*. Bristol, UK: Policy Press.

Favell, Adrian. 1998. *Philosophies of Integration*. London: MacMillan.

Geddes, Andrew. 2000. "Lobbying for Migrant Inclusion in the European Union: New Opportunities for Transnational Advocacy?" *Journal of European Public Policy* 7(4): 632–649.

Givens, Terri E. and Adam Luedtke. 2004. "The Politics of European Union Immigration Policy: Institutions, Salience, and Harmonization." *Policy Studies Journal* 32(1): 145–165.

Givens, Terri E. 2005. *Voting Radical Right in Western Europe*. New York: Cambridge University Press.

Green, Simon. 2007. Divergent traditions, converging responses: Immigration and integration policy in the UK and Germany. *German Politics* 16(1): 95–115.

Groenendijk, Kees. 2004. "Legal Concepts of Integration in EU Migration Law." *European Journal of Migration and Law* 6(2): 111–126.

Guiraudon, Virginie. 2000. "European Integration and Migration Policy: Vertical Policy-Making as Venue Shopping." JCMS: *Journal of Common Market Studies* 38(2): 251–71.

Guiraudon, Virginie. 2001. "Weak Weapons of the Weak? Transnational Mobilization around Migration in the European Union." In Doug Imig and Sydney Tarrow, Editors, *Contentious Europeans: Protest and Politics in an Emerging Polity*. Lanham, MD: Rowman and Littlefield.

Isensee, J. 1974. "Die staatsrechtliche Stellung der Ausländer in der Bundesrepublik Deutschland." *Veröffentlichungen der Vereinigung der Deutschen Staatsrechtslehrer* 32.

Joppke, Christian. 1999. *Immigration and the Nation-State*. New York: Oxford University Press.

Lahav, Gallya. 2004. *Immigration and Politics in the New Europe: Reinventing Borders*. New York: Cambridge University Press.

Lavenex, Sandra. "Towards the constitutionalization of aliens' rights in the European Union?." Journal of European Public Policy 13, no. 8 (2006): 1284–1301.

Leitner, Helga. 1997. "Reconfiguring the Spatiality of Power – The Construction of a Supra-National Migration Framework for the European Union." *Political Geography* 16(2): 123–143.

Münz, Rainer and Ralf E. Ulrich.1998. "Changing Patterns of Immigration to Germany, 1945–1997." *Research and Seminars* 4(4): Working paper. University of California (System). Berkeley: Center for German and European Studies, 4.14.

Oezcan, Veysel. 2004. "Germany: Immigration in Transition." http://www.migrationinformation.org/Profiles/display.cfm?ID=235, accessed on 8/14/2019.

Perlmutter, Ted. 2014. "Italy." In James F. Hollifield, Philip L. Martin, and Pia M. Orrenius, Editors, *Controlling Immigration: A Global Perspective*. Palo Alto, CA: Stanford University Press.

Schmid-Drüner, Marion. 2018. *Fact Sheets on the European Union: Immigration Policy*, Brussels: European Commission http://www.europarl.europa.eu/factsheets/en/sheet/152/immigration-policy, accessed 10/11/2018.

Schneider, Jan and Peter Scholten. 2015. "Consultative Commissions and the Rethinking of Integration Policies in the Netherlands and Germany: The Blok Commission and the Süssmuth Commission Compared." In Peter Scholten, Han Entzinger, Rinus Penninx, and Stijn Verbeek, Editors, *Integrating Immigrants in Europe: Research-Policy Dialogues*. London: Springer-Verlag.

Schwerdtfeger, G. 1980. "Welche rechtliche Vorkehrungen empfehlen sich, um die Rechtstellung von Ausländern in der Bundesrepublik Deutschland angemessen zu gestalten?" In *Verhandlungen des Dreiundfünfzigsten deutschen Juristentags Berlin 1980, Vol. II*. Munich: C. H. Beck.

Sitkin, Lea. 2019. *Re-thinking the Political Economy of Immigration Control: A Comparative Analysis*. New York: Routledge.

Tooze, Adam. 2018. "The Forgotten History of the Financial Crisis: What the World Should Have Learned in 2008." *Foreign Affairs*, September/October. https://www.foreignaffairs.com/articles/world/2018-08-13/forgotten-history-financial-crisis, accessed 8/14/2019.

6

PARTY POLITICS

Introduction

Political parties play a significant role in determining agendas for policy and politicians, as they compete for votes and control of governments. As noted in Chapter 1, political scientists began to pay more attention to the politics of immigration in the mid-to-late 1990s. One argument that was made at this time was that left parties tend to focus more on immigrant integration, whereas right parties tend to focus on immigration control. Money (1999) found that, in general, there was consensus among parties on the need for immigration control, but that left parties tended to be more open to immigrant integration. This has been a major focus in the study of party politics and immigration since that time. Left parties tend to see immigrants as potential voters and try to recruit them to their parties as they become citizens. Right parties have tended to focus more on immigration control and appealing to voters who feel threatened by immigration.

In this chapter, we examine political parties in more detail, focusing on how parties on the left (i.e., social democratic, or in the case of the U.S., the Democratic party) have positioned themselves on immigration policy, as compared with conservatives or the Republican party. We also examine more extreme parties, particularly **radical right parties** that tend to take a strong anti-immigrant position, and in the European case, have more recently focused on Muslim immigrants. The position taken by some European politicians can be compared with the position that many American politicians have taken toward Hispanic or Spanish-speaking immigrants. In a seminal article, Zolbert and Woon (1999) described the perceived similarities regarding integration of the two groups by asking the following question: "[w]hy does the principal focus of contentious debates over immigration and its sequels [sequelae] center on religion in Europe and language in the United States?" (p. 7). Spanish speakers were seen as being resistant to integration in the U.S., whereas Muslim migrants were seen as being resistant to integration in Europe because of their religious differences. The authors explain how different types of integration may play out for both native-born citizens and immigrants and how that changes with successive generations. For politicians on the right, these groups have become the focal point of political rhetoric and campaigns to attract white working-class voters.

One reason that left parties tend to focus more on immigrant integration is that they are more likely to be able to attract immigrant voters, who tend to be ethnic minorities. This has certainly been the case in the United States. In the wake of the civil rights movement, more immigrants came to the U.S. from places like Africa, the Caribbean, Asia, and other places outside of Europe. As these groups became enfranchised, it was not necessarily the case that they would lean toward the Democratic party over the Republicans, given that many of these groups came from more socially conservative backgrounds. However, over time, particularly in presidential contests, immigrant groups have tended for vote in larger number for Democratic versus Republican candidates. This leftist preference is not a given outside of the United States. There are many motivations for voting for a particular party, and in multi-party systems, voters have more choices than U.S. voters do in general elections, although factions like the Tea Party Republicans in the House of Representatives have had an outsized influence on immigration policy, acting as a veto player in rejecting legislation under both President Obama and President Trump.

Political parties play a key role in the politics of immigration. In general, left parties have focused more on immigrant rights, whereas right parties tend to focus their policy proposals around border security and limiting immigration. This chapter examines differences between left and right parties on immigration issues, paying particular attention to how parties have converged on the issue of immigration control but have diverged on issues of citizenship and immigrant rights.

The chapter goes on to examine anti-immigrant far right and nativist parties and their influence on party politics in several countries. We argue that the impact can often lead to more restrictive policies, but it can also spur left parties to pursue antidiscrimination policies. The chapter concludes with an examination of immigrants as politicians and their impact on party strategies and development as immigrant and ethnic communities increase in numbers and influence.

From an ideological perspective, left parties and right parties differ in their approaches to immigration and immigrants. Left parties usually work toward social equality and solidarity, and thus favor policies that achieve these goals. They also tend to support legislation that grants immigrants access to political, economic, or social structures in efforts to stimulate their integration into broader society. With this intent to include immigrants within these social structures, left parties generally can appeal directly to immigrants and they are more prone to see immigrants as constituents or potential constituents. Messina (2007) argued that "the left's traditional policy agenda tends to dovetail with the perceived interests of immigrants" (p. 208). On the other hand, right parties tend to favor more restrictive legislation on immigration. This stems from a range of conservative concerns about the effects of immigration on the economy (particularly strains on social services), crime and terrorism, or national identity. Unlike left parties that emphasize greater access, right parties tend to favor policies that either restrict immigration flows with heightened border security or encourage greater self-sufficiency and market-based incentives for immigrants already in the country. Right parties also may benefit from the fact that the median voter in most advanced democracies tends toward restrictionism. Therefore, unlike left parties, catering to anti-immigrant sentiment and more exclusive forms of nationalism is a common strategy among right parties.

In recent decades, new parties on the right and left of the political spectrum in Europe have influenced these configurations, however. A number of scholars have examined the rise of radical right parties (including Betz 1994; Art 2011; Mudde 2007). Because these parties appeal to voters with a staunch anti-immigrant message, many mainstream, right parties risk losing constituents to these more extreme parties if they do not adopt more anti-immigrant positions themselves. Interestingly, leftist parties are also affected by these radical right parties. Leftist parties rely on both the native-born working class and those with immigration backgrounds, and those parties that favor immigrant issues at the expense of native-born working-class issues may risk losing the latter to the radical right. Alonso and Fonseca (2011) even concluded that the radical right's "main impact is not on the mainstream Right but on the Left" (p. 880). The study of radical left parties remains in its early stages, but the rise of parties such as the Greens further complicates these dynamics for mainstream left parties as well. Because they advocate for even stronger forms of social equality, access, immigrant rights and multiculturalism than mainstream left parties, these radical left influences challenge those of the mainstream left and may likewise shift their stances in a more immigrant-friendly direction.

When immigration became a more salient, high-profile political issue in the late 1800s in the U.S., the political parties at the time staked out positions based on their positions on civil rights – for example, Radical Republicans were opposed to immigration restriction, whereas Democrats were for ethnic based restrictions (Tichenor 2002). Specific parties develop at the time in response to Chinese immigration in California, for example, the Know Nothing Party, which wanted to restrict immigration and citizenship for non-white immigrants. In general, extreme parties have been short-lived in the United States. In both the U.S. and Germany, tendencies toward anti-immigrant sentiment have generally been subsumed by mainstream parties. In this chapter, we focus mainly on the rise of the far right in Europe, with a review of the role of far-left parties, and a discussion of the results of the 2016 elections.

Radical Right Parties

Radical or far right parties gained attention in Europe with parties like the French **National Front (FN)** and the German *Republikaner* (**Republicans**) in the 1990s gaining votes and more recently with the **Alternative for Germany (AfD)** gaining seats in the German parliament. The study of these parties took off in the mid-1990s with several books which focused on how and why radical right parties were finding success in Europe. Part of the challenge was defining these parties: For example, in his book *The Radical Right in Western Europe*, Kitschelt (1995) focused on the type of approach a party took (e.g., populist or more extremist) that determined whether it won votes. Other studies focused on what defined a "breakthrough" for a particular party, whether it was winning a local election, a national election, or just getting the attention of the mainstream parties.

Heading into the late 1990s and early 2000s, radical right parties began to go beyond winning votes and actually winning seats in legislatures in Europe. For example, the **Austrian Freedom Party** went from being a consistent third party in the Austrian party system, to winning second place in the 1999 Austrian parliament election and joining a government coalition for the first time. The party's leader, Joerg Haider, was highly controversial and had made statements that were considered anti-immigrant and anti-European Union (EU), but he personally remained outside of the government. Although the party's participation in the government coalition led to a diplomatic backlash from the rest of the EU member states, the party remained in government.

In studies in the early 2000s, one of the key themes was comparing radical right parties across countries in Europe and trying to determine what were the main factors for the success of parties in some countries (e.g., the Austrian Freedom Party) or their lack of success in others (e.g., the *Republikaner* in Germany). Many of these studies focused on party strategies (both the mainstream parties and their radical right challengers), and the context in which they competed for votes. The rise of parties in Western Europe which generally had an anti-immigrant message led to a debate, particularly in the late 1990s, on how these parties should be defined. Some authors have referred to these parties as "extreme-right" and considered them to be anti-system (Ignazi 1992; Fennema 1997). These authors tended to see these parties as a continuation of fascist tendencies which developed during the interwar period and anti-system in the sense that they were viewed as outside of and challengers to the mainstream party system. Others have used terms such as "far right" (Cheles et al. 1995) or "new right" (Minkenberg 1997) to describe the same set of parties, with an emphasis on the fact that these parties represented a new type of right party that had little or no connection to the fascist past. These differences in terminology are an example of the difficulty researchers have had in classifying these parties.

Despite varied labels, most authors agree that radical right parties do have certain characteristics in common. For example, Swank and Betz (1995) noted that "[c]oncretely, RRWP [Radical Right-Wing Parties] combine radical free market programmatic commitments with xenophobic and strident anti-establishment positions" (p. 1). In a survey of political experts by Huber and Inglehart (1995), these parties (except for the NPD, which was not included) are placed on the **extreme right**. Although there may be different labels for these parties, they can be placed into a particular ideological category that is different from the center and far left parties. As Givens (2005) explained in her book on the radical right, most of these parties can be described by the following characteristics:

- They take an anti-immigrant stance by proposing stronger immigration controls, the repatriation of unemployed immigrants, and call for a national (i.e., citizens only) preference in social benefits and employment ("welfare chauvinism").
- In contrast to earlier extreme right or fascist parties, they work within a country's political and electoral system. Although they do not have the goal of tearing down the current political system, they are anti-establishment. They consider themselves "outsiders" in the party system, and therefore are not tainted by government or mainstream parties' scandals (p. 20).

More recent analyses of the radical right have focused on factors such as the attitudes and motivations of radical right voters. For example, Art (2011) developed "a tripartite typology of radical right activists: *moderates, extremists,* and *opportunists*" (p. 20) and argued that these differences in approach have an impact for party development. Some, particularly those who are well educated, benefit from party building, whereas others do not. Mudde (2007), who has written broadly on populism and the radical right, develops a conceptual framework for defining populist radical right parties across Europe, which focuses on not only their nationalism, but also their acceptance of democracy. His book examined the failures and successes of these parties across Europe and examines potential avenues of future research.

The positions of particular parties will shift and adjust over time as issues change, for example, some have taken on more **Euroskeptic** positions, and then shifted to a more anti-immigrant approach, whereas others have come and gone as their political agendas and leaders have become more or less popular. It is clear however that populist radical right parties have become a fixture in European politics.

Immigration and Party Politics in Europe

As described in Chapter 4, European immigration policy was impacted by several factors, such as the oil shocks of the early 1970s that forced labor-importing countries to break from their relatively liberal and non-committal immigration regimes, whereas the integration questions of the 1980s, asylum problems of the 1990s, and national security concerns of the 2000s have spurred more critical debate and action. In this section, we examine more directly the linkage between party politics and immigration policy, with a focus on Britain and France as examples of the policy concerns of left and right parties and the impact of the radical right, drawing on the work of Givens (2012).

Britain

Britain grappled earlier than other European countries with immigration control and immigrant integration issues. As a result of the post-World War II labor shortage, hundreds of thousands of immigrants arrived to take up jobs in Britain between the late 1940s and early 1960s (Bleich 2003, p. 37). Initially, many came from Ireland and the "Old Commonwealth" (Canada, Australia, and New Zealand) and other non-Commonwealth countries. Later groups came from "New Commonwealth" countries that comprised of primarily non-white populations.

On the political front, it was clearly the right that was in favor of more control of immigration, while it was only under **Labour Party** governments that antidiscrimination or "race relations" legislation was passed. Freeman (1979) argued that the **Conservative Party** went against its own economic interests in supporting control legislation, as it is clear that anti-immigrant elements of the party were able to hold sway in the passage of legislation.

As race and color became a part of the public consciousness, immigration increasingly became a subject of public and political debate. As the numbers of ethnic minority immigrants rose, the balance shifted between those who favored an inclusive policy toward members of the Commonwealth and colonies and those who argued for restrictions (Bleich 2003, p. 39) The electorate began to put more pressure on mainstream politicians to halt the influx of immigrants (Money 1999). Therefore, unlike in France and

Germany where the 1970s oil shocks were the main catalyst, the issue of restricting or somehow curbing immigration became part of the political agenda much sooner in Britain, mainly due to race, which is clearly delineated by Freeman (1979).

During this time period, fear of a clampdown generated a surge of ethnic minority immigrants, as individuals from the Commonwealth and colonies rushed to Britain to "beat the ban" announced by the Conservative government in 1961. New Commonwealth immigration rates in 1960 were 57,700 and increased in 1961 to 134,600. During the first six months of 1962, the number was 94,900 (Layton-Henry 1992, p. 13). Later that year, the Conservative government introduced legislation to control immigration from other parts of the Commonwealth. The Labour Party resisted what would be called the Commonwealth Immigrants Act, saying that the bill was embodying pure race restrictions not only because it came in response to public statements about preserving British "whiteness" but also because it exempted the Irish from immigration control (even though hundreds of thousands of them were entering during the same era) (Bleich 2003, 45).

Although Britain didn't have a radical right party at this time, there were members of the Conservative Party who expressed fairly extreme views on immigration. For example, on April 20, 1968 Enoch Powell (a member of the Conservative shadow cabinet) pronounced his famous "rivers of blood" speech in Birmingham in which he articulated in inflammatory rhetoric a doomsday scenario for Britain's multiracial future. He believed that Commonwealth immigrants would not integrate into British society and that the Race Relations Bill would entrench this problem (Bleich 2003, p. 74). Despite the positive response Powell's speech received in some quarters, the Labour government continued to pursue measures to help immigrant communities.

The Labour Party lost control of government in the election of 1970. The Conservative government of Edward Heath was elected partially due to its promise to bolster controls on Commonwealth immigration. The result was the Immigration Act of 1971, with a new category of "patrials," persons allowed free entry into the U.K. whose parent or one grandparent was born in the U.K., thus restricting the entry of persons from the "New" Commonwealth. The Labour Party opposed the act and reaffirmed that, while controlling immigration on the basis of labor demand was sound, doing so on the basis of race was unacceptable

Freeman (1979) argued that the Labour Party was in essence caught between a rock and a hard place – "between the dictates of its conscience, ideology, and militants, and the imperatives of a winning electoral strategy" (p. 158). Being a working-class party, it could not ignore the xenophobic and racist inclinations of its constituents if it were to win elections, while at the same time its roots were in the workers' movement grounded in theories of worldwide solidarity. Freeman concludes that it is unclear whether its acquiescence in a racially restrictive immigration regime helped it any at the polling stations, after all they did lose the 1971 election to the Conservatives, but what is clear is that "it seriously damaged the leadership's standing among the 'Labor Left'" (Freeman 1979, p. 158). Joppke (1999) similarly argued that the Labour Party quite often fell under the sway of illiberal opinion.

During the 1980s and 1990s British policy continued to demonstrate the balancing act between immigration control and immigrant integration. The next important stage for British policy began in the late 1990s. The rise of radical right parties across Europe included the **British National Front** and the **British National Party (BNP)**, in the 1980s and the **United Kingdom Independence Party (UKIP)** in the 1990s. However, these parties had little influence on electoral politics in Britain until the late 1990s. As Hansen noted (2000), "[t]he National Front collapsed in the 1979 General Election, earning less than 2 per cent of the vote; since then the BNP's support in any electoral contest has almost always been below 5 per cent of the vote" (p. 224). Neither the National Front nor BNP has had much influence on immigration policy, although Hansen also noted that this does not mean that black Britons have no experience with racist attacks. UKIP, however, has had a different trajectory.

The UKIP was founded on September 3, 1993 at the London School of Economics by members of the Anti-Federalist League. From the beginning the party had defined as its foremost goal the reestablishment of U.K. independence by withdrawal from the EU. UKIP participated in the 1994 European Parliament election, but received less than 1 per cent of the vote and did not win any seats under the first past the post electoral rules. In Britain's first European Parliament election using PR in 1999, UKIP received 7 per cent of the vote and won three seats.

Following its humble beginnings, UKIP more than doubled its result in the 2004 European Parliament elections. The 2004 European Parliament elections took place in the United Kingdom on June 10, 2004. UKIP, thought of as simply a fringe party of the right, won 12 seats (78 Members of the European Parliament come from the United Kingdom) with 17 per cent of the vote.[1]

UKIP is often considered a single-issue party with their main focus on the United Kingdom's immediate withdrawal from the EU (which has now become a reality). However, UKIP has also made the argument that the British population is overflowing and the infrastructure of the state cannot handle an influx of new immigrants. UKIP sees an EU takeover of immigration policy as a disaster for Britain. Although UKIP does not adhere to the overt racism of the BNP (Fieschi 2004), its platform is also anti-immigrant. Margetts et al. (2004) noted that "one of the party's five manifesto pledges is 'Freedom from overcrowding,' arguing that immigration was clogging up roads, railways, doctors' surgeries and hospitals, and even the countryside" (p. 5). Although the main raison d'être of UKIP is a deeply-embedded Euro-skepticism, the xenophobia of the party cannot be dismissed as insignificant when attempting to understand the support it received at the 2004 elections.

In a European election exit poll, British National Party (BNP) and UKIP voters were the most likely to respond that immigration was "the most important issue facing Britain today" (Margetts et al. 2004, p. 11), with 77 per cent of BNP voters and 53 per cent of UKIP voters choosing this option. This compares with 24 per cent of Conservative and Liberal Democratic voters and 10 per cent of Labour Party voters. Clearly, UKIP was attracting voters that had strong (generally negative) opinions about immigration.

After the 2004 European Parliament election, the Conservative Party, getting over the shock of UKIP's performance, set out to win back supporters who had defected. A *Guardian*/ICM poll conducted shortly after the 2004 EP Election showed that a strong plurality of UKIP voters defected from the Conservative ranks. In total, 45 per cent of UKIP's voters had voted Conservative in the 2001 General Election, whereas 20 per cent cast their ballots for Labour and 11 per cent for the Liberal Democrats.[2] By early September 2004, the Conservative Party co-chairman, Liam Fox, was reported as stating to a closed meeting that the "number one issue to get UKIP voters back to the Conservatives is immigration and asylum. If we had a tougher line on immigration and asylum, they would come back."[3] If the Conservatives did not feel the need to adapt their stance to stem the UKIP tide, then that all changed with the result of the Hartlepool by-election on September 30, 2004. In a shocking result, the Conservative candidate finished in fourth place behind the UKIP representative. According to the *Guardian* newspaper, "it was the first time since the middle of the last century that the main opposition party had sunk to fourth place in an English parliamentary election."[4] Within a week of the result, the shadow home secretary, David Davis Member of Parliament (MP), was calling for substantial curbs on immigration to the United Kingdom because it endangered British values.[5] Although this announcement caused uproar in the more moderate wing of the Conservative Party, the die had been cast.

By the end of January 2005, in anticipation of the General Election, Conservative Party leader Michael Howard announced strict new controls on immigration and asylum if his party won the General Election. This platform was aimed at taking over the ground cultivated by UKIP at the 2004 European Parliament election.[6] After the announcement of the election, the complete immigration package of the Conservatives came into full view. They aimed to withdraw from the 1951 UN

Refugee Convention in order to impose limits on asylum seekers, whereas Mr. Howard claimed that Britain would face fresh race riots and the unwitting admittance of terrorists if immigration was not brought under control.[7]

The most significant policy change in the early 2000s was the commitment to enact "planned migration" in order to boost primarily labor migration. The highly skilled migrant program that began in the summer of 2002 would allow Britain to compete with other developed countries for skilled labor. This was a significant break from the established British approach of maintaining a "no migration" policy. A strategy of this new approach has been the intention to retain international students, especially those in sciences and engineering. Furthermore, some suggest that Prime Minister Tony Blair's government was consistently more restrictive with regard to asylum seekers in part because of a populist backlash against an asylum system that was seen as broken and exploited by illegitimate asylum seekers (Seldon 2005). Overall, in pursuing these reforms, Blair's government faced very little opposition from the Conservatives who limited "their attacks to competence rather than policy direction" (Somerville 2007), thus reaffirming Freeman's (1979) assessment that the British Labour Party holds considerable anti-liberal views toward immigration.

Despite these new policies, Blair and his governing Labour Party were considered to be weakest on the immigration issue, a fact even pointed out by news outlets in the United States (Cowell 2005). The Conservative Party's strategy also emanated from a desire to take back voters lost in the 2004 EP Election and the 2004 Hartlepool by-election. Given polling data that showed a high percentage of UKIP's support coming from traditional Tory backers, the Conservative Party was determined to win back these voters. The success of radical right parties (in this case UKIP) is often dependent upon the response by the mainstream parties. Once immigration was spotlighted by the mainstream Conservatives, UKIP's remaining unique trait with which to contest the election was its hard version of Euroskepticism.

The Conservatives' strategy was not successful in keeping the radical right from gaining seats during the 2009 European Parliament election. The BNP won its first seats ever in a national election and UKIP increased its seat share from 12 to 13. The election was more of a referendum on the government in power, however. Labour's 15 per cent of the vote compared with the Tories 28 per cent and UKIP's 16 per cent was more of a slap in the face to the Brown government. The right performed well across Europe in this election, during a time of great economic uncertainty which has been shown to aggravate popular concerns related to immigration in the past.

As both internal EU migrants and flows of refugees from Syria and other conflict areas were highlighted in the media, the U.K. Conservative government continued to pursue a policy of discouraging immigrants, as noted in this article in the *Guardian* newspaper, which stated "Theresa May was two years into her job as home secretary when she told the Telegraph in 2012 her aim 'was to create here in Britain a really hostile environment for illegal migration.'"[8] These policies continued as **Brexit** became the focus of the government's attention in 2018 and 2019. Immigration politics remained high on the agenda for politicians, as described in Goodfellow's (2019) book, *How Migrants Became the Scapegoats of Contemporary Mainstream Politics*. Immigrants were blamed for a host of ills despite multiple studies confirming that immigration was not damaging the U.K.'s economy. As we describe later in the chapter, Brexit would be partially driven by anti-immigrant sentiment, but it was also a referendum on the United Kingdom's ongoing membership in the EU.

France

Unlike Britain, French politicians did not focus as directly on immigration control and integration issues until the late 1960s. Miller (1981) argued that the Left Wing in France, and especially its civil society branches, was much more pro-immigrant, therefore indicating a higher level of contestation between political parties. Miller asserted that the government wanted to regain control over immigration from employers as early as the mid-1960s under Prime Minister Pompidou during the de Gaulle Presidency. In 1966 the Directory for Population and Migrations was created within a new ministry that combined those of labor, public health, and population. Miller argued that "the guiding idea behind immigration policy modifications at this juncture was to assert governmental control through compliance with the law instead of further acquiescence to a de facto reversion to employer monopoly over foreign worker recruitment" (Miller 1981, p. 14). Miller argued that one of the main reasons behind this effort was government desire to curb legalizations of workers. Therefore, prior to 1968, a watershed year for so many policies in France, government employed a laissez-faire approach toward immigration, due to the needs of business.

Regarding the position toward immigrants of the non-governmental sector, Freeman (1979) pointed out how both the Communist party dominated Confédération Générale du Travail, CGT (General Confederation of Labor) and the Socialist party dominated Confédération Française Démocratique du Travail CFDT (French Democratic Confederation of Labor) alternated in their views towards immigration, from initial support for controls to an approach favoring ameliorating the situation of immigrants already in France. The two federations have often worked together to address the issue of immigration, signing joint accords and communiqués in 1966 and 1971. Freeman (1979) noted how the unions have adopted typical class arguments in dealing with the issue of immigration. He continued on to explain their position in the late 1970s:

> The basic premise of the unions with regard to immigration regulation is that a failure of planning and adequate controls has caused present French policy to be extremely exploitative. Only a carefully planned policy which guarantees each worker a job, adequate housing, and equal working conditions can ensure that migrants will not be used to weaken the position of indigenous workers. Toward that end, both confederations endorse the principle of restoring the National Immigration Office to its monopoly over-all immigration into France.
>
> (Freeman 1979, p. 160)

Hargreaves offered many examples from the early 1980s where the politicization of immigration often descended into a competition over who could be "tougher" on immigrants, regardless of party lines (Hargreaves 1995, p. 182). Hargreaves argued that the mainstream parties agreed on three points: that immigration should be forcefully curtailed, that immigrants should be encouraged and supported to return to their countries of origin, and that the immigrants already in France should be assisted in their efforts to assimilate into French society. The truce was accomplished as the Right withdrew its policy of mass repatriation while the Left dropped its "flirtation with multiculturalism" (Hargreaves 1995, p. 188).

Perhaps one of the most important impacts of immigration and the radical right has been in agenda setting. Immigration politics were impacted in the 1980s by the rise of the radical right *Front National* (FN) led by Jean-Marie Le Pen. The FN had an electoral breakthrough in 1983 elections in the town of Dreux, which was followed by success in European Parliament elections. At the legislative level, the FN has won as much as 15 per cent of the vote in the 1997 election but was only able to win one seat in the French Assembly. As Givens (2005) argued, the unwillingness of the French mainstream right to coordinate with the FN made it difficult for the party to win seats. However, this did not mean that the mainstream right ignored the issues raised by the FN.

In the 1984 European Parliament elections the FN won 11 per cent of the vote and ten members of the European Parliament – the same percentage of the vote as the French Communist party. In 1988 Le Pen received 14.4 per cent of the vote in the presidential election and had an equally impressive showing in the 1995 presidential election. The FN received 9.6 per cent of the vote in the first round of the 1988 legislative elections and 12.5 per cent of the vote in the first round of the 1993 legislative elections.

The FN also played a role in agenda setting when the **RPR** (**Rally pour la Republique**) and **UDF** (**Union Democratique Française**) government became concerned about the impact of anti-immigrant sentiment.

> Anxious to staunch the loss of their supporters to the FN, the traditional centre-right parties hardened their policy platform on immigration and related issues. After gaining a narrow election victory in March 1986, they formed a government ... who announced that the government would introduce legislation ending the automatic acquisition of French nationality by people of foreign origin.
>
> (Hargreaves 1995, p. 169)

In 1986, Chirac had to pull back his reform, since his government only had a slim majority in Parliament and opposition to the change was fierce. In 1993 Balladur had a landslide majority and the anti-racist movement was on the decline. Thus, the political opportunity structure was such that policy change was possible in 1993.

The FN saw its best result in a legislative election in 1997. The snap election called by Chirac was a dismal defeat for the mainstream right parties. Chirac had hoped to consolidate his control of the legislature, but instead was faced with a rejuvenated Socialist party, and his very unpopular prime minister, Alain Juppe, was unable to lead the right parties to victory. In the first round of voting, the FN received 14.9 per cent of the vote. Although 76 FN candidates were able to compete in the second round of voting, only one candidate was able to win a seat.

In terms of representation, the FN was more successful at the regional level, due to the proportional representation electoral system used for these elections. This highlights the impact of political institutions on the success of radical right parties. In the 1998 regional elections, the FN won 15.3 per cent of the vote and gained many seats in the regional councils. This led to a crisis for the mainstream right parties, which had to rely on FN votes in several regions to be able to elect rightist regional presidents.

After the 1999 European election, Le Pen worked to consolidate the FN's position in anticipation of the 2002 national elections. The 2002 election was the first election after the presidential term was reduced from seven years to five years. It was also expected to be Jean-Marie Le Pen's last stand as the leader of his party. Le Pen stunned France and the rest of Europe by taking second place in the first round of the presidential election and qualifying for a run-off with President Jacques Chirac. After two weeks of anti-Le Pen protests, Chirac trounced Le Pen with 82 per cent of the vote.

The FN hoped to gain some momentum from the presidential election, but their result in the first round of the legislative election was a disappointing 11 per cent. The FN was able to field 37 candidates in the second round but did not win any seats. The mainstream right refused to work with the FN, and this time their strategy worked. The RPR and UDF won an overwhelming majority of seats in the Assembly and controlled the executive and legislature.

With the FN in decline, a change in focus occurred with the adoption on July 25, 2006 of a new immigration law (loi relative à l'immigration et à l'intégration). The law moved France toward a more selective immigration system that "(1) emphasizes employment-drive immigration at the expense of the 113,000 immigrants who arrive in France annually for family-related reasons and (2) that carries out a robust campaign against illegal migration" (Murphy 2006). This law is very similar to the one that Britain passed under New Labor, where the focus is on importing highly skilled labor. The law also created strict limits on family reunification and a new "welcome and integration contract" (contrat d'accueil et d'intégration) (Engler 2007). The new law allows the government to deport migrants who have had their stay in France refused, or those foreigners who are deemed to be "delinquent."

The law was very controversial and took over 300 amendments in both the National Assembly and the Senate before the bill finally passed. Nicolas Sarkozy, Minister of Interior at the time of the bill's passing, said of the new law that "selective immigration... is the expression of France's sovereignty. It is the right of our country, like all the great democracies of the world, to choose which foreigners it allows to reside on our territory" (Murphy 2006). The concern of the legislature was that, much like in Germany, family reunification had overtaken labor migration after the early 1970s oil shocks forced France to cut down on labor migration. Family reunification accounted for nearly 65 per cent of immigration to France, a much higher figure than in both the U.K. and Germany.

The new law was clearly an attempt to bring France in line with the new British law and create a "selective migration" policy. Recruiting skilled workers, while simultaneously curbing family reunifications was at the forefront. With Islam becoming a new focal point of discrimination in Europe, there is definite evidence that the U.K. and France are converging on a set of policies that seeks to restrict immigration, even family reunifications, while promoting integrationist criteria for residency and citizenship. However, it is also important to note that France, along with Britain and Germany, is competing for the same set of skilled workers as the United States and felt the need to make their policies more attractive to these workers who can be important for economic growth.

The FN had a major shift with the rise of its most recent leader, Marine Le Pen, the daughter of Jean-Marie Le Pen. The party's representation in the European Parliament dropped from seven seats to three in the 2009 EP election. However, the French political system received a shock in 2014 when the FN came in first in the 2014 European Parliament election, winning 24 seas. The party has focused more on Muslim immigration and did win representation in the French Assembly in the 2016 parliamentary election, but the result was well below expectations given the results of the European Parliament election. The focus on immigration continues with Syrian refugees entering the EU in high numbers and conflicts in the Middle East that continue to put pressure on migration flows more generally.

The Populist Left: An Antidote to the Far Right?

Although much of the academic research done on populism has focused on the far-right, there are also populist left parties that have been growing in power and influence. Like many of their far-right counterparts, they are Euroskeptic, anti-establishment, and disrupt the traditional left/right divide of politics. Unlike the movements on the far right, however, they do not attempt to restrict citizenship, attack immigrants, or use xenophobic rhetoric; instead, they seek to incorporate immigrants into a broad-based working-class movement. Rather than attempting to cast blame on immigrants or exclude them, these parties identify global capitalist systems as the cause for high unemployment, refugee crises, and the erosion of the social safety net. In the U.S., this movement was captured by Bernie Sanders' run for the Democratic nomination for president; in Europe, the focal points have been Podemos ("We Can") in Spain and Syriza in Greece.

Although far-right populists have seen electoral victories, the far left has also seen electoral gains. In the 2014 EU Parliamentary elections, the European United Left/Nordic Green Left won 52 seats; the Europe of Freedom and Democracy group, which represents many national far-right populist groups won 48. Syriza, a leftist and anti-austerity party, was ushered into power as the head of a coalition government with the Party of Independent Greeks after the January 25, 2015 Greek election. They won 36 per cent of the votes and gained 149 MPs (151 MPs were needed for a majority). In Spain, Podemos won 69 seats (20.66 per cent of the vote) in Congress in the December 20, 2015 election and 71 seats (21.1 per cent of the vote) in the second election held on June 26, 2016, making it the third largest party in the Congress. This is in stark contrast to the last election held in 2011, when the third largest party in Congress only won 16 seats, or 4.17 per cent of the vote.

Many academics who study populism warn that there is a dark side to the emerging left populism. For example, Müller (2016) argued that what underlies all populist movements is their rejection of pluralism and their claims to be the only true representative of the "people." This focus, whether from the right or left, leads to the exclusion of those not considered "the real people" and allows for the party to engage in anti-democratic behavior. This argument is echoed by Mudde who stated that "While leftwing populism is often less exclusionary than rightwing populism, the main difference between them is not whether they exclude, but whom they exclude, which is largely determined by their accompanying ideology."[9]

The 2016 Election Cycle

Several major elections in 2016 saw populists make gains in many European countries as well as in the United States. In a blow to the EU, the U.K. voted to leave the EU in the Brexit vote; radical right parties made gains in France, the Netherlands, and Eastern Europe; and reality TV star Donald Trump was elected president in the U.S. on a wave of populist sentiment (coupled with Russian interference in the election). There were many causes for this chain reaction of electoral results, but perhaps the most telling was the vote of white males: Across Europe and the United States, voters expressed their frustration with the status quo, particularly immigration and multiculturalism that was eating away at the cultural hegemony that the white majority had come to expect.

Left parties across Europe and the Democratic party in the U.S. were left licking their wounds. With no clear path forward, the parties looked to understand why white, working-class voters had abandoned them. Of course, this was a process that had been developing for some time. It has become clear that an important turning point was the 2007–2008 fiscal crisis. The fiscal crisis opened up fault lines among EU countries like Greece, Spain, and Ireland, who were hit hard by the need to take on austerity measures to avoid defaulting on loans taken after they joined the Euro zone, and countries like Germany, France, and other Northern European countries who felt their EU compatriots had taken advantage of easy credit and deserved the harsh austerity measures being imposed (Tooze 2018; Wöhl et al. 2019). Amidst the major changes to fortunes, populists on the left and right moved to take advantage of a volatile political situation. Anti-immigrant sentiment rose as the Arab Spring[10] devolved into regional conflicts, leading to massive flows of refugees, particularly into Europe.

Terror attacks also played a role in raising the profile of Muslim migrants in Europe. An attack on the satirical magazine *Charlie Hebdo* in Paris led to the deaths of ten journalists, two policemen, and three days of terror in Paris and the surrounding area. The magazine had been a source of controversy with its cartoons depicting the Prophet Mohammed, which is considered blasphemy by many Muslims. Although the leaders of the attack were born and raised in France,[11] the fact that they were of Muslim origin raised many issues about Muslim immigrants in Europe.

A series of attacks that followed, including one at a music hall in Paris, the Brussels Airport, and several truck attacks, kept the issue of Muslim terror and immigration high on the agenda for voters and politicians. The rise in terror attacks and increased flows of refugees from the Middle East created fertile ground for the rhetoric of anti-immigrant politicians and even led some parties to shift their focus. For example, the AfD party started out with a focus on taking Germany out of the Eurozone, but shifted its focus to immigration and managed to get 11 per cent of the vote in the September 2016 Bundestag election – the highest percentage for a far-right party since World War II.[12] Other parties like the French National Front and the Dutch Freedom party also saw their vote totals increase in their respective 2016 legislative elections.

With the U.K. vote to leave the EU in 2016, it was clear that immigration was a clear factor in the "Leave" vote.[13] Many voters felt that Britain had accepted too many immigrants from other EU countries and free movement was having a negative impact on their own prospects for economic prosperity. Long-time UKIP party leader Nigel Farage led the party to a third place showing (but only won one seat) in the 2015 parliament election on the basis of support for the referendum. He would leave the party in 2018 as he felt it had gone too far to the extreme right,[14] but remained a supporter of the "Leave" campaign as the country worked toward a complicated departure from the EU.

Similarly, in the U.S., Donald Trump was able to tap into voter concerns about immigrants, particularly from Mexico, in his bid for the presidency. His call for building a wall between the U.S. and Mexico, and his depiction of Mexicans, "[s]ome are good, and some are rapists and some are killers. We don't even know what we're getting," was controversial for many, but clearly hit fertile ground for others.[15] When Trump won the election in November 2016, to the surprise of most observers, it signaled a new era of restrictive immigration policy for the U.S. and a major shift for the Republican party to a much more restrictive approach to immigration policymaking.

As president, Trump has signed several executive orders that targeted both Muslim and vulnerable undocumented immigrants. A ban on refugees and immigrants from particular countries (mainly in the Middle East) which was billed as a measure to increase security, was initially nullified by the courts as it was seen to target Muslims. Trump also put a time-limit on one of President Obama's signature executive orders, the Deferred Action for Childhood Arrivals (DACA), calling on Congress to come up with a comprehensive approach to the issue, but leaving those who were in this status in a state of uncertainty. Despite having control of both houses of Congress and the Presidency, the Republican party seemed to have difficulty in the first year of Trump's presidency to address major issues, particularly those related to immigration, through legislation. Splits within the party on how to respond to refugees, DACA recipients, and labor issues left the party unable to take quick action on immigration reform.[16]

Despite major differences in policy goals, when they were at an impasse with Congress, both Obama and Trump attempted to handle immigration through executive action. This strategy turns out to have been easier said than done. The challenges facing DACA in 2018 show that policies are much more likely to survive with Congressional support. Despite that constitutional scholars generally agree that the president has wide latitude when it comes to handling both immigration and national security, the Trump White House faced multiple setbacks from federal courts, which were skeptical that Trump's executive orders were non-discriminatory.[17]

Conclusion

The late 20th and early 21st centuries saw a great deal of focus on immigration in Europe and the United States. The impact of terror attacks played an important role in the positions that many parties took on immigration policy. Undocumented immigration from Mexico and Central America helped to fuel anti-immigrant sentiment in the U.S., whereas the growth in flows of Muslim immigrants and refugees fueled anti-immigrant sentiment in Europe. Political parties on the right and left called for control, but parties on the right tended to take a stronger position on immigration control, calling out issues such as immigrant criminality, and this anti-immigrant sentiment led to, in many cases, more restrictive immigration policies.

Immigration policy, as well as the integration of immigrants, is likely to stay high on the agenda for political parties in Europe. More recent policies on immigrant integration show a tendency toward connecting immigration control and immigrant integration. It is clear that security concerns and public attitudes remain a factor in the development of immigration policy, and it is likely that radical right parties will be able to tap into these issues in order to challenge mainstream parties. The European Parliament elections of 2015 were a turning point for several radical right parties, and they are clearly keeping the focus of mainstream parties on control issues, despite efforts of non-governmental organizations and left parties to focus on issues such as discrimination. It remains to be seen if immigrants themselves will be able to play more of a role in these political systems and if that might impact the discourses surrounding immigration flows.

KEY TERMS

AfD (Alternative for Germany)   The AfD was formed in 2013 as an anti-EU party, focusing particularly on the Euro currency. The party shifted to an anti-immigrant position and gained over 12 per cent of the vote in the 2017 parliament election.

Austrian Freedom Party   The Austrian Freedom Party is the main radical right party in Austria. They were founded in 1956 as a liberal party and became identified with the radical right when Joerg Haider became party leader in 1986. The party was known as being anti-EU as well as anti-immigrant.

Brexit Britain voted in a referendum in 2016 to leave the EU. The exit from the EU was termed *Brexit* (British Exit), and the passage of the referendum led to a series of negotiations by then Prime Minister Theresa May.

British National Front The British National Front party was a nativist, anti-immigrant party that attempted to contest elections in the 1970s, with little success.

British National Party (BNP) Like the British National Front party, the BNP is a nationalist, nativist party that had very little electoral success in Britain and had little impact on immigration policy.

Conservative Party In the United Kingdom, the Conservative Party is also known as the Tories. They are the mainstream right-wing party that has alternated in power with the Labour Party.

Euroskeptic Political parties who take an anti-EU or anti-Euro position are known as Euroskeptic. They tend to call for more national sovereignty and less control by the EU or may even call for an end to the EU. Often this position is taken in regard to immigration policy, for example in the case of UKIP and Brexit, particularly intra-EU immigration, focused on people moving from Eastern Europe to the United Kingdom.

Extreme Right Extreme right parties tend to take on extreme positions out of the mainstream, such as glorifying the Nazi era, and extreme racist positions. They often commit acts of violence against Jews and immigrants in Europe.

Front National (National Front – FN) The FN was led by Jean-Marie Le Pen from its founding in the 1970s until his daughter Marine Le Pen took over leadership of the party in 2011 The party has taken a consistent anti-immigrant position and become more focused on Muslim immigrants since Marine Le Pen took over the party.

Labour Party The British Labour Party is the mainstream social democratic or left-leaning party and has alternated in power with the Conservative Party.

Radical Right Radical right parties tried to distance themselves from more extreme right groups. They work within the existing party system but take a strong anti-immigrant position and are often also anti-EU.

Republikaner **(Republicans)** The Republikaner were a radical right party that had some success at the state level in Germany in the 1990s.

RPR (Rally pour la Republique) The RPR was a moderate right-wing party led by conservative politicians like Jacque Chirac. The party considered itself the heir to France's resistance leader during World War II, Charles De Gaulle. The party has disappeared for the most part since the 2002 legislative election.

UDF (Union Democratique Française) The UDF was a mainstream liberal party – that is, they were moderate on social issues and pro-business on economic issues. The party was also a casualty of voter shifts in the early 2000s.

United Kingdom Independence Party (UKIP) UKIP was formed in 1993 as an anti-European Union party, and has grown in influence over the years, leading up to its support for Brexit in 2015.

NOTES

1 See "Main Parties Rattled by UKUP Surge in the Euro Vote." *The Telegraph* published 5/14/2004 https://www.telegraph.co.uk/news/worldnews/europe/1464433/Main-parties-rattled-by-UKIP-surge-in-Euro-vote.html, accessed 1/12/2020.

2 See "Poll shows UKIP Will Split Tory Vote." *The Guardian* published 6/15/2004. https://www.theguardian.com/politics/2004/jun/15/uk.eu, accessed 10/13/2019.

3 See "Signs of Desperation." *The Guardian* published 1/24/2005. https://www.theguardian.com/politics/2005/jan/24/immigration.immigrationandpublicservices, accessed 9/29/2019.

4 See "Battered Tories Face Pressure to Change." *The Guardian* published 10/2/2004. https://www.theguardian.com/politics/2004/oct/02/uk.byelections1, accessed 10/13/2019.

5 See "Tory Alarm at Immigration Plans." *The Guardian* published 10/7/2004. https://www.theguardian.com/society/2004/oct/07/asylum.politics, accessed 10/12/2019.

6 See "Howard Plays the Immigration Card." *The Scotsman* published 1/24/2005. https://www.scotsman.com/news/politics/howard-plays-the-immigration-card-1-672514, accessed 9/29/2019.

7 See "Weak Immigration Laws Let in Terrorists – Howard." *The Scotsman* published 4/11/2005. https://www.scotsman.com/news/politics/weak-immigration-laws-let-in-terrorists-howard-1-707316, accessed 9/29/2019.

8 See "Hostile Environment: Anatomy of a Policy Disaster." *The Guardian* published 8/28/2018. https://www.theguardian.com/uk-news/2018/aug/27/hostile-environment-anatomy-of-a-policy-disaster, accessed 7/14/2019.

9 See "The Problem with Populism." *The Guardian* published 2/17/2015. https://www.theguardian.com/commentisfree/2015/feb/17/problem-populism-syriza-podemos-dark-side-europe, accessed 10/13/2019.

10 See "Arab Spring: Timeline of the African and Middle East Rebellions." *The Telegraph* published 10/21/2011. https://www.telegraph.co.uk/news/worldnews/africaandindianocean/libya/8839143/Arab-Spring-timeline-of-the-African-and-Middle-East-rebellions.html, accessed 10/7/2018.

11 See "Charlie Hebdo Attackers: Born, Raised and Radicalised in Paris." *The Guardian* published 1/12/2015. https://www.theguardian.com/world/2015/jan/12/-sp-charlie-hebdo-attackers-kids-france-radicalised-paris, accessed 10/25/2018.

12 For an analysis of the impact of the Syrian refugee influx on German electoral politics, see Mader and Schoen 2019. https://doi.org/10.1080/01402382.2018.1490484, accessed 8/8/2019.

13 See "3 Reasons Brits Voted for Brexit" *Forbes* published 7/5/2016. https://www.forbes.com/sites/johnmauldin/2016/07/05/3-reasons-brits-voted-for-brexit/#6f1a17b21f9d accessed 10/25/2018.

14 See "Nigel Farage Quits UKIP over Its Anti-Muslim 'Fixation'" *The Guardian* published 12/4/2018. https://www.theguardian.com/politics/2018/dec/04/nigel-farage-quits-ukip-over-fixation-anti-muslim-policies, accessed 9/29/2019.

15 See "What Donald Trump Has Said About Mexico and Vice Versa." *CNN* published 8/31/2018. http://www.cnn.com/2016/08/31/politics/donald-trump-mexico-statements/index.html, accessed 10/25/2018.

16 For more background see "Trump Tries to Unite His Fractured Party Behind His Broad Immigration Plan." *Washington Post* published 2/1/2018. https://www.washingtonpost.com/powerpost/no-issue-divides-the-gop-like-immigration-at-party-retreat-its-not-on-the-agenda/2018/02/01/d511405e-0752-11e8-b48c-b07fea957bd5_story.html?utm_term=.3a35426779fb; "It's Not Illegal Immigration That Worries Republicans Anymore. The Trump-era GOP Cares More About the National Origin and Race of Immigrants Than the Methods They Used to Enter the United States." *The Atlantic* published 8/2/2018. https://www.theatlantic.com/politics/archive/2018/02/what-the-new-gop-crack-down-on-legal-immigration-reveals/553631/; and "The Immigration Battle Donald Trump Has Already Won." *Vox* published 2/14/2018. https://www.vox.com/2018/2/14/17012358/immigration-congress-trump-daca all articles, accessed 10/13/2019.

17 See "Trump's Travel Ban Wins a Round in Court." *The Atlantic* published 3/28/2017. https://www.theatlantic.com/politics/archive/2017/03/how-trumps-travel-ban-could-be-upheld/520995/; and "Key Justices Seem Skeptical of Challenge to Trump's Travel Ban." *New York Times* published 4/25/2018. https://www.nytimes.com/2018/04/25/us/politics/trump-travel-ban-supreme-court.html both articles, accessed 10/25/2018.

REFERENCES

Alonso, Sonia and Sara Claro da Fonseca. 2011. "Immigration, Left and Right." *Party Politics*, 18(6), 865–884.

Art, David. 2011. *Inside the Radical Right: The Development of Anti-Immigrant Parties in Western Europe*. New York: Cambridge University Press.

Betz 1994 - Betz, Hans-Georg. 1994. Radical Right Wing Populism in Western Europe. New York: St. Martin's Press.

Bleich, Eric. 2003. *Race Politics in Britain and France: Ideas and Policymaking since the 1960s*. New York: Cambridge University Press.

Cheles, Luciano, Ronnie Ferguson, and Michalina Vaughan. 1995. *The Far Right in Western and Eastern Europe*. New York: Longman.

Cowell, Alan. 2005. "British Election Debates Spotlight Immigration Fears." *New York Times*. Retrieved from https://www.nytimes.com/2005/04/24/world/europe/british-election-debates-spotlight-immigration-fears.html

Engler, Marcus. 2007. "Länderprofil: Frankreich." *Focus Migration*, 2 (March). Hamburg: Bundeszentrale für politische Bildung.

Fennema, Meindert. 1997. "Some Conceptual Issues and Problems in the Comparison of Anti-Immigrant Parties in Western Europe." *Party Politics*, 3(4): 473–492.

Fieschi, Catherine. 2004. "The New Avengers." *The Guardian*.

Freeman, Gary P. 1979. *Immigrant Labor and Racial Conflict in Industrial Societies: The French and British Experience, 1945–1975*. Princeton, NJ: Princeton University Press.

Givens, Terri E. 2005. *Voting Radical Right in Western Europe*. New York: Cambridge University Press.

Givens, Terri. 2012. "Immigrant Integration." In Marc Rosenblum and Daniel Tichenor, Editors, *The Oxford Handbook of the Politics of International Migration*. New York: Oxford University Press.

Goodfellow, Maya. 2019. *Hostile Environment: How Migrants Became the Scapegoats of Contemporary Mainstream Politics*. New York: Verso.

Hansen, Randall. 2000. *Citizenship and Immigration in Post-War Britain: The Institutional Origins of a Multicultural Nation*. New York: Oxford University Press.

Hargreaves, Alec G. 1995. *Immigration, 'Race' and Ethnicity in Contemporary France*. London: Routledge.

Huber, John and Ronald Inglehart. 1995. "Expert Interpretations of Party Space and Party Locations in 42 Societies," *Party Politics*, 1(1): 73–111.

Ignazi, Piero. 1992. "The Silent Counter-Revolution." *European Journal of Political Research*, 22: 3–34.

Joppke, Christian. 1999. *Immigration and the Nation-State*. New York: Oxford University Press.

Kitschelt, Herbert. 1995. *The Radical Right in Western Europe*. Ann Arbor, MI: University of Michigan Press.

Layton-Henry, Zig. 1992. *The Politics of Immigration: Race and Race Relations in Postwar Britain*. London: Wiley-Blackwell.

Mader, Matthias and Harald Schoen. 2019. "The European Refugee Crisis, Party Competition, and Voters' Responses in Germany." *West European Politics*, 42 (1): 67–90.

Margetts, Helen, Peter John, and Stuart Weir. 2004. "Latent Support for the Far-Right in British Politics: The BNP and UKIP in the 2004 European and London Elections." Paper presented at the PSA EPOP Conference, University of Oxford, Oxford, England, September 10–12.

Messina, Anthony. 2007. *The Logics and Politics of Post-WWII Migration to Western Europe*. New York: Cambridge University Press.

Miller, Mark J. 1981. *Foreign Workers in Western Europe: An Emerging Political Force*. Westport, CT: Praeger Publishers.

Minkenberg, Michael. 1997. "The New Right in France and Germany: Nouvelle Driote, Neue Rechte, and the New Right Radical Parties." In Peter H. Merkl and Leonard Weinberg, Editors, *The Revival of Right-Wing Extremism in the Nineties*. Portland, OR: Frank Cass.

Money, Jeannette. 1999. "Defining Immigration Policy: Inventory, Quantitative Referents, and Empirical Regularities." Paper presented at the Annual Meeting of the American Political Science Association, Atlanta, GA, September 2–5.

Mudde, Cas. 2007. *Populist Radical Right Parties in Europe*. New York: Cambridge University Press.

Mudde, Cas. 2019. *The Far Right Today*. New York: Polity Press.

Müller, Jan-Werner. 2016. *What Is Populism?* Philadelphia: University of Pennsylvania Press.

Murphy, Kara. 2006. "France's New Law: Control Immigration Flows, Court the Highly Skilled." Migration Policy Institute. https://www.migrationpolicy.org/art icle/frances-new-law-control-immigration-flows-court-highly-skilled, accessed 9/ 29/2019.

Rosenblum, Marc and Daniel Tichenor, Editors. 2012. *The Oxford Handbook of the Politics of International Migration*. New York: Oxford University Press.

Rydgren, Jens, Editor. 2018. *The Oxford Handbook of the Radical Right*. New York: Oxford University Press.

Seldon, Anthony. 2005. *Blair*. London: Gardners Books.

Somerville, Will. 2007. "The Immigration Legacy of Tony Blair." Migration Policy Institute. http://www.migrationinformation.org/Feature/display.cfm? ID=600, accessed 10/7/2018.

Swank, Duane, Hans-Georg Betz, "Globalization, the welfare state and right-wing populism in Western Europe," Socio-Economic Review, Volume 1, Issue 2, May 2003, Pages 215–245.

Tichenor, Daniel. 2002. *Dividing Lines: The Politics of Immigration Control in America*. Princeton, NJ: Princeton University Press.

Tooze, J. Adam. 2018. *Crashed: How a Decade of Financial Crises Changed the World*. New York: Viking.

Tyson, Adam. 2001. "The Negotiation of the EC Directive on Racial Discrimin- ation." *European Journal of Migration and Law*, 3(2): 199–229.

Wöhl, Stefanie, Elisabeth Springler, Martin Pachel, and Bernhard Zeilinger, Editors. 2019. *The State of the European Union: Fault Lines in European Integration*. London: Springer-Verlag.

Zolberg, Aristide R. and Long Litt Woon. 1999. "Why Islam Is Like Spanish: Cultural Incorporation in Europe and the United States." *Politics and Society*, 17(1): 5–38.

7

POLITICS OF LABOR MIGRATION

Introduction: Employers vs. Unions and Workers

Labor migration is a difficult subject for politicians in most countries of immigration. Business interests tend to want a more expansionist immigration policy, whereas unions and workers often want to limit immigration unless they can see some benefit to organizing immigrant workers. Even though the economic rationale for allowing immigrant labor into a country may be sound, it often conflicts with a variety of concerns about cultural homogeneity and changing demographics. Experiences with guest worker programs often lead to unintended consequences, such as poor working conditions or guest workers staying on as residents, both legal and undocumented.

In terms of rhetoric, labor issues are often at the top of the agenda for politicians. Some politicians argue that immigrants take jobs away from native-born workers, regardless of the true economic impact, whereas others point out that immigrants are doing jobs that native-born workers do not want or seek, such as working in agricultural or service jobs. The debate is not limited to low-skilled migrants; high-skilled migrants are often attacked as well. For example, the H1-B Visa Program in the U.S. is criticized as a way for employers to use visas to import high-skilled workers who earn lower wages than their native-born counterparts. The tech sector has become a lightning rod for this issue, with many claiming that the regulations put in place to ensure visa recipients are not lowering overall wages is ineffective.[1]

Although both the gap hypothesis and client politics theories tend to fit the model of labor migration for certain periods of time, they do not provide long-term explanations for policymaking in this area. In discussing labor immigration policy, sometimes big business wins, yet at other times restrictionists triumph. This is due to several factors that the gap hypothesis and client politics theories tend to gloss over. First, the power and size of coalitions shift and, sometimes, wane over time. Employers, unions, and political parties' positions change over time, depending on the particulars of the economy, previous policy actions, and the role that advocates on various sides play in the political debate. Second, immigration policymaking is not solely about facts – it is often about perceptions, including fears that migrants are taking jobs away from native-born workers.

Currently, all developed nations, regardless of their labor importation system, face mismatches between their labor pool and their labor needs. In addition to dealing with this mismatch, they must also deal with visa overstayers and those who have been trafficked into the country to work under inhumane conditions. Politicians also must deal with internal politics, political legacies of previous policymakers, and how prior policies shape the current immigration debate.

To examine this debate and how the politics of labor migration play out in countries today, we first turn to two cases from history. We begin by looking at Chinese exclusion and the Bracero Program to understand why these policies passed – even though one is expansive and the other restrictive. We then consider Germany, where a temporary guest worker program was created in the post-WWII years to address labor shortages, with the expectation that the workers' stays would be temporary.

Building on this history of guest worker policies, we then discuss the role of labor unions and business associations in creating immigration policy both in the United States and in Europe. Finally, we discuss current immigration debates, including whether policymakers should focus on stemming the flow of migrants or stopping the demand for their labor, public opinion regarding labor migration and migrants, and differences between family- and employer-driven systems.

For most countries, as noted in Chapters 3 and 4, immigration policy has more recently revolved around family reunification versus the importation of labor. Family reunification policies, exemplified by the United States, prioritize visas for family members of immigrants currently in the country rather than focusing on the skills of the immigrants or labor needs of business. Other systems, such as the points systems of Canada and Australia, prioritize importing immigrants with certain skill sets, awarding "points" based on education, skills, and labor needs of the business community. A second type of system that prioritizes importation of labor are employer-led selection programs, like the H1-B program in the United States, and similar policies in Spain, Sweden, and Norway. In these systems, employers extend job offers to certain workers, who then apply for visas, following the governmental rules set for their respective visa category.

Finally, we look at the economic impact of immigration, including that on native wages, and discuss labor migration in an increasingly global age.

Why have governments agreed to the free movement of goods while show-ing intense resistance to the free movement of people? Is there a disparity between highly skilled "global citizens" and low-wage immigrants?

Historic Immigration Policy: Restrictions for Some, Encouragement for Others

Although countries allowed immigrants to enter in order to provide labor during worker shortages, leaders of these countries were also careful to encourage the "right" type of migrants through policy and public state-ments. Migrants who were considered less-desirable (typically non-white or non-European migrants) were encouraged in both overt and covert ways to make their stays temporary. For example, because of the post-World War II labor shortage, hundreds of thousands of immigrants arrived to take up jobs in Britain between the late 1940s and early 1960s (Bleich 2003, p. 37). Initially, many came from Ireland and the "Old Commonwealth" (Canada, Australia, and New Zealand) and other non-Commonwealth countries. Later groups came from "New Commonwealth" countries, comprising pri-marily non-white populations (Layton-Henry 1992). After public discus-sion about the "best" immigrants for Britain, the first boatload of Jamaicans sailed into Britain on the *Empire Windrush*. Bleich noted that "The Minister of Labour, despite a shortness of workers, hoped, 'no encouragement is given to others to follow their example'" (Foot 1965, as cited in Bleich 2003, p. 38), an early indication of the role that race would play in the politics of immigration after the war.

Case Study: The United States

Historically, the politics of labor migration in the United States was intrinsically tied to racial categories, the political power of business, and whether immigrants were viewed as permanent new settlers or temporary guests. In the Southwest, where borders were fluid, agriculture and busi-ness strong, the attitude toward migration was permissive; Mexicans were allowed to come and go in order to provide cheap labor. The key point was that they would eventually leave. These workers were seen as tempor-ary labor that could provide labor surpluses when needed and then would return home when the work was finished. This stood in stark contrast to the immigrants that crossed oceans to arrive in the United States. Although still fulfilling very real labor needs, these immigrants were seen as threats because of the permanent nature of their move.

Chinese exclusion was one of the first immigration policies pursued in the U.S. on a federal level. Despite that a coalition of business interests pre-ferred the continued migration and employment of Chinese laborers, a coalition of politicians and nativists in California were able to influence national level policy. In his seminal work, Tichenor (2002) described this as "a formidable political alliance of classic exclusionist favoring racial cleansing, and egalitarian nationalist of a nascent labor movement seeking protection from Chinese contract labor" (p. 88). In addition to this powerful coalition, popular opinion was against the inclusion of Chinese immigrants. Both the Democratic and Republican parties at the time took strong anti-Chinese positions to attract voters in a newly competitive postbellum world. This combination of electoral politics, cross-class alliance, and legislative control over the issue easily defeated the less well-organized employer and religious groups.

With the closing of borders after the 1920s and the need for labor during and after World War II, the U.S. looked to the south to find a source of labor, especially in the agricultural sector. Unlike in the 1880s and 1890s, Franklin D. Roosevelt attempted to keep immigration away from both the public and Congress, choosing instead to use executive orders to shape policy (Tichenor 2002, p. 13). By April 1943, the Bracero Program was put in place, allowing for migrant workers from Mexico to work in the southwestern United States. This program included a bilateral treaty with the U.S. and Mexican governments which required the Mexican government to recruit the workers. To ease concerns in the U.S., policymakers claimed that the workers would be easily repatriated when the need for their labor decreased (Tichenor 2002, p. 173); to ease concerns about worker abuse, policymakers told the Mexican government that the working conditions of the workers would be equal to that of American workers. However, neither proved to be the case (Tichneor 2002).

Eventually the program was ended in 1963 after years of lobbying by unions, religious groups, and civil rights organizations when it failed to get Congressional reapproval. Overall, 4.6 million work contracts were signed through this program.[2] However, while it was in force, many workers did not leave the country as expected. Rather, the U.S. government created deportation programs such as the infamous "Operation Wetback" in 1954, which deported not only Braceros on expired contracts, but also their U.S.-born children and other legal residents (Tichenor 2002). Although organized labor protested strongly against this program from the beginning, the parties no longer had an incentive to court public opinion on this issue. Parties could have their cake and eat it too; they were able to restrict European immigration to satisfy an anti-immigrant public in the East, but by allowing "returnable" Mexican guest workers in the Southwest, they also appeased a powerful and rich agricultural lobby.

German Guest Worker Recruitment: 1960–1973

In 1960, the number of job vacancies exceeded the number of registered unemployed, and German employers requested permission to recruit additional foreign workers. There were four major reasons why recruiting guest workers seemed to be the best option (Bohning 1984). First, the German labor force was shrinking in the early 1960s because of a delayed baby boom that limited female labor force participation, the greater availability of educational opportunities that kept more youth in school, and better pensions that prompted earlier retirements. Second, leaders who had experienced post-war privation were reluctant to risk what was still perceived to be a fragile economic recovery on risky mechanization/automation alternatives to foreign workers (Kindleberger 1967). Unions did not oppose recruiting foreign workers in this era of full employment, especially after the government and employers promised to ensure that foreign workers would be treated equally in wages and work benefits.

Third, a keystone of the European Community (EC) was worker freedom of movement, so recruiting guest workers allowed Germany to regulate the mobility expected to occur with the implementation of the treaty in January 1968. Fourth, European currencies were undervalued in the early 1960s, which made Germany and other European nations magnets for foreign investment, creating jobs.

Guest worker recruitment expanded faster than anticipated and by 1960, there were 329,000 foreign workers in Germany. After the building of the Berlin Wall in 1961 made East–West migration more difficult, Germany signed recruitment agreements with seven non-EC recruitment countries: Greece, Morocco, Portugal, Spain, Tunisia, Turkey, and Yugoslavia. The number of guest workers employed in Germany first topped a million in 1964, and, after a dip during the 1966/67 recession, the employment of foreign workers in Germany climbed to a peak 2.6 million in 1973, when foreign workers were 12 per cent of wage and salary workers. Many guest workers were employed in agriculture in their countries of origin, although there were also semi-skilled and skilled Turks and Yugoslavs who moved to Germany to fill jobs in construction, mines, and factories, earning three to five times more than they could earn at home.

The German government required employers to try to recruit German workers before giving them permission to recruit foreigners. After receiving permission to hire foreign workers, most German employers used the public Employment Service (ES) to find migrant workers; the German ES established offices abroad and selected workers from the lists of Turks and Yugoslavs who had registered to work in Germany. Guest workers could sometimes jump the queue by having family and friends already in Germany persuade German employers to recruit them by name, while others went to Germany as tourists and found employers to hire them (Turks did not need visas to travel to Germany in the 1960s).

Guest worker recruitment peaked between 1968 and 1973, when the migrant work force rose from a million to 2.6 million (Martin 1981). Two widely shared assumptions discouraged planning for the integration of guest workers and their families: rotation and return. The *Rotationsprinzip* (Rotation Principle) assumed that, after completing a year of work, and perhaps another two years for especially good workers, guest workers would return to their countries of origin with savings to finance upward mobility. If guest workers were still needed, another Turk or Yugoslav would have the opportunity to earn higher wages in Germany.

Business and Labor: Foes or Strange Bedfellows?

It is easy to understand why business wants to import labor. The argument is that immigrants not only work for less but that they will do jobs that native-born workers will not do (or jobs that native-born workers will not do at the wages employers are offering). Immigration allows for business to fill labor shortages, obtain skilled employees that the native market does not provide, and, yes, possibly lower wages. Given that, it can be strange to think that trade unions might end up in the same coalition as business on the issue of immigration policy. Yet that is exactly what happens time and time again, as labor and business often end up supporting the same types of immigration bills.

Trade unions have been on both sides of the immigration debate. At the start of union power until the 1960s, unions opposed immigration under the argument that immigrants drive down native-born worker wages (Tichenor 2002; Freeman 2004; Fine and Tichenor 2012). Over time, unions shifted, their position, not only because of ideas of equality and human rights, but also because of worker solidarity and to recruit new members (Donnelly 2016).

In the U.S., this shift is best identified by the move of the American Federation of Labor (AFL) from a strict restrictionist position to an expansionary one that matched the pro-immigrant position of the Congress of Industrial Organizations (CIO) when the two organizations merged in the 1950s. In Europe, a similar pattern emerged. During the era of labor importation post-WWII, the relatively stronger unions in Europe generally did not look to unionize immigrant workers. Their positions shifted only when it became apparent that these "temporary" immigrants were anything but and amidst the beginning of the decline in union membership. In the U.K., the Trades Union Congress also followed a similar path as the AFL.

In France, the Confédération Général du Travail (CGT) and Confédération Française Démocratique de Travail (CFDT) shifted from wanting to protect the domestic market to issuing joint statements in 1966 and 1971 focusing on working class solidarity (Freeman 2004); while they shifted back towards restriction, their focus in the mid-1990s was on preventing the exploitation of immigrant workers via stronger use of workplace inspection, rather than the expulsion or punishment of unauthorized workers (Fine and Tichenor 2012). Today these unions, especially the

CGT, push for expansionary immigration and integration policies based on human rights.

Yet, despite the similarities in the direction of these policy shifts, there are important historical and nation-specific factors that explain both how the shift occurred and why it occurred when it did in individual countries. Tichenor and Fine (2004) argued that, in the case of British, American, and French trade unions, their shifts in policy preferences cannot be reduced to a change in ideology; the policy shifts were also the result of specific contextual factors. Changes in the structure of the labor market, state capacity, and racial attitudes all interacted to create different paths and timelines for change. Whatever the causal mechanisms for this change, it is clear that most unions in the U.S. and the EU currently support generous immigration and integration polices (Baldwin-Edwards and Kraler 2009).

Unions also face similar dilemmas about quotas, temporary worker programs, legalization of unauthorized workers, and how to deal with employers that violate hiring laws (Fine and Tichenor 2012). These issues all come down to the question of how you protect workers' rights, prevent exploitation, and welcome newcomers into society – three very complex topics with no simple answer.

Labor Immigration Systems Today

Skilled labor became a focus of immigration policy in the 1960s in countries like the U.S. and Canada. However, as the high-tech era moved into full-speed during the 1980s and 1990s, European countries began to see the need to compete for high-skilled workers from places like India, Russia, and China. This competition for high-skilled workers set off controversy about what type of immigrants to encourage and which systems to utilize to ensure receiving countries were getting skilled laborers immigrating in.

High-Skilled Versus Low-Skilled Versus Family Migrants: Points Systems Versus Employer-Based Systems

Some governments prefer policies that focus on importing high-skilled migrants, whereas others focus on family reunification, which allows for more low-skilled migrants to enter their country.[3] These systems are generally referred to as skills-based and family-based immigration systems respectively. There are two types of skills-based immigration systems currently in use. The first, developed originally in Canada, is referred to as the "points system," whereas the second is described by researchers at the Migration Policy Institute as employer-led programs (Papademetriou and Sumption 2011). Much of the support of points systems comes from the idea that these systems are clear, transparent, and easily adjustable. Systems such as those in Denmark, New Zealand, Australia, and Canada award a certain amount of points to each immigrant, based on education, language fluency, savings, and other skills. These schemas are easily located online, and it is very clear for what points are awarded and from where the final score comes. Potential immigrants must meet a certain threshold of points to become eligible for a visa.

Those opposed to this system have pointed out that, traditionally, the immigrants who enter with "points" are not required to have a job offer. Governments cannot assess non-quantifiable skills – such as interpersonal skills, fit, etc. – of immigrants who will be looking for work. There are also complaints that the points system is unable to actually fill labor shortages; although it leads to the importation of skilled workers, these people may not be workers skilled in the ways needed to fill job vacancies. Several studies have shown that underutilization of skills costs Canada several billion dollars per year, and it is one of the largest complaints immigrants have about their experience in Canada (Reitz 2014). The definition of "skilled workers" also varies greatly by country (Boucher 2019).

Employer-led systems overcome these problems by having employers extend a job offer to a potential immigrant, then the immigrant applies for a visa. However, critics of this system fear that immigrants are ripe for exploitation, as they are not competing with native-born workers on the open market, and their visa status is tied to their employers. If an immigrant wants to switch jobs or finds themselves in an undesirable working situation, they must also find a new visa sponsor in order to stay in status. Others also warn that this system could cause discrimination among local native-born workers, as employers may first search outside the country for new employees so as to hire "cheaper" labor. Both of these programs are criticized for overlooking low-skilled workers. Typically, most discussions of employment-based immigration focus on highly skilled workers.

Some proposed fixes include a hybrid system where extra points are awarded for job offers (Canada and New Zealand) or they require both a job offer and a certain point level (United Kingdom). Others also call for employer-based systems to have an easier transition from short-term employment visas tied to employers to longer term visas or citizenship that would allow immigrants to change jobs or employers.

Comparing Family Reunification Systems to Skills-Based Systems

The aforementioned systems also stand in contrast to the family reunification systems currently used in the United States. Presently, there is a debate over ending the contemporary family-based immigration system and replacing it with a point system or an employer-based system (see the following "What Is Chain Migration?" section). Yet this debate is not as clear cut as it seems. Ending a system that is predominantly family-based does not mean an end to family migration. As noted in the preceding text, most systems are mixed; rather than being either/or, they tend to be mostly one type or the other. Canada and Australia still allow for family reunification, even though their respective policies are typically seen as points systems. Canada allows permanent residents and citizens to sponsor their parents, grandparents, and other relatives who meet certain conditions, although these are more limited than in the United States.[4] Yet, even though there are fewer options to sponsor relatives in the Canadian system, the rates of family immigration are about the same in the United States and Canada (about 2.0 per 1,000 residents in 2013); however, the rate of employment-based migrants is much higher in Canada (0.48 for the U.S. and 4.5 for Canada in 2013; see Griswold 2017). In other words, the rate of family-based migration is about the same for the U.S., Australia, and Canada; however, the latter two countries, overall, allow many more employment-based immigrants (Griswold 2017).

Restricting family migration to convert to a points-based system could have unintended consequences by deterring otherwise qualified immigrants. Given the choice between a country that allows them to bring their family and one that does not, it is possible that the country that allows family re-unification will be more attractive to higher skilled workers, and also encourage higher levels of integration (Chang 2000, p. 218).

What Is Chain Migration?

This once scholarly term has been popularized by President Trump, who uses it to describe family reunification systems, and has been echoed by others in the Republican Party (Lehman 2017). However, this usage of the term **chain migration** to refer to family-based migration is quite different from how scholars of immigration use the term. This term was originally developed to describe the idea that immigrants do not randomly settle in a new country; instead they typically move to areas where other migrants from their sending countries now live (for an early use of this definition, see MacDonald and MacDonald 1964). This creates communities like Vietnamese in the Gulf South, Iranians in California, and Scandinavians in Minnesota.

According to a White House website, the Trump Administration defines chain migration as "the process by which foreign nationals permanently resettle within the U.S. and subsequently bring over their foreign relatives, who then have the opportunity to bring over their foreign relatives, and so on, until entire extended families are resettled within the country."[5] Although it is theoretically possible that this could occur, it would require both a very long time and a large amount of money. Because of the limitations discussed subsequently, studies have shown that those who immigrated between 1996 and 2000 sponsored 3.45 family members, whereas those who immigrated earlier between 1981 and 1985 sponsored 2.60 (Carr and Tienda 2013).

Income is one limitation of sponsorship, as the original immigrant must show that he or she would be able to support anyone they sponsor. This is met by showing they have a household income 125 per cent of the poverty line (in this case, "household" includes the potential new immigrant). For example, if you have a spouse and two children (i.e., a household of four) and you wish to sponsor your parent, you must show that you earn at least $31,375 per year; if you wished to sponsor both of your parents and your spouse wanted to sponsor theirs, this would be considered an eight person household, thus you would have to show that you earn at least $52,975 per year (USCIS 2018a).

Next, green card holders can petition only for spouses, dependent children, and unmarried children to enter the U.S. as permanent residents (USCIS 2015). To petition for others to enter as permanent residents, the petitioner must be a U.S. citizen, which typically requires five years of permanent residency, three years as a permanent resident if the petitioner is married to a U.S. citizen, qualifying service in the U.S. Armed Forces, or the petitioner is a child of a U.S. citizen who was born outside the U.S. and who meets certain requirements (USCIS 2018b, USCIS 2018c).

Finally, the current immigration system in the U.S. includes country limits and allows for unlimited visas for immediate family members only – a group limited to spouses, dependent children, and the immigrant's parents. As a result of the limit on other family members and current country limits, there is often a large backlog of visa petitions. In fact, in July 2018, USISC was processing applications for unmarried sons or daughters of U.S. citizens who applied in March 2012; yet there are even more drastic delays for those who are from Mexico (September 1998) or the Philippines (February 2008). The processing backlog is even greater for other categories (Bureau of Consular Affairs 2018).

Unauthorized Labor Migration: Stemming the Flow Versus Stopping Demand

Aside from debates on which sort of system governments should use to regulate the influx of migrants, politicians must also deal with those who come illegally. Is it better to harden the border, thereby stemming the flow, or is it better to punish companies that employ unauthorized migrants, thereby stopping the demand for workers?

Often referred to as employer sanctions, these punitive measures taken against employers can include fines, workplace shutdowns, and other punishments. Understandably, business interests tend to oppose these measures; however, unions and immigrant rights groups often oppose them as well. There is a fear that these sanctions could lead to discrimination where employers refuse to hire members of groups associated with immigration or foreign-born residents. Workforce sanctions could still harm workers if raids and deportations are the primary enforcement mechanisms and could even be used in retaliation if employers wish to punish or remove unauthorized workers who complain about wages or working conditions (see Bacon and Hing 2010 for a discussion of union and worker rights groups' position on this issue). Despite these complaints, many nations have created some form of workplace sanction. France imposed fines and even prison terms for those who employed unauthorized workers in the 1980s, modifying their policies over the years (Fine and Tichenor 2012). The United Kingdom first required employers to verify employee's immigration status in the Asylum and Immigration Act of 1996, increasing these penalties in the 2006 Immigration, Asylum and Nationality Act, expanding it past the hiring phase to require employers to check throughout the period of employment. In the United States, employer sanctions were first passed in the 1986 Immigration Reform and Control Act (IRCA), yet critics have pointed out that these measures seem designed to allow employers to circumvent them. For example, as Fine and Tichenor (2012) noted, although the law required employers to ask for documents showing work authorization, they did not have to take any steps to verify said documents. Others have criticized these policies on the basis that the fines and punishments levied against employers are too light to provide an effective deterrent.

The fear that employer sanctions could lead to discrimination was realized in the United States, where a General Accounting Office (1990) report found that – whereas it was difficult to determine if IRCA was directly responsible for the situation – persons of Hispanic and Asian decent suffered higher levels of discrimination after the Act was passed.

What about stopping the employment of unauthorized migrants by preventing them from entering the country or deporting them when they are found? A study by Cornelius (2005) suggested that border hardening policies, such as those utilized by the United States between 1993 and 2004, changed only the patterns of entry, increased associated costs and migrant deaths, and resulted in workers staying for longer durations because the crossing and re-entry became more difficult. In his cross-national study, Wong (2015) suggested that increasing restrictions, as measured by the number of deportations, "is not significantly related to immigrant inflows and is only weakly related to asylum inflows," suggesting that though these policies may be popular with politicians, their effectiveness in stopping immigration is not supported by the empirical evidence (p. 26).

Public Opinion

Current research has suggested that public opinion on immigrants has little to do with native-born workers' fears that immigrants will "take their jobs," concerns that immigrants will drive up the cost of the social safety net, or that foreign-born workers will affect the personal economic situations of native-born workers. For example, in their review of over 100 studies on public opinion on immigration, Hainmueller and Hopkins (2014) outlined two broad explanations for public opinion toward immigrants and immigration: one is politico-economic and the other socio-psychological. In their review, the authors found little support for political economic explanations of opinion, stating there is "little accumulated evidence that citizens primary form attitudes about immigration based on their personal economic situations" (p. 227). Rather, what they did find is that views about the country's economic situation on the whole, cultural fears, a native-born person's education level – or all three – matter much more in attitude formation than does his or her personal economic situation. Support also is not predicated on the native-born person's skill level; rather the immigrant's skill level is what matters, suggesting it is not a straightforward fear of personal competition driving opposition to immigration (Dancygier and Donnelly 2012; Hainmueller, Hopkins, and Yamamoto 2014).[6]

As a result, it appears that public opinions on immigrants and their contribution to the economy differ based on the type of immigrant discussed and the native-born person's perception of the national economy. The public thinks about high- and low-skilled migrants differently; but are the fears of native-born citizens about low-skilled immigrants borne out by the evidence?

Economic Impact of Immigrants

Overall, most economic studies show that immigrants help grow the economy. As Smith and Edmonston (1997) showed, and as Martin (2014) subsequently noted, immigrants added a net $8 billion to the U.S. economy in 1996 and that the economy was $200 billion larger because of immigration on the whole. Although Smith and Edmonston found that immigrants depressed wages by an estimated three per cent, this finding has been challenged by later work.[7] Most recent economic studies show no downward effect on native-born workers' wages (Hainmueller and Hiscox 2010; Hainmueller, Hopkins, and Yamamoto 2014; Orrenius and Zavodny 2012; Tingley 2013).[8]

Another large question about the economic impact of migrants focuses on their contribution via taxes versus their costs to social services.[9] According to one major study, the average immigrant and his or her children were expected to pay $80,000 more (in 1996 U.S. dollars) than they used, assuming they followed similar taxation and usage patterns of Americans in general (Smith and Edmonston 1997). A report from The National Academies of the Sciences, Engineering and Medicine (2017) found a more complicated picture, which suggested that although first-generation immigrants typically cost more at the outset, especially at the state and local level, this cost was offset by the contributions of their children, the second generation, who eventually pay more in taxes than their parents and native-born citizens.

Even when focusing on unauthorized migrants, studies have shown that these migrants do pay taxes.[10] For example, an actuarial note from the Social Security Administration (Goss et al. 2013) estimated that there were about 3.1 million unauthorized immigrants working and paying Social Security taxes in 2010. These workers paid over $12 billion to the Social Security fund in excess of benefits paid in 2010, and the office expected the positive impact to continue. In general, however, the research record shows that unauthorized immigrants, like low-skilled native-born workers and low-skilled authorized immigrants, tend to pay less in taxes than they use in public services. Yet, because most unauthorized immigrants are not eligible for social welfare programs, they may have a smaller impact than do low-skilled authorized migrants (Orrenius and Zavodny 2013).

These findings are echoed in other economies, with economic research in Scandinavian countries showing little impact on native-born worker wages or unemployment, while showing that immigrants contribute more to social security programs then they use (Wadensjö 2014). Economic growth was also echoed in Spain, where the government claimed that foreign workers contributed to upward of 50 per cent of the GDP growth between 2000 and 2005 and that immigration between 1996 and 2005 helped to reduce structural unemployment (Hazán 2014). Once again, immigrants were shown to contribute more to the social security system then they took out.

The Mariel Boatlift: A Natural Experiment on Wages

In the spring of 1980, the famous "Mariel Boatlift" created an influx of Cuban immigrants into Miami, with about 125,000 Cubans arriving in a six-month period, causing the workforce in Miami to grow by eight per cent. Due to Cold War politics, if Cubans reached the U.S. territorial waters at this time, unlike other immigrant groups, they were allowed to stay in the country and typically would qualify for an expedited legal permanent resident status. This created an unprecedented natural experiment, allowing economists and political scientists to investigate the following question: Does a large increase in immigrants push down native-born workers' wages? According to the first major study on the effects of the Boatlift (Card 1990), there were no differences in ages or employment trends in Miami after the Boatlift when compared with other cities. In 2015, two studies emerged reconsidering this issue. The first was by Borjas (2017), who challenged Card's findings; the second was by Peri and Yasenov (2018), who confirmed Card's findings. How do we reconcile these contradictory studies?

The reason the respective authors arrived at these two different conclusions was due to the assumptions each team of economists made regarding the data. Card (1990) looked at wages of U.S. workers who had a high school education or less; Borjas (2017) and Peri and Yasenov (2018) studied those who did not finish high school. However, Borjas defined the group of American workers that would be affected by the newcomers even more strictly: He focused only on non-Hispanic men between the ages of 25 and 59 without high school diplomas, which derived a sample of 17 workers. With this sample, he showed that wages fell for this group of workers but rose for other low-skilled workers, including other Hispanics, which was a finding not explained by economic theory. A recent article – published in the same journal in which Borjas' article was published – by economists Clemens and Hunt (2019) discussed the conflicting findings on the Boatlift and expanded their discussion to include studies on three other refugee waves that occurred in France, Israel, and Europe. The authors concluded that the evidence from these four waves "reinforces the existing consensus that the impact of immigration on average native-born workers is small."[11]

Labor Mobility, Trade, and Globalization

Classical economic theories would predict that in a world free of immigration restrictions, labor migration would flow to the places with higher wages, leading to net increases in wages around the world. However, immigration restrictions distort the market, leading to "a misallocation of labor among countries, thereby wasting human resources and creating unnecessary poverty in labor-abundant countries" (Chang 2000, p. 207). Of course, free movement of immigrants would lead to both gains and losses across the labor-lacking countries, but, on the whole, economic theory predicts that there would be a net economic gain for native-born people. However, despite predictions culled from economic theories and empirical evidence, which suggests – at worst – mixed results on native salaries, the idea of the free movement of people have not been politically popular. Rather, what is more common is a protectionist type of immigration system in many places, where policies are "designed to protect natives from foreign competition" (Chang 2000, p. 212).

Although we did see some movement toward the free labor movement with the rise of the EU and the EC in the late 20th century, this policy was driven less by economic factors and more by security concerns and the desire to make inter-European war an impossibility (Miller and Stefanova 2006). However, third-country nationals (those from outside the EU or EC) were still incredibly limited in their ability to emigrate, even though European countries lacked labor. On the other side of the Atlantic, the

North American Free Trade Agreement (NAFTA) was negotiated in the 1990s and was created with the goal to balance the single European market and provide greater economic benefits to Mexico, the United States, and Canada. Although this program pushed for the free movement of goods, there was only a single minor clause in the treaty that discussed migration, with migration itself being seen as a "poison pill" (Miller and Stefanova 2006, p. 560). Even in the EU there were fears that the free movement of labor would help to push the U.K. out of the EU through Brexit (Ipsos MORI 2016).[12] Furthermore, though the EU allows for the free movement of its citizens, the EU has little involvement in regulating the movement of third-country nationals (Boswell and Geddes 2011). When it comes to other than EU migration, policy is firmly in the hands of national governments, despite the EC's attempts to promote harmonization of immigration policy.

What leads to this divide for pro-free trade, but hesitance to endorse freedom of movement? Many people blame public opinion; the idea of the Polish plumber or the immigrant "taking our jobs" has rhetorical impact on the debate. Another explanation is that rather than being complements of each other, free trade can actually substitute for more open immigration. In other words, increasing free trade can actually increase firm resistance to open immigration as governments would no longer need to import workers; rather, they can export production to the places where labor is abundant (Peters 2015). Either way, despite increasing globalization in trade, there is no movement to liberalize labor movement in the same way.

Conclusion

Despite the gap between labor needs and available workers and the large power of business and agricultural interests, decisions by politicians do not always fit economic realities. Policies in countries such as Italy and Spain encourage workers to come, but they do not encourage them to stay (Calavita 2005); such policies allocate too few visas to fill the number of vacant positions or encourage immigrant workers in sectors where they are not needed.

Is it possible to have a successful labor immigration policy? First, in order to say a policy is a success, we must define success. Some have argued that policies that encourage unauthorized entries and employment are actually successes, contradictory as that may seem. Although the policies may appear tough on paper, they were never meant to be seriously enforced; this leads to a situation where the government can take credit for "doing something" yet it does not actually disrupt the steady stream of cheap labor. Others have pointed out the problem of basing judgements on the success of policies by asking if they meet their stated objectives, arguing that policymakers may not always be honest about their true goals (Castles 2004; Boswell and Geddes 2011).

However, most would probably suggest that a successful policy allows for worker shortages to be met in both high- and low-skill positions, while making legal entry more attractive than illegal entry. It would decrease the pull effect of illicit employment, but at the same time it would ensure that the influx of immigrant labor would not displace native labor or decrease wages. Is such a policy possible? And if a policy could achieve these objectives, would such a policy be accepted and subsequently implemented by elected officials? Or would the various stakeholders and opposing interests involved in the debate preemptively doom such a policy? Thus far in the 21st century, it appears that such policies are, in fact, doomed, as the trend has been toward retrenchment on immigration control policies in the U.S. and Europe that directly affect labor migration. In Chapter 8, we examine the policies that impact the possibilities for citizenship for immigrants.

KEY TERMS

Bracero Program A U.S. program that allowed for Mexican workers to work in the U.S. Southwest from 1943 to 1963. During this time, 4.6 million work contracts were signed through the program.

Chain Migration A currently contested definition originally used to describe the idea that immigrants do not randomly settle in a new country; instead they typically move to areas where there are other migrants from their sending countries. The Trump Administration uses this term to describe family-based migration.

H-1B Visa Program A type of visa created under the Immigration and Nationality Act, section 101(a)(15)(H), that allows for temporary employment of foreigners in specialty occupations. H1-Bs were limited to 65,000 for FY2020, with an extra 20,000 allowed for those with an advanced degree above a bachelor's.

North American Free Trade Agreement (NAFTA) A trade agreement among the United States, Canada, and Mexico to establish a free trade zone in North America. The agreement came into force on January 1, 1994 and is expected to be replaced by the United States–Mexico–Canada Agreement (USMCA), which has been signed and is expected to go into effect in the summer of 2020.

Rotationsprinzip **(Rotation Principle)** A key assumption underlying German migration policy in the 1960s and 1970s. This idea held that after guest workers completed a year or two of work, the foreign workers would return to their home country and be replaced by another guest worker.

NOTES

1 For a typical example of press coverage of this issue, see Preston, Julia. 2015. "Large Companies Game H1-B Visa Program, Costing the U.S. Jobs." *New York Times* published 11/10/2015. https://www.nytimes.com/2015/11/11/us/large-companies-game-h-1b-visa-program-leaving-smaller-ones-in-the-cold.html, accessed 10/25/2018.

2 See "Bracero History Archive: About." Center for History and New Media. http://braceroarchive.org/about, accessed 10/29/2019.

3 Note that outside of family reunification policies, most Western countries, including the U.S., have no way for low-skilled migrants to permanently enter their country despite a need for these migrants in service industries and agriculture. There is no "line" for low-skilled migrants to get in to enter these countries legally.

4 See "Family Sponsorship." Government of Canada last revision 7/26/2019. https://www.canada.ca/en/immigration-refugees-citizenship/services/immigrate-canada/family-sponsorship.html, accessed 10/13/2019.

5 See "It's Time to End Chain Migration." The White House published 12/15/2017. https://www.whitehouse.gov/articles/time-end-chain-migration/, accessed 10/13/2019.

6 For a discussion on the effects of labor demand rather than labor supply on anti-immigrant feelings, see Pardos-Prado and Xena 2019.

7 Martin (2014) pointed out that the reason studies on immigrant effects on native wages is inconclusive is due to the assumptions that researchers make. For example, in his 2003 work, Borjas assumed that foreign-born and U.S.-born workers are interchangeable, whereas others such as Doncquier, Ozden, and Peri (2010) have viewed foreign-born workers as complements to U.S.-born workers.

8 See Orrenius and Zavodny (2012) for an in-depth discussion on the different models used to answer this question and how they may affect the answers researchers find.

9 In addition to academic and government studies, think tanks have also issued reports on this issue, especially as it pertains to unauthorized migrants. Whereas all find that unauthorized immigrants pay taxes, their estimation of how much social services unauthorized migrants use tends to fall along partisan lines. This difference can be attributed to how the institutes define social or public services and if researchers count services used by unauthorized immigrants' children who are citizens of the United States.

10 See Orrenius and Zavodny (2012) for a review of research on the net economic effect of unauthorized migrant contributions and the assumptions this research requires.

11 For more accessible discussions on this debate, see Michael Clements, "There's No Evidence That Immigrants Hurt Any American Workers." *Vox* published 6/23/2017, https://www.vox.com/the-big-idea/2017/6/23/15855342/immigrants-wages-trump-economics-mariel-boatlift-hispanic-cuban, and Ben Leubsdorf, "The Great Mariel Boatlift Debate: Does Immigration Lower Wages?" *Wall Street Journal*, https://www.wsj.com/articles/the-great-mariel-boatlift-experiment-1497630468; both articles accessed 10/13/2019.

12 For more information on attitudes impacting the Brexit vote see, "BBC Newsnight Post-Referendum Research." https://www.ipsos.com/sites/default/files/migrations/en-uk/files/Assets/Docs/Polls/newsnight-post-referendum-poll-charts-2016.pdf, accessed 10/9/2018.

REFERENCES

Bacon, David, and Bill O. Hing. 2010. "The Rise and Fall of Employer Sanctions." *Fordham Urban Law Journal*, 38(1): 77–105.

Baldwin-Edwards, Martin and Albert Kraler. 2009. "REGINE: Regularisations in Europe." Vienna: International Centre for Migration Policy Development.

Bleich, Eric. 2003. *Race Politics in Britain and France: Ideas and Policymaking Since the 1960s*. New York: Cambridge University Press.

Böhning, W. R. 1984. *Studies in International Labor Migration*. London: Macmillan.

Borjas, George J. 2003. "The Labor Demand Curve Is Downward Sloping: Reexamining the Impact of Immigration on the Labor Market." *Quarterly Journal of Economics*, 118(4): 1335–1374.

Borjas, George J. 2017. "The Wage Impact of the Marielitos: A Reappraisal." *ILR Review*, 70(5): 1077–1110.

Boswell, Christina and Andrew Geddes. 2011. *Migration and Mobility in the European Union*. New York: Palgrave Macmillan.

Boucher, Anna Katherine. 2019. "How 'Skill' Definition Affects the Diversity of Skilled Immigration Policies." *Journal of Ethnic and Migration Studies*, 1–18.

Bureau of Consular Affairs. 2018. *Immigrant Numbers for July 2018*. Washington DC: U.S. Department of State. https://travel.state.gov/content/dam/visas/Bulletins/visabulletin_July2018.pdf, accessed 9/29/2019.

Calavita, Kitty. 2005. *Immigrants at the Margins: Law, Race, and Exclusion in Southern Europe*. New York: Cambridge University Press.

Card, David. 1990. "The Impact of the Mariel Boatlift on the Miami Labor Market." *Industrial and Labor Relations Review*, 43: 245–257.

Carr, Stacie and Marta Tienda. 2013. "Family Sponsorship and Late-Age Immigration in Aging America: Revised and Expanded Estimates of Chained Migration." *Population Research and Policy Review*, 32(6): 825–849.

Castles, Stephen. 2004. "Why Migration Policies Fail." *Ethnic and Racial Studies*, 27(2): 205–227.

Chang, Howard F. 2000. "The Economic Analysis of Immigration Law." In Caroline Brettell and James F. Hollifield, Editors, *Migration Theory: Talking Across Disciplines* (1st ed.). New York: Routledge.

Clemens, Michael A. and Jennifer Hunt. 2019. "The Labor Market Effects of Refugee Waves: Reconciling Conflicting Results." *ILR Review*, 72(4): 818–857.

Cornelius, Wayne A., 2005. "Controlling 'unwanted' immigration: Lessons from the United States, 1993–2004." *Journal of Ethnic and Migration Studies*, 31 (4): 775–794.

Dancygier, Rafaela M. and Michael J. Donnelly. 2012. "Sectoral Economies, Economic Contexts, and Attitudes Toward Immigration." *The Journal of Politics*, 75(01): 17–35.

Docquier, Frédéric, Çalar Özden, and Giovanni Peri. 2010. "The Wage Effects of Immigration and Emigration." NBER Working Paper 16646. Available at www.nber.org/papers/w16646

Donnelly, Michael J. 2016. "Competition and Solidarity: Union Members and Immigration in Europe." *West European Politics*, 39(4): 688–709.

Ellermann, Antje. 2019. "Human-capital citizenship and the changing logic of immigrant admissions." *Journal of Ethnic and Migration Studies*. Advance online publication. https://doi.org/10.1080/1369183X.2018.1561062

Fine, Janice, and Daniel J. Tichenor. 2012. "An Enduring Dilemma: Immigration and Organized Labor in Western Europe and the United States." In Marc R. Rosenblum and Daniel J. Tichenor, Editors, *Oxford Handbook of the Politics of International Migration*. New York: Oxford University Press.

Freeman, Gary P. 1995. "Modes of Immigration Politics in Liberal Democratic States." *International Migration Review*, 29(4): 881–902.

Freeman, Gary P. 2004. "Immigrant Incorporation in Western Democracies." *International Migration Review*, 38(3): 945–969.

General Accounting Office. 1990. "Immigration Reform: Employer Sanctions and the Question of Discrimination." Report to Congress, GAO/GGD-90-62. Available at https://www.gao.gov/assets/110/103126.pdf

Goss, Stephen, Alice Wade, J. Patrick Skirvin, Michael Morris, K. Mark Bye, and Danielle Huston. 2013. *Effects of Unauthorized Immigration on the Actuarial Status of the Social Security Trust Funds*. Actuarial Note 151. Baltimore, MD: Social Security Administration, Office of the Chief Actuary.

Griswold, Daniel T. 2017. "Reforming the US Immigration System to Promote Growth." *SSRN Electronic Journal*. Mercatus Research Paper. https://www.ssrn.com/abstract=3066361, accessed 6/24/2018.

Hainmueller, Jens, and Michael Hiscox. 2010. "Attitudes Toward Highly Skilled and Low-Skilled Immigration: Evidence from a Survey Experiment." *American Political Science Review* 104(01): 61–84.

Hainmueller, Jens and Daniel J. Hopkins. 2014. "Public Attitudes Toward Immigration." *Annual Review of Political Science* 17(1): 225–249.

Hainmueller, Jens, Daniel J. Hopkins, and Teppei Yamamoto. 2014. "Causal Inference in Conjoint Analysis: Understanding Multidimensional Choices via Stated Preference Experiments." *Political Analysis* 22(01): 1–30.

Hazán, Miryam. 2014. "Spain." In James F. Hollifield, Philip L. Martin, and Pia M. Orrenius, Editors, *Controlling Immigration: A Global Perspective*. Palo Alto, CA: Stanford University Press.

Ipsos MORI. 2016. "Britain Remains Split as 9 in Ten Say They Would Not Change Their Referendum Vote." https://www.ipsos.com/ipsos-mori/en-uk/britain-remains-split-9-ten-say-they-would-not-change-their-referendum-vote, accessed 6/24/2018.

Kindleberger, Charles. 1967. *Europe's Postwar Growth: The Role of Labor Supply*. Cambridge, MA: Harvard University Press.

Layton-Henry, Zig. 1992. *The Politics of Immigration: Race and Race Relations in Postwar Britain*. London: Wiley-Blackwell.

Lehman, Charles Fain. 2017. "Sen. Perdue: Ending Chain Migration a 'Top Priority' for Republicans." *Washington Free Beacon*. http://freebeacon.com/issues/sen-perdue-ending-chain-migration-top-priority-republicans/, accessed 6/24/2018.

MacDonald, John S. and Leatrice D. MacDonald (1964). "Chain Migration, Ethnic Neighborhood Formation and Social Networks" *The Milbank Memorial Fund Quarterly*, 42(1): 82–97.

Martin, Philip L. 1981. Germany's Guestworkers. *Challenge*, 24(3): 34–42.

Martin, Philip L. 2014. "The United States." In James F. Hollifield, Philip L. Martin, and Pia M. Orrenius, Editors, *Controlling Immigration: A Global Perspective*. Palo Alto, CA: Stanford University Press.

Miller, Mark J. and Boyka Stefanova. 2006. "NAFTA and the European Referent: Labor Mobility in European and North American Regional Integration." In Anthony M Messina and Gallya Lahav, Editors, *The Migration Reader: Exploring Politics and Policies*. Boulder, CO: Lynne Rienner Publishers.

National Academies of Sciences, Engineering, and Medicine. 2017. *The Economic and Fiscal Consequences of Immigration*. Washington, DC: The National Academies Press.

Orrenius, Pia M., and Madeline Zavodny. 2012. "Economic Effects of Migration: Receiving States." *Oxford Handbook of the Politics of International Migration*.

Orrenius, Pia M., and Madeline Zavodny. 2013. *Immigrants in the US Labor Market*. Working Paper 1306. Dallas, TX: Federal Reserve Bank of Dallas, Research Department.

Papademetriou, Demetrios G, and Madeleine Sumption. 2011. "Rethinking Points Systems and Employer-Selected Immigration." Migration Policy Institute. Available at https://ec.europa.eu/migrant-integration/librarydoc/rethinking-points-systems-and-employer-selected-immigration.

Pardos-Prado, Sergi, and Carla Xena. 2019. "Skill Specificity and Attitudes Toward Immigration." *American Journal of Political Science*, 63(2): 286–304.

Peri, Giovanni, and Vasil Yasenov. 2018. "The Labor Market Effects of a Refugee Wave: Synthetic Control Method Meets the Mariel Boatlift." Advance online publication. *Journal of Human Resources*. http://dx.doi.org/10.3368/jhr.54.2.0217.8561R1

Peters, Margaret E. 2015. "Open Trade, Closed Borders Immigration in the Era of Globalization." *World Politics*, 67(114): 114–154.

Reitz, Jeffrey G. 2014. "Canada." In James F. Hollifield, Philip L. Martin, and Pia M. Orrenius, Editors, *Controlling Immigration: A Global Perspective*. Palo Alto, CA: Stanford University Press.

Smith, James and Barry Edmonston, Editors. 1997. *The New Americans: Economic, Demographic, and Fiscal Effects of Immigration*. Washington, DC: National Research Council.

Sumption, Madeleine. 2019. "Is Employer Sponsorship a Good Way to Manage Labour Migration? Implications for Post-Brexit Migration Policies." *National Institute Economic Review*, 248(1): R28–R39.

Tichenor, Daniel J. 2002. *Dividing Lines: The Politics of Immigration Control in America*. Princeton, N.J.: Princeton University Press.

Tingley, Dustin. 2013. "Public Finance and Immigration Preferences: A Lost Connection?" *Polity*, 45(1): 4–33.

United States Customs and Immigration Services. 2015. "Permanent Residents (Green Card Holders) Helping Family Members to Immigrate." https://www.uscis.gov/family/family-green-card-holders-permanent-residents, accessed 10/14/2019.13

United States Customs and Immigration Services (USCIS). 2018a. "2018 HHS Poverty Guidelines for Affidavit of Support." https://www.uscis.gov/sites/default/files/files/form/i-864p.pdf [2018 version no longer available online].

USCIS. 2018b. "Family of U.S. Citizens" https://www.uscis.gov/family/family-us-citizens, accessed 10/14/2019.

USCIS. 2018c. "How to Apply for Naturalization." USCIS. https://www.uscis.gov/us-citizenship/citizenship-through-naturalization, accessed 10/14/2019.

Wadensjö, Eskil. 2014. "Commentary: Swenden and Scandinavia." In *Controlling Immigration: A Global Perspective*, eds. James Frank Hollifield, Philip L. Martin, and Pia M. Orrenius. Stanford, California: Stanford University Press, 302–7.

Wong, Tom K. 2015. *Rights, Deportation, and Detention in the Age of Immigration Control*. Palo Alto, CA: Stanford University Press. http://clcjbooks.rutgers.edu/books/rights-deportation-and-detention-in-the-age-of-immigration-control/, accessed 8/18/2018.

8

IMMIGRATION AND CITIZENSHIP

Introduction

Citizenship is a political institution that regulates who belongs in a country and who does not. The politics of citizenship center on deciding this question: how should members of the political community be welcomed or limited, and by what criteria should these members be selected? Obviously, this question is critical to sovereign states, and has therefore been a hotly debated political issue in many nation-states across the world and across the years. The origins of citizenship and the policies that regulate it derive from centuries of national self-understanding as well as historical ties to countries via colonial legacies. This chapter seeks to uncover the origins and development of different models of citizenship across different countries and the politics that have shaped specific citizenship policy in recent decades.

The concept of the nation-state was developed in Europe, although countries have different self-conceptions that are linked to their political development. There is much truth to the conventional wisdom that speaks of two archetypes, the "cultural nation" and "state-nation," which are exemplified by the two polar opposites, France and Germany. Brubaker (1992) illustrated this in his seminal book *Citizenship and Nationhood in France and Germany*. Germany's long-standing contention that it is not a country of immigration is linked to the idea that there is a need to foster an ethnically German nation. However, even in France, a country that prides itself on its motto of *liberté, egalité, fraternité* (liberty, equality, and brotherhood), the revolution resulted in the enforcement of the Parisian identity over the rest of the country.

The concept of citizenship is complex, and we cannot fully cover all the nuances in this chapter. There are, however, two basic definitions of citizenship that tend to guide policymaking. The first is that those who are born on the territory of a country or are born to parents who are citizens of a country are automatically conferred citizenship, which is known as *jus soli* – this is the type of citizenship we have in the United States. The second is that only those who are born to citizens or can trace their lineage to citizens of a country are conferred citizenship, which is known as *jus sanguinis*. The two exemplars of these types of citizenship in Europe have been France and Germany. Brubaker (1992) offered a deep historical analysis of the differences in French and German citizenship laws, comparing the development of French *jus soli* (i.e., law of the soil, or birth right citizenship) and German *jus sanguinis* (law of the blood, or citizenship passed down by parents).

Until the 1990s in France, those who were born to immigrants automatically became French citizens; however, this was not the case in Germany. Brubaker's (1992) conclusion is that the French **assimilationist** view of citizenship allows for the eventual integration of its North African migrants, whereas Germany was unable to do the same with its large Turkish population. However, his historical analysis – as he pointed out – could not predict future changes in law: "I should emphasize that I am not trying to account for the fine details of particular policy outcomes. Clearly these depend on a host of factors unrelated to patterns of national self-understanding. The policymaking process is highly contingent" (Brubaker 1992, p. 185). We provide a more detailed discussion of policy changes in these countries, and in Britain, in the following text.

The focus of this chapter is on citizenship policy in Europe, given that there hasn't been much change in citizenship policy in the U.S. in the last century. The last important change to U.S. policy was the **14th Amendment** to the Constitution which gave citizenship rights to African Americans. In the United States, anyone born on its territory is considered a citizen. This policy has been a focus of critique in more recent years due to concerns about people coming to the U.S. and having children to take advantage of the citizenship that would be conferred on the child. This concept of "anchor babies" has led to a push to rethink birthright citizenship by some commentators (Fix 2015), and in the Fall of 2018, President Trump announced plans to change birthright citizenship through executive order, although this would face major hurdles because of Constitutional issues, and the consensus of legal scholars is that it would take a Constitutional amendment to do away with birthright citizenship.[1]

The issue of citizenship arose prior to the 2020 U.S. Census as the Trump Administration planned to include a question on citizenship. Many cities, counties, and states sued to keep the question off the census due to concerns that it would keep people from filling out their census forms, given the Administration's hard line on immigrants. Every ten years, the results of the census determine the distribution of hundreds of billions of federal dollars, the boundaries of voting districts, and each state's share of seats in the U.S. House. Citizenship is not a requirement for receiving federal benefits, but the impact on the results would have long-lasting impact on states with large immigrant populations. There were also concerns that the question was designed for partisan reasons, to aid Republicans in maintaining control over districts with changing demographics.[2]

Citizenship Policy in Europe

Citizenship policy in Europe has been much more malleable than that in the United States. Many of these countries have only been in existence in their current form since the 19th century, or even since World War II. Citizenship is a much more politically fraught issue as ethnicity and historic ethnic ties come into play. Immigration has had a major impact on citizenship policy, particularly since World War II, and the countries we describe subsequently have gone through significant changes in policy in response to new migration flows.

Britain

Historically, British citizenship policy has derived from its experience with its overseas Empire. Prior to 1945, Britain had no defined citizenship policy, and the country accepted migration liberally throughout the 19th century. Subjects of the British Empire were considered citizens of the empire and faced few formal obstacles to migration within the empire. During the development of the empire, the concept of British "subject," that is, a person born or naturalized in the United Kingdom or one of the colonies under the control of the British Empire, became the way to deal with geographic diversity. This concept of citizenship became much more complicated with independence and the end of the British Empire as we describe in the following text.

There is a great deal of overlap between Britain's citizenship, immigration, and race relations policies. It was only when the Empire began to break down and immigration from former colonies to the "motherland" increased that Britain began to reform its citizenship policy. Britain was forced to develop a more coherent citizenship policy when the influx of Commonwealth immigrants after World War II made it an imperative. The British colonial Empire forced the creation of an imperial British citizenship model, but it only became necessary to define who was "British" once the Empire collapsed.

The 1948 British Nationality Act, passed by a Labour government, created a British citizenship synonymous with Commonwealth citizenship, thus allowing "some 800,000,000 subjects of the crumbling empire, inhabiting a quarter of the earth's land surface, with the equal rights of entry and settlement in Britain" (Joppke 1999, p. 101). In this context, the tumult of decolonization in the years after World War II, as well as the resurgent need for cheap and flexible labor in the post war years, led to rapid increases in migration flows from the former colonies and newly independent states to the British motherland. Britain had a New Commonwealth population (those considered non-white residents of the former British Empire) of 218,000 in 1951; by 1971, that number had increased to 1.2 million.

Although the 1948 Act was initially welcomed because of the need for labor in the 1950s, Britain experienced tensions with its migrants earlier than France and Germany due to the racial makeup of most of its migrants, particularly those from the Caribbean. The problem Britain faced initially was how to juggle the domestic front where controls for immigration were called for and the idea of the Commonwealth, which was still held on to as a substantive link between the former Empire and its colonies (Panayi 1999). The act came under greater scrutiny as race riots of 1958 in Nottingham and Notting Hill, combined with the Civil Rights unrest in the United States, brought forward the issue of race.

Commonwealth citizenship and immigration were greatly curtailed by Conservative governments in the 1960s and 1970s (with the passing of the 1962 Commonwealth Immigration Act and the 1971 Immigration Act) with fears that immigration from the colonies, especially the Caribbean and former British India (including Bangladesh, India, and Pakistan), would overflow in Britain. (Boyce 1999, pp. 249–251). The 1968 Commonwealth Immigrants Act, passed by a Labour government, introduced the concept of patriality, which was meant to allow overseas British subjects with demonstrable links to the British Isles – such as those who had at least one parent or grandparent born in the United Kingdom – to be allowed entry into the United Kingdom. The policy was strengthened in the 1971 Immigration Act which officially created the distinction between the *patrials*, that is "people with a parent or grandparent born in the UK" (Hussain 2001, p. 24) and non-patrials. Patrials were allowed to enter the United Kingdom and were free of immigration control, but non-patrials were asked to obtain a 12-month work visa.

The goal of hanging onto the relationships with Commonwealth countries for political and foreign policy ends delayed the development of British citizenship policy. As Karatani argued, "Previous works on postwar immigration policy in Britain have mainly focused on the way in which it became racially discriminatory. They have not asked why British governments delayed until 1981 before creating the status of British citizenship and have remained silent about the fact that the status of British citizenship, unlike the citizenship of other Western democratic countries, is still not defined by nationhood" (Karatani 2003, 106). Karatani emphasized the point that it was the "global institution," that is, the British Empire followed by the Commonwealth, which was the focal point for British citizenship policy and not only the domestic impact of immigration that led to the development of British citizenship in 1981.

The British Nationality Act (BNA) of 1981 finally created a category of "British Citizenship," although it also expanded it to include the **British Dependent Territories Citizenship (BDTC)** and **British Overseas Citizenship (BOC)**. Hussain (2001) argued that the act provides the strongest proof that citizenship and immigration are highly linked in Britain. The point of the act was essentially to restrict immigration by defining "nationality narrowly" (p. 26). The Act superseded the liberal and Commonwealth British Nationality Act of 1948 with the three categories of which the last, BOC, was about as useful to its holders in the Commonwealth for entry into the United Kingdom as a greeting card from Hyde Park. The second category, BDTC, entrenched the concept of patriality hinted at by the 1968 Immigration Act and entrenched by the 1971 Immigration Act.

The 1981 BNA continues to define the parameters of citizenship in Britain today. British citizenship remains a complicated concept given the relationship between the components of the United Kingdom and its Commonwealth. As in France, Britain has birthright citizenship (*jus soli*), but unlike the United States, persons born to parents in the country illegally are not automatically granted citizenship.

France

In comparison with Britain and Germany, France has a unique conceptualization of citizenship, it being political rather than ethnic (Germany) or pseudo-territorial (Britain). The French Revolution was essentially about human rights, not national identity as a biological postulation. Although, it should be noted, the French Revolution did ultimately produce a strong centralized state that imposed a central Iles-de-France identity on the nation. In fact, as Brubaker posited, "modern national citizenship was an invention of the French Revolution" (p. 35).

Assimilation is therefore not a novel concept for the French, having played a crucial role in the birth of the French nation as various regional identities, (e.g., Bretagne, Provencal, Burgundian) as well as urban were subsumed into the coherent core. The French Revolution broke down the system of privileges that defined pre-Revolutionary Europe. Brubaker (1992) explained just how revolutionary the Revolution truly was in creating the modern conception of citizenship:

> As a bourgeois revolution, the French Revolution established civil equality, realizing in a few weeks what the absolutist monarchs had struggled for over centuries. As a democratic revolution, the French

Revolution institutionalized political rights as citizenship rights, transposing them from the plane of the city-state to that of the nation-state, and transforming them from a privilege to a general right.

(p. 44)

However, this modern citizenship also created what Brubaker (1992) referred to as the "national revolution." For France, "the development of national citizenship represents a displacement of personal boundaries – that is, boundaries between personal statuses – from within to between nations" (Brubaker 1992, p. 45). For the first part of that evolution – replacement of boundaries between personal statuses and privilege – to be accomplished, the centralized state had to adopt an assimilationist attitude that to this day characterizes French ideology of citizenship. The first French Constitution of 1791 extended all French laws to foreigners, and the subsequent 1793 Constitution even extended them some political rights (Brubaker 1992, p. 45). The counterrevolutionary period and its xenophobic paranoia drew back many of these cosmopolitan privileges.

The French approach to citizenship lies in the French understanding of the concept of citizenship as one that is inherently political in nature. As Brubaker (1992) posited, Germany and France, in their primordial forms of early statehood, essentially understood that citizenship was separate from nationhood and – "paradoxically," as Brubaker characterized it – more firmly so in early Prussia than France. The French Revolution was intensely national, as it essentially created modern nationalism. However, Brubaker explained how it was the novelty of the act of creating the concept of citizenship that left those involved in the process intensely aware of its political nature:

It is true that nation and state, nationality and citizenship have always been more closely integrated in France than in Germany. Yet precisely the early and stable fusion of nation and state shaped the French understanding of nationhood as an essentially political fact, unthinkable apart from the institutional and territorial framework of the state. French citizenship has been national, even nationalist, since its inception... the specifically political and statist quality of French nationalism has permitted, even required, a citizenship law that would transform migrants into Frenchmen.

(p. 51)

France ultimately adopted *jus soli* principle for transforming its second-generation migrants into citizens in the late 19th century. Ironically, *jus soli* came to be the law exactly because of resentment against migrants. As Brubaker (1992) recounted, citizen resentment in frontier departments of France rose as non-citizens were excused from universal conscription and military service. The policy that was adopted in this context – *jus soli* – therefore flowed from the already established assimilationist conception of the state. As Brubaker posited, "[t]he decisive extension of *jus soli* in 1889 can be explained only with reference to a distinctively state-centered and assimilationist understanding of nation-hood, deeply rooted in political and cultural geography and powerfully reinforced in the 1880s by the Republican program of universal primary education and universal military service" (pp. 85–86).

In the 19th century, labor immigration was quite prominent and pronounced in France, further accelerated following the demographic catastrophe of WWI. In the 1920s, the *Societe Generale d'Immigration* was created by officials in order to increase immigration from Belgium, Sweden, Yugoslavia, Italy, and Poland. In fact, according to the demographer Tribalat, "French population today would be 10 to 12 million less had there been no immigration from the mid-19th century and onwards" (as cited in Schnapper, Krief, and Peignard 2003, p. 18). However, it is obvious that "[t]he French pattern of integration… is characterized by a tension between 'universalistic principles' and the (more or less unofficial) departures from these principles" (Schnapper et al. 2003, p. 17).

In comparison with Britain and Germany, France has a unique conceptualization of citizenship, it being political rather than ethnic (Germany) or pseudo-territorial (Britain). The French approach to citizenship lies in the French understanding of the concept of citizenship as one that is inherently political in nature.

An important element of French immigration policy is nationality law. According to Article 44 of the Nationality Code, the children of immigrants born in France become French citizens if they reside in France at the age of majority. The ordinance of October 19th, 1945 inaugurated the *Code de la Nationalite Francaise*. It adds to Article 44 that the children of foreigners must have also resided in France or at least five years preceding their majority. Amendment of 1973 also allowed them to receive French nationality before the age of 18 if they requested it (Schnapper et al. 2003, p. 22).

The influx of migrants, particularly of those from its former colonies, has had a profound impact on the French conception of citizenship much as it did with the British. Brubaker argued that the reconstitution of French citizenship, and particularly the "challenge to *jus soli*" came about due to the following:

> The emergence of a large population of second-generation North African immigrants, many possessing dual citizenship; increasing concern about the emergence of Islam as the second religion of France; a Socialist government perceived as 'soft' on immigration;

the emergence on the left of a 'differentialist,' cultural-pluralist discourse on immigration [and] the rise of the National Front.

(Brubaker 1992, p. 138)

In the mid-1980s, according to Brubaker (1992), the principle of *jus soli* came under considerable attack from the Far Right. In part as a response to this attack, the right-wing RPR governments of Edouard Balladur and Aain Juppe made it mandatory that French-born persons between the ages of 16 and 21 make a special request known as the "demonstration of the will" (*manifestation de la volonte*). The new socialist government of Lionel Jospin rescinded this law on September 1, 1998. Therefore, unlike the pure *jus soli* principle of the United States, France places great emphasis on *socialization*. One must become socialized, a Jacobin principle, through education, in order to become French. Schools are therefore an integral part of becoming French.

A law of November 2003 further introduced restrictive conditions to obtaining French nationality for the foreign spouses of French citizens. The minimum length of marriage before one could apply for French citizenship was extended from one to two years, plus the married couple had to prove that they were living together and that they had a good knowledge of the French language. Nonetheless, as an OECD (2006) report on global migration illustrated, "the number of foreigners obtaining French nationality has significantly increased in the last two years. This is mainly due to the implementation since January 2003 of the Action Plan for the simplification and acceleration of the process to obtain French nationality. As a consequence, the average time taken to examine an application has been reduced to one month" (p. 98).

Germany

What is unique to Germany, as opposed to Britain and France, is the explicit understanding in German discourse of what it means to be "German" in terms of citizenship. The mixing of ethno-nationalism and the legal definition of citizenship is not unique to Germany, but in the context of this study it certainly sets Germany apart from the other two examples. Ironically, early citizenship laws of Prussia (the administrative and geopolitical predecessor to Germany) were as devoid of an ethno-national component as had laws in France. This changed in 1913 when citizenship was firmly defined in terms of *jus sanguinis*, primarily as a way to facilitate "the preservation of citizenship by *Auslandsdeutsche*" (German expatriates or *Aussiedler*), Germans who had migrated to German territories (Brubaker 1992, p. 115). This is a critical point – Germany's conception of citizenship is predicated on the idea that it is defined by German blood. Without a similar assimilationist and statist tradition as France, the solution that Germany came to in the early 20th century was markedly ethno-nationalist and did not even take *jus soli* to be within the realm of the possible (Brubaker 1992, pp. 120–121). Brubaker argued that

> [t]he new law marked the nationalization, even the ethnicization, of German citizenship. While late nineteenth-century French nationalism, state-centered and confidently assimilationist toward foreigners, permitted, even required, the transformation of immigrants into citizens, turn-of-the-century German nationalism, ethnoculturally oriented and 'dissimilationist' toward immigrants from the east, required their civic exclusion.
>
> (Brubaker 1992, p. 114)

Two further historical contexts in Germany meant that the strict jus sanguinis approach was never seriously threatened. First, the German state was formed almost 100 years following the French Revolution. The French Revolution created the modern conception of nationalism and of the nation. Whereas the French Revolution created both the citizenship and the nation in a comprehensive manner, the German nation was to a large extent already developed as a principle by 1871, in no small part due to the influences of the French Revolution. Because the nation came before the state, it is only natural that it is prime in the conceptualization of citizenship. The "understanding" that Brubaker posited as having existed in France (i.e., that nationality is inherently a political conception) did not exist in Germany exactly because the political conceptualization flowed out of the understanding of the nation. The second context for Germany was its *Polenpolitik* (**Polish policy**), the struggle to stem the immigrant tide of Slavs and Jews from the East. As Brubaker (1992, pp. 128–137) posited, this policy became increasingly ethno-nationalist in nature and moved away from the original statist Prussian approach of assuring loyalty of the Polish citizens in Germany (an assimilationist approach) towards an increasingly exclusionary approach in the early 20th century.

Because of its limited colonial history, the German conception of the nation state based on *jus sanguinis* was never truly challenged by a large pool of migrants until well into the 1970s. In fact, much more important for the eventual conceptualization of its citizenship policy is the fact that Germany is considered the "Fatherland" of all Germans, and, as such is open to migration of Germans, particularly from Eastern Europe and the former Soviet Union. The focus of German governments on retaining connections to people of German heritage in former territories is therefore an important aspect of its citizenship formulation. Germany in fact constitutionalized a right to return for all *Aussiedler* after World War II, meaning that individuals of German descent who lived in Communist Eastern Europe and the Soviet Union would have the right of citizenship upon their return to Germany. Following World War II, nearly eight million took advantage of this right. And after the collapse of the Soviet Union many more did so. These people were granted full citizenship rights.

By contrast, the guest worker program begun by Germany after the war was considered temporary and framed in the terms of a labor policy. Even though these people may have resided in Germany for years, they were denied citizenship over Germans who had previously never stepped foot in the country. In contrast to Britain, where political elites tried to hold on to the liberal idea of nondiscrimination and enact a discriminatory immigration policy, the Germans had no qualms about their citizenship policy.

German law has historically made it very difficult for guest workers as well as the children of guest workers to obtain German citizenship. Over the last 25 years, political elites have attempted to modify these rules. In 1990, the conservative Kohl government reformed Germany's naturalization law after the fall of the Berlin Wall with reunification in mind. As a result, after 15 years of residence, non-ethnic Germans could naturalize and acquire German citizenship. This reform forbade dual citizenship, an element of the policy that was strictly enforced. The issue of citizenship and dual citizenship was of particular importance to Turkish immigrants, who wanted to maintain ties to Turkey. In 1999, the naturalization law was amended to accord children born in Germany dual citizenship until the age of twenty-three, at which time they must choose one nationality. In order to qualify, the child must have at least one parent who has resided in Germany for at least eight years.

A major shift in policy occurred with the election of the SPD/Green government in 1998. Gerhard Schroeder, the new chancellor, pledged to move away from the former government's "not a country of immigration" stance. A change in the citizenship law was proposed in October 1998 and became law on January 1, 2000. The new naturalization law introduced a limited form of *jus soli* citizenship and reduced the requisite length of legal residency from fifteen to eight years. Children born in Germany to parents who had lived in the country for eight or more years automatically obtained conditional German citizenship, which could be held alongside citizenship in another country. However, between the ages of 18 and 23, these individuals must choose their citizenship. By failing to declare their German citizenship by age 23, they automatically lose it. In addition, children under the age of ten could, upon their parents' application, be eligible for German citizenship so long as their parents satisfied the legal requirements and applied before December of 2000. A number of additional requirements and responsibilities accompanied these reforms. These reforms acknowledged that Germany is a country of immigration and that foreigners may join the political community.

Italy

Citizenship in Italy is mainly based on the principals of jus sanguinis, while allowing some to claim membership under *jus soli* in specific circumstances. Regulated by Law No. 91 of 1992 and the implementing regulations set out by Decree No. 572 of 1993 and Decree No. 362 of 1994, the citizenship law of Italy covers issues of citizenship by birth, dual citizenship, and reclaiming of lost citizenship (Governo Italiano, Ministero degli Affari Esteri e della Cooperazione Internazionale 2018). First, Italy recognizes multiple citizenship, and does not require renunciation of previous citizenships. Italian citizenship is automatically conferred if: you are born to an Italian citizen (or are the minor child of someone who became a citizen); you are born in Italian territory to stateless parents or parents who cannot transmit their citizenship; or if you are adopted by a citizen as a minor.

There are also several ways to obtain citizenship, such as marriage or birth in the country followed by continuous residence via a naturalization process. You may also gain Italian citizenship if at least one grandparent was an Italian citizen born in Italy, if you join the military, or meet certain employment or residential requirements. These measures allow those in the Italian diaspora to reclaim citizenship that was lost before the government recognized dual citizenship.

Spain

Like most other European countries, Spanish citizenship is based on the principals of jus sanguinis, with limited situations that allow for *jus soli* claims. The post-Franco Constitution of 1978, Article 11 establishes that it is the role of the Spanish Civil Code to define and regulate citizenship which it does in articles 17 to 28 (Cortes Generales and the Congress of Deputies 1978). These articles were most recently modified by Law 36 of 2002 (Ministerio de Justica 2018). One interesting aspect of Spanish citizenship is recent attempts to allow former citizens and their descendants who were exiled to reclaim it. While allowing those whose families fled because of the civil war and Franco regime to reclaim citizenship via the Law of Historical Memory (Ministerio de Justica 2007) might not raise eyebrows, the government also allowed Sephardic Jews to apply for citizenship in 2015 in recompense for the 1492 expulsion of the Jews from Spain (Ministerio de Justica 2018).

There are three types of Spanish citizens: natural-born Spaniards (Nacionalidad para Españoles de Origen), Spaniards by option (Nacionalidad por opción), and Spaniards by choice (Nacionalidad por residencia and others; see Ministerio de Justica 2010). Natural-born Spaniards are those who are born to a Spanish parent, are born in Spain to a couple where at least one parent was also born in Spain, or were born in Spain to parents who are stateless or cannot transmit citizenship. Foreign minors can apply for natural born citizenship if they are adopted by Spaniards. If you are born to a Spaniard outside of Spain or to someone who was born in Spain, you may apply for nationality by option. Nationality by choice (based on residency) can be met by meeting residency requirements and living in Spain (residence requirements vary based on country of origin, with former colonies and Portugal having shorter requirements), marriage, or by being born abroad to a Spanish citizen who was also born outside of Spain. There is another option to gain nationality via Royal Decree for exceptional circumstances (Nacionalidad por carta de naturaleza).

Spain recognizes some dual citizenships. If you are a natural born Spaniard, you cannot lose your citizenship if you gain citizenship elsewhere, but, unless that country has a treaty with Spain on citizenship, you must declare your desire to retain your Spanish nationality within three years. For naturalized citizens, they must renounce their previous citizenship unless they are natural born citizens of Latin America, Andorra, the Philippines, Equatorial Guinea, or another country Spain has a treaty with.

European Citizenship

With the advent of the European Union (EU), the possibility of a new type of citizenship emerged: that of the transnational citizen. These citizens, while retaining their nation-based citizenship, also became European citizens, allowed to work and travel freely across the EU with the advent of the Maastricht Treaty, which came into force in 1993, and the Schengen agreement, which allowed for free movement, but was not signed by all EU members.

Although some optimistically considered the right of free movement to be the start of decoupling citizenship from the nation, in hindsight, this turned out not to be the case. While we have seen increased interest in the free movement of goods and capital from different geographic trading blocks, free movement has not accompanied these treaties. With the confusion over Brexit, the role of a transnational citizenship seems even further away. Not only is freedom of movement being questioned, it is also unclear what will happen to those EU nationals currently residing in the United Kingdom and those U.K. nationals residing in the EU. Whereas the Home Office had developed a program, the EU Settlement Scheme, to address the visa status of EU nationals within its borders, the government announced in August 2019 that it would seek to end freedom of movement on October 31, 2019.[3] As for the British nationals living in the 27 EU countries, a patchwork system is being enacted. Some countries, such as Portugal and France, have created legislation to deal with these citizens, but at the time of writing, it is unclear what the future of citizenship will look like in the EU and beyond.[4]

Conclusion

What the move away from the strict *jus sanguinis* model in Germany characterizes is the limits of the culturalist approach since national culture changes relatively slowly and so offers an insufficient explanation of sudden policy change. As one studies the modern development in migration/citizenship policy, one realizes that there are now considerable departures from the original French (assimilationist) or German (disimilationist) models and that the case studies in this book seem to be converging on a similar model in which citizenship offers some avenue for naturalization but is restrictive in immigration policy other than for skilled migrants.

Nonetheless, as Brubaker (1992) illustrated in late 19th century France and early 20th century Germany, when citizenship debates did crop up, the cultural/ideological frameworks available to policymakers set the available options for reform. France opted for *jus soli* as a way to resolve resentment against migrants not because it was deemed the best possible option, but because it was first deemed as an option to begin with, and second, because it fit the country's assimilationist and statist conception of itself. In Germany, *jus soli* did not even come up for debate when the 1913 citizenship law was promulgated.

As these cases show, citizenship policy can change over time, along with conceptions of who should be a member of a country. Even in the U.S., it took the 14th Amendment to the constitution to get to full citizenship for previously enslaved African Americans. Whether those decisions should be revisited is a political question that should be done with a great deal of care and thought as to the consequences.

KEY TERMS

14th Amendment   One of the three Reconstruction amendments, the 14th Amendment was passed in the wake of the U.S. Civil War. The amendment extends citizenship to all those born in the United States with very few exceptions.

Assimilationist   An approach that assumes that immigrants will, over time, integrate and adopt the culture, norms, and values of their new country, becoming indistinguishable from mainstream culture.

British Dependent Territories Citizenship (BDTC)   One of the three categories of citizenship created by the British Nationality Act of 1981.
This category applied to citizens of the United Kingdom and colonies
that had a close connection with one of the U.K.'s Dependent Territories,
granting them British and Commonwealth nationality, but not British
citizenship. This category was renamed British Overseas Territories
Citizenship (BOTC) in 2002.

British Overseas Citizenship (BOC)   One of the three categories of citizenship created by the British Nationality Act of 1981. This category
applied to citizens of the United Kingdom and colonies who did not
have the right of abode in the United Kingdom or qualified as
a BDTC. Like BDTC, it does not confer British citizenship.

Jus Sanguinis   Latin for law of the blood. Used to describe cases where
citizenship is based on ancestry.

Jus Soli   Latin for law of the soil. Used to describe cases where citizenship
is based on place of birth. Also referred to as birth right citizenship.

Polenpolitik (Polish Policy)   German government efforts to stop the flow
of Slavs and Jews from Eastern Europe, particularly Poland.

NOTES

1 See "Trump Says He Will Void Birthright Citizenship Law Through Executive Order." *NPR* published 10/30/2018. https://www.npr.org/2018/10/30/
662043904/trump-says-he-will-void-birthright-citizenship-law-through-execu
tive-order; and "Trump's Birthright Citizenship Proposal Is at Odds With
Legal Consensus." *NY Times* published 10/30/2018. https://www.nytimes.
com/2018/10/30/us/politics/birthright-citizenship-executive-order-trump.html,
accessed 10/30/2018.

2 See "A Republican Operative Figured a Citizenship Question on the Census
Would Help Republicans. Here's How." *Washington Post* published 5/30/
2019. https://www.washingtonpost.com/politics/2019/05/30/republican-operative-
figured-citizenship-question-census-would-help-republicans-heres-how, accessed
6/17/2019.

3 See "EU Settlement Scheme Rolled Out to Public Test Phase." Gov.uk. https://
www.gov.uk/government/news/eu-settlement-scheme-rolled-out-to-public-test-
phase; and "Media Factsheet: EU Citizens and Freedom of Movement." https://
homeofficemedia.blog.gov.uk/2019/08/19/media-factsheet-eu-citizens-and-free
dom-of-movement/, accessed 9/18/2019.

4 See "Brexit: What Are EU Countries Doing to Prepare for No Deal?" *BBC
News* published 9/4/2019. https://www.bbc.com/news/world-europe-
46064836, accessed 9/18/2019.

REFERENCES

*References marked with an asterisk are sources that can be used for further research and information

Boyce, D. George. 1999. *Decolonization and the British Empire*. New York: St. Martin's Press.

Brubaker, Rogers. 1992. *Citizenship and Nationhood in France and Germany*. Cambridge, MA: Harvard University Press.

Cinalli, Manlio and David Jacobson. 2020. "From Borders to Seams: The Role of Citizenship." In Maurizio Ambrosini, Manlio Cinalli, and David Jacobson, Editors, *Migration, Borders and Citizenship. Migration, Diasporas and Citizenship*. Cham, Switzerland: Palgrave Macmillan,.

Cortes Generales and the Congress of Deputies. 1978. *Spanish Constitution*. http://www.congreso.es/portal/page/portal/Congreso/Congreso/Hist_Normas/Norm/const_espa_texto_ingles_0.pdf, accessed 9/30/2018.

Finotelli, Claudia, Maria Caterina La Barbera, and Gabriel Echeverría. 2018. "Beyond Instrumental Citizenship: The Spanish and Italian Citizenship Regimes in Times of Crisis." *Journal of Ethnic and Migration Studies*, 44(14): 2320–2339.

Fix, Michael. 2015. "Repealing Birthright Citizenship: The Unintended Consequences." Migration Policy Institute. http://www.migrationpolicy.org/news/repealing-birthright-citizenship-unintended-consequences, accessed 10/1/2018.

Governo Italiano, Ministero degli Affari Esteri e della Cooperazione Internazionale. 2018. *Citizenship*. https://www.esteri.it/mae/en/servizi/italiani-all-estero/cittadinanza.html, accessed 9/30/2018.

Harpaz, Yossi and Pablo Mateos. 2019. "Strategic Citizenship: Negotiating Membership in the Age of Dual Nationality." *Journal of Ethnic and Migration Studies*, 45(6): 843–857.

Hussain, Asifa Maaria. 2001. *British Immigration Policy under the Conservative Government*. Burlington, VT: Ashgate.

Joppke, Christian. 2019. "The Instrumental Turn of Citizenship." *Journal of Ethnic and Migration Studies*, 45(6): 858–878.

Karatani, Rieko. 2003. *Defining British Citizenship: Empire, Commonwealth and Modern Britain*. New York, NY: Routledge.

Martill, Benjamin, and Uta Staiger, Editors. 2018. *Brexit and Beyond: Rethinking the Futures of Europe*. London: UCL Press.

*Ministerio de Asuntos Exteriores, Union Europea y Cooperacion. 2018. *Spanish Nationality*. http://www.exteriores.gob.es/Portal/en/ServiciosAlCiudadano/InformacionParaExtranjeros/Paginas/Nacionalidad.aspx, accessed 9/30/2018.

Ministerio de Justica. 2007. *A Descendientes de Españoles*. https://leymemoria.mjusticia.gob.es/cs/Satellite/LeyMemoria/es/concesion-nacionalidad/descendientes-espanoles, accessed 9/30/2018.

Ministerio de Justica. 2010. *¿Cómo se Adquiere la Nacionalidad Española?* http://www.mjusticia.gob.es/cs/Satellite/Portal/en/areas-tematicas/nacionalidad/nacionalidad/como-adquiere-nacionalidad/modos-adquisicion, accessed 9/30/2018.

Ministerio de Justica. 2018. *Tabla normativa: Legislación Sobre Nacionalidad y Estado Civil*. http://www.mjusticia.gob.es/cs/Satellite/Portal/1292428740247?blobheader=application%2Fpdf&blobheadername1=Content-Disposition&blob

headervalue1=attachment%3B+filename%3DTabla_normativa%3A_Legisla
cion_sobre_Nacionalidad_y_Estado_Civil.PDF, accessed 9/30/2018.

Ministerio de Justica. 2018. *Trámites y Gestiones Personales Concesión de la Nacionalidad a Sefardíes Originarios de España.* http://www.mjusticia.gob.es/cs/Satellite/Portal/es/ciudadanos/tramites-gestiones-personales/concesion-nacio nalidad, accessed 9/30/2018.

OECD. 2006. *International Migration Outlook.* Paris: SOPEMI.

Panayi, Panikos. 1999. *An Ethnic History of Europe Since 1945: Nations, States and Minorities.* New York: Routledge.

Schnapper, Dominique, Pascale Krief, and Emmanuel Peignard. 2003. "French Immigration and Integration Policy. A Complex Combination." In Friedrich Heckman and Dominique Schnapper, Editors, *The Integration of Immigrants in European Society.* Stuttgart, Germany: Lucius and Lucius.

9

IMMIGRANT INTEGRATION
From Migrant to Settler

Introduction

As we have explained throughout this book, labor migrations in Europe, and long-term immigration flows in the United States have led to significant foreign and immigrant-origin populations. Once arrived in their new countries, these immigrants are expected to become part of society, except in the case of temporary workers. In the U.S., integration is often taken for granted, whereas in Europe, it is often overlooked that one of the motivations for immigration reform has been the perceived inability of "foreign" populations to assimilate or of immigrants to **integrate** into receiving societies. Researchers have observed that since the end of the Second World War, the Western European experience in dealing with immigrant integration has largely converged to a set of policies and policy challenges that are similar across the cases. Despite considerably divergent starting points, France, Britain, and Germany (as well as the other Western and Southern European countries) have all been struggling with the task of integrating, socially and economically, their immigrant and foreign-born populations. We introduce a new European country case, the Netherlands, as it has been a model for its **multicultural** approach to immigrant integration in the 1990s, and the shift to **civic integration** in the early 2000s. Although Britain didn't follow the lead of the Netherlands on civic integration, France and Germany certainly followed their lead on this policy.

Immigrant integration has come to the forefront as a policy issue in the last few decades, particularly after events like the attacks of 9/11 and the series of terror attacks in Europe. These events have also led to a focus on immigration and religion, particularly the growth of Islam in Europe. As Muslims have become more defined as a group, rather than as part of their respective nationalities and ethnicities, they have become the target of restrictive immigration policies, punitive integration measures, and citizenship tests designed to test for "anti-liberal" values. In the U.S., integration policy has focused more on refugees, but there have been measures at the state level that have been designed to limit bilingual language programs and make English the official language, focusing primarily on Spanish-speaking migrants.

In general, integration policy is not a response to the needs of immigrants. Integration policy is considered a need when a newer group of immigrants is seen as not fitting in with existing populations. However, this has been the general trend for first and second-generation immigrants. New migrants take time to learn the language and make their way in society. As immigration flows increase or the issue becomes more salient, politicians tend to link immigration and integration policy. Policy then tends to focus on controlling immigration and developing policies to integrate those who are already settled in the country.

Integration is a component of policy processes related to immigration, which takes place after a person has settled in a country. Other terminology for it includes **assimilation**, incorporation, inclusion, and multiculturalism. These terms describe a broad range of policies that include economic, social, and political integration. Often these types of integration are uneven and experienced in different ways by immigrants. Countries like the U.S. and the U.K. have not had integration policies that are as explicit as many European countries, but immigrant integration is still an important consideration when determining immigration policy. Particularly in past immigration debates, the suitability of particular groups of migrants has been determined on the basis of their perceived ability to integrate. Even more recent policies target particular countries on the basis of their perceived security risk, or the fact that the majority of migrants are Muslim, for example, the Trump Administration's so-called Muslim ban[1] which restricted migrants and asylum seekers from predominantly Muslim countries.

Another factor in the more recent politics of integration is the perceived "failure" of integration policy which has been expressed by many European governments, particularly the Netherlands and Sweden, countries which were considered fairly successful in their "multicultural" approach to immigrant integration. The multicultural approach emphasized the retention of cultural practices of individuals while teaching the language and civics of the host country. As Joppke (2007a) noted, "[e]ven in states long believed to adhere to articulate and coherent national models of immigrant integration, such as the multicultural Netherlands, and assimilationist France, this sense of failure is strong" (p. 1). Part of this has to do with the rise in Islamic radicalism and violence in Europe, but it also has to do with politics and the rise of radical right parties that influenced the development of more punitive integration policies. On the other hand, it is important to note the role of antidiscrimination policy as a counter to the rise of the radical right, as in the case of the EU's **Racial Equality Directive (RED)**, which was passed in 2000.

Another important component of immigrant integration is political participation. As immigrant communities have become settler communities, more attention has been paid to their political participation and behavior. The first issue is the extent to which immigrants become voters and involved in politics as party members and eventually candidates. The second issue is if there are partisan differences for immigrants as a whole and for particular immigrant groups. In general, immigrants have been seen as being more likely to vote for left-leaning parties, but this is not always the case.

In the next section, we examine how researchers have examined and explained immigrant integration and the processes countries have used to deal with the issues surrounding the settlement of new populations. We then examine how the issues of race and religion have impacted the policy processes related to immigrant integration. We then examine country cases, including those who have taken an approach referred to as civic integration.

What Is Immigrant Integration?

As noted in the Introduction, immigrant integration consists of the processes that take place after an immigrant has moved to and settled in a new country. As Freeman (2006) pointed out, integration is often the intersection of migrants' strategies with regulatory frameworks which were not particularly designed as immigrant incorporation mechanisms, such as welfare regimes. Integration is also considered to be a two-way process, requiring accommodation on the part of both the native and the immigrant populations. Ireland (2004) described it as a process directed toward overall social cohesiveness. Authors have used terms such as *assimilation, incorporation,* and *multiculturalism* to describe the processes that lead to an immigrant becoming an integrated part of his or her adopted community. However, these are ambiguous concepts, mainly used by policymakers to describe a particular policy outcome (i.e., immigrants who can speak the language; are sending their children to school; and, in general, are not causing problems in a society).

In the United States, immigrant integration has not been seen as a formal process. As Jiménez (2011) reported, "[w]ith the exception of refugees, immigrants receive relatively little federal funding for integration programs. This laissez faire approach to immigrant integration has in the past relied primarily on a strong labor market and high-quality public education to provide opportunities for integration" (p. 1). Immigrant integration can take a great deal of time, but the process of newcomers and existing society adjusting to each other is seen as a relatively uncomplicated process. That is not to say that there aren't issues for new arrivals and their children, but immigrant integration is rarely considered to be a high priority on the agenda of politicians in the United States.

On the other hand, immigrant integration is seen as a very important issue in Europe. Since the early 2000s, most European countries are looking at how they have integrated immigrants in the past, and how they might change their policies to avoid some of the problems exhibited in immigrant and minority communities today. Immigrants tend to face higher levels of unemployment than the general population, as well as exclusion from many aspects of society, particularly as non-citizens. Discrimination and issues of racism, including the rise of anti-immigrant radical right parties, have become critical issues, as evidenced in part by the passage of the European Union's RED in 2000. The RED was largely driven by calls for greater "social cohesion and solidarity" but its passage was also a political response to the entry of the radical right Austrian Freedom Party into government in 2000. The RED addresses racial discrimination in the areas of social protection, housing, education, and associations, as well as in employment (Givens and Evans Case 2014). More recently, immigrants have formed new organizations in the social and political spheres to advocate for themselves, with the support of government and EU institutions.

The direction of integration policies, and anti-discrimination policies, is often dependent on politics, as in the case of the RED. Parties have certainly used immigration as an issue in electoral campaigns. However, this factor is not always taken into consideration when examining immigrant integration. Many political scientists and sociologists instead have examined "modes of immigrant integration" in order to develop country typologies.

Research dating back to the 1990s has worked to identify various models of incorporation to explain the policies of different countries and differences in outcomes for immigrants (Castles, de Haas, and Miller 2014; Schain 2008; Favell 1998). According to this approach, cultural idioms and philosophies broadly structure the immigration and incorporation of newcomers. Yet in light of recent policy shifts in many countries, a number of scholars have offered critiques of these model-centered approaches to integration policy (Howard 2009; Joppke 2007a). Many have noted that national approaches to immigration and integration show little correspondence with the messy institutional reality of these countries' policy efforts. Bertossi (2011) claimed that these "highly stylized national models, as we often imagine them, have never existed... for the simple reason that they were never institutionalized or internalized on the basis of stable, univocal, and coherent normative systems over the last 30 years" (p. 1571). Instead, as Freeman (2004) argued, these models "do not represent self-conscious, deliberate choices so much as the unintended consequences of subsystem frameworks that are weakly, if at all, coordinated... particular states possess a patchwork of multidimensional frameworks that hardly merit the appellation 'regime' or 'type'" (p. 946). Consequently, a focus on national approaches as objects of analysis causes us to overlook how these approaches are translated into institutional and bureaucratic reality.

A few authors have engaged the topic of the immigrant integration, conducting in-depth studies which explore the politics of integration in a comparative and systematic way. For example, Messina (2007) argued, "as immigration has evolved as a policy challenge in each of its distinct but interrelated phases, that is, labor immigration, secondary immigration and illegal/humanitarian immigration, it has been driven and dominated by a political logic, a logic that has superseded and trumped economic and humanitarian imperatives whenever these imperatives conflict with the goals and interests of politics" (pp. 10–11). This "political logic" varies over time and across cases. Freeman (1979) described British policy as "a tale of the descent of a government from a heady and idealistic image of itself as the center of a vast Common-wealth – 'the greatest multi-racial association the world has ever known' – to the unembarrassed announcement that 'our first duty is to consider the interests and wishes of our own people'" (pp. 43–44).

The recent literature in political science has focused on whether or not integration policy is converging. For example, Joppke (2007b) found that countries more recently are all moving to similar policies on citizenship, and family reunification. In the case of immigrant integra-tion, particularly antidiscrimination policy, he also argues that this is due to the impact of the EU. Although Joppke mentioned the role of radical right politics, there is no clear linkage between mainstream party politics and integration policies. But how did we get here, and what were the catalysts for these policies?

In general, there has been a lack of focus on the politics impacting policy. Penninx, Spencer, and Van Hear (2008) have examined the state of research on migration and integration in Europe and found that "[a]nalysis of the mismatch between policy evaluation and advice and actual political processes is lacking and it is not clear how political processes originate and develop in the field of immigration and integration as well as what is the role of different actors (e.g., governments – central, regional, local, trade unions, NGOs, individuals)" (p. 7). In analyzing the politics of immigrant integration, it is important to note that it is inextricably intertwined with immigration policy.

In response to the rise of integration as a distinct policy area in Europe, another strand of the integration literature on the subject has begun to investigate the actual policies that states employ to manage immigrant integration. Unlike the control-focused literature, however, this body of work has produced a promising array of quantitative tools for comparing integration approaches and policies. These range from indices coding civic integration policies (Goodman 2010) to citizenship policy indices (Howard 2009; Janoski 2010). Among the many projects that seek to measure immigrant integration policy, the Migrant Integration Policy Index (MIPEX) is one of the most ambitious. In 2010, MIPEX coded 148 aspects of integration policy in (then) all 27 member states into six "strands": (1) labour market mobility, (2) education, (3) political participation, (4) long-term residence, (5) access to nationality, and (6) anti-discrimination. These strands attempt to capture the extent to which "integration policies provide the conditions for promoting legal integration and to what extent these conditions are closer to or further away from the highest equality standards" (Huddleston, Niessen, Chaoimh, and White, 2011, p. 5).

Niessen (2009) argued that these "[p]olicies set favorable conditions as long as they tackle to [sic] access to the labour market, secure residence status, ensure family reunion, offer political participation, encourage acquisition of nationality, and prohibit discrimination" (p. 3). However, these categories emphasize the positive side of integration, as the author confirmed. Using the 2014 MIPEX, Table 9.1 indicates how the case study countries rank and their score, in comparison to Sweden with the top ranking, and Austria, which is currently ranked 24 out of 31 countries. There is clear variance across countries, indicating differences in how each country is assessed in terms of these benchmarks.

In Europe, immigrants are often referred to as third country nationals (TCNs) that is, they are not from the country they are living in, and not from another EU country, so they are from a third country.[2] On their website, the European Network Against Racism (ENAR) characterizes the issue of integration in the EU as follows:

> [w]hen it comes to the integration of migrants, many restrictive measures are in place – for instance with regard to family reunification conditions, accessing citizenship or voting rights, transition of work/residence permits. The focus on security measures is also undermining the integration process and integration policies in place.
>
> A number of discriminatory and exclusionary practices prevent migrants from effectively participating in society, resulting in a waste of many talents.[3]

The situation described is part of the focus on "civic integration," which is a series of policies that focus on requirements that an immigrant must learn to be considered eligible to acquire a visa or stay in a country. As described by Carrera and Wiesbrock (2009),

[t]he civic dimension of integration requires TCNs to demonstrate that they know, understand and respect the receiving society's history and institutions, as well as its common shared values and way of life (and even in some cases that they adhere to these latter aspects). The predominantly nationalistic, and to a certain extent patriotic, and subjective (indeterminate) juridical nature of the concept of civic integration allows member states to exercise even more discretion when deciding whether to grant EC rights and freedoms to TCNs as envisaged in EC immigration law.

(p. 2)

TABLE 9.1 Migrant Integration Policy Index (MIPEX) 2014 Overall Rankings

Rank	Country	MIPEX 2014 score	Change from MIPEX 2011
1	Sweden	80	−3
5	Netherlands	61	−7
6	Belgium	70	+3
12	Germany	63	+6
12	United Kingdom	56	−1
	EU-15 average		
		61	+9
15	France	54	+3
24	Austria	48	+6

Note. The source of these data is the Migrant Integration Policy Index (see http://mipex.eu/). EU = European Union.

These types of analyses lead one to see that immigration has led to an inconsistent set of policies designed to integrate immigrants in a difficult political context.

This approach also raises the question whether this focus on civic integration keeps policymakers from focusing on issues of discrimination. For example, in the case of Germany, the focus on integration put minorities on the defensive and created the kind of exclusive communalism that politicians claimed they wanted to avoid. More generally, pro-immigrant discourses found on the left tend to emphasize the rights of immigrants (to work, to be free from discrimination, to family reunification, to participation in politics, and so on) while anti-immigrant discourses found on the right tend to emphasize their responsibilities (to enter legally, to follow the law, to learn the local language, to follow local customs, and so on). We discuss more of the specifics of the country cases in the following text.

Integration Policy

Many Western European countries experienced high levels of migration following World War II, but they did not adopt similar policies or even address immigrant integration at similar times. Britain began to focus on integrating its immigrants soon after citizens from new commonwealth countries began entering the country in large numbers in the 1950s and 1960s. Despite inflows from their colonies, France and the Netherlands did not focus on the integration of immigrants until the 1970s. Germany only admitted it was a country of immigration in the late 1990s and still struggles with integration policy. Countries focus on immigrant integration at different times in part due to the times that the main flows of immigrants entered the country. However, the salience of the issue is also a factor. When Muslim immigrants became a concern in the late 1990s, the focus on immigrant integration focused on civic integration as we explain in the following text.

In the case of Britain, the immigrants from the "New Commonwealth" (i.e., recently de-colonized countries in the Caribbean, Africa, and Asia) were considered neither temporary nor assimilable, due to the fact that they were from parts of the former empire which were considered culturally incompatible with the mainland. Early moves to control immigration focused on the conflicts that arose between new arrivals and working-class whites. However, the Left in Britain saw immigrants as potential voters and exchanged "race relations" antidiscrimination policy for more immigration control policies in the 1960s and 1970s (Givens and Evans Case 2014).

Race had very high salience early in the immigration debate in Britain. In France, by contrast, labor immigrants were considered temporary until after the immigration stop in the 1970s. Although they were considered assimilable, race (and religion) began to play more of a role over time, particularly with the rise of the anti-immigrant Front National in the 1980s. However, although race became more salient, the Left did not respond with antidiscrimination policy since even those of immigrant origin who were citizens did not have much of a voice in politics, as we describe below. In Germany, immigrants were considered temporary guest workers (*Gastarbeiter*) and could not easily become German (at least until the late 1990s). Race was not an issue, particularly because there was no chance that immigrants would have a role to play in politics. Immigrants (i.e., *Ausländer* or foreigners) tended to be classified by nationality rather than ethnic origin (Green 2004). In the Netherlands, religion became a much larger issue than race, prompting a focus on educating immigrants around civic norms and language, and this focus was taken on by other countries in the early 2000s.

Citizenship policy also played an important role in the status and approach to these populations. In Britain, the fact that many of the immigrants had citizenship, or they and their children could acquire citizenship, created a potential pool of voters. This potential was not as critical in France, given the nature of the political system which made it difficult for ethnic minorities to gain political clout, despite having citizenship, and was non-existent in Germany where it was very difficult for immigrants to get citizenship until recently. The Netherlands took a more mixed approach, making citizenship accessible to immigrants from former colonies and relatively less accessible for those from other parts of the world.

Between 1950 and 1994, immigration accounted for 80 per cent of Germany's population growth (Joppke 1999). Although origin rarely entered the discourse on immigration explicitly, the emphasis on German nationality (particularly on the Right) allowed the government to pursue restrictive policies towards foreigners. The courts were the only recourse for immigrants, at least until the change in citizenship law in 2000 allowed more Turks to naturalize. Germany would have to face the immigrant integration issue more directly.

Despite these differences in the emphasis placed on race, the outcomes for immigrants and ethnic minority citizens have been similar in each of these countries. They face high unemployment, residential segregation, and difficulties with the educational systems in each country. Because of colonial linkages and citizenship issues, Britain grappled early with the issue of race. After World War II, it is clear that economic priorities drove the policies that led to the importation of labor in France and Germany. After labor was no longer being encouraged to migrate, the social issues related to these groups became more of a priority.

It can help to examine the differences between general and targeted policies as delineated in Table 9.2, because many of the policies which impact immigrants are also targeted at citizens as well, although they may be targeted at those with "an immigration background." This is sometimes referred to as "indirect immigration" policy (Doomernik 2003; Doomernik and Bruquetas-Callejo 2016). We would expect right parties to be more likely to introduce exclusionary policies and left parties more inclusionary policies. Though "contingent" policies may be favored by either right or left, they may be implemented in a more inclusionary way under a left government and a more exclusionary way under a right government. Many European countries are beginning to focus on women and integration related to the veil and burqa issue, particularly in France.

Inclusionary policies, such as antidiscrimination policy, have been pursued at the EU level, and incorporated at the national level in all EU countries, with mixed results (Givens and Evans Case 2014). As concerns about immigrant integration became connected to terrorist attacks in the Netherlands, U.K., and France, integration became more connected to control-related measures.

TABLE 9.2 General and Targeted Integration Policies

Types of policies	General	Targeted
Inclusionary	Antidiscrimination policy (housing, employment, etc.) Human rights policies	Family reunification Voting rights
Mixed or contingent	Education policies Welfare	Language courses Integration contract Visa policies Citizenship policies Residence permits Work permits
Exclusionary	Language requirements Racial profiling	Limits on family reunification Veil ban Welfare restrictions

Civic Integration

In 2009, Carrera and Wiesbrock (2009) recognized "civic integration" as a new approach to immigrant integration policy. They describe it as

> the organisation of integration courses or introductory/orientation programmes, tests and contracts. These compel TCNs to demonstrate that they know, understand and respect the host society's history and institutions, along with the common shared values (and symbols) of the nation-state and in some cases even those of the EU.[3] Civic integration therefore confers strong cultural and identitarian connotations on the juridical framing of the phenomena of human mobility and diversity. It can be considered a new discursive line intending to hide the much-contested classical logics of assimilation or acculturation.[4]
>
> (p. 3)

This concept of integration is assuming a role formerly played by nationality laws, chiefly as a condition for naturalization. As noted in Table 9.1, these types of policies tend to be more exclusionary, and have become the preferred approach in countries like the Netherlands, which had focused on a more multicultural approach to immigrant integration in the 1990s.

Netherlands

The case of the Netherlands is an important one for immigrant integration. As is explained in the following text, the country was considered the main example of a multicultural approach to immigrant integration up through the late 1990s, then became the testing ground for the new civic integration. Many countries have emulated policies developed in the Netherlands, and the EU has also taken on the civic integration approach in its broader policymaking around immigrant integration.

After World War II, the Netherlands was in a much different position than the other country cases. Rather than importing labor, the Netherlands was initially concerned with a growing population and, due to the lack of industrial expansion, the government pursued "a vigorous emigration policy" (Bagley 1973, p. 33). Most of the immigration to the Netherlands from 1945 to 1963 was the result of refugees from Indonesia and other colonies as they went through their processes of independence after World War II. As with France and Algeria, "[t]he Dutch lost Indonesia after a bloody and humiliating struggle" (Bagley 1973, p. 49).

The Dutch government focused on providing services and support for these migrants immediately after the war. A variety of welfare services were provided and these immigrants were expected to assimilate quickly,

> [t]he social services for the care of migrants evolved in 1949; their emergence followed the whole-hearted decision of the Dutch Government, supported by all sections of intellectual and business opinion, to accept the migrants...Critics of the Government's policy based their objections on grounds of the over-rapid and perhaps forced assimilation of Indonesian migrants into Dutch life
>
> (Bagley 1973, p. 79).

In 1954 citizens of former colonies were able to become citizens of the Netherlands.

By the 1960s, new groups of immigrants were beginning to arrive in the Netherlands, and the government also recruited guest workers from Turkey and Morocco while still encouraging emigration. The approach toward these immigrants was much different than that toward the Indonesians as "[s]ocial policy on how to treat the immigrant workers has developed quite slowly. None of the elaborate social welfare facilities used for the reception of the immigrants from Indonesia was used, and the arrival of these workers, in small groups, did not attract attention" (Bagley 1973, p. 150). With Surinamese independence in 1975, migration from the former colonies in Indonesia declined, and the recruitment of guest workers had stopped with the oil crisis in the early 1970s, but the Dutch government did not encourage return migration.

By the early 1980s, the government had developed a minority integration policy which established that the government should facilitate the integration of those who wished to stay and the return of those who wished to return. Marginalization was to be avoided and group/cultural autonomy was to be respected. The rights of those who were legal residents were similar to those of full citizens; after five years, non-national legal residents could apply for citizenship (Doomernik 2003).

The Ministry of Interior's integration portfolio was created in 1980, with a focus on Moluccans immigrants and the potential for terrorist attacks. Although there were only a few thousand that came in the late 1940s, they remained a separate community because they wanted to be independent from Indonesia and hoped to return to an independent Molucca. The Dutch government allowed them to live together as a reward for their service in the military in Molucca. Moroccans started moving into their neighborhoods and this led to conflicts between the two groups. Municipal authorities couldn't handle the problems which developed and looked to the central government for support with housing, education, and unemployment.

In the 1990s the government introduced a variety of "discouragement policies" to limit further immigration. However, political correctness tended to be the rule – politicians preferred multiculturalism, even though it wasn't supported by the public. An important issue was how to deal with the language problem, since many immigrants weren't learning French or Flemish. By 1996 there was the passage of the *Inburgeringsbelied,* a law aimed at the integration of newcomers (with exceptions for guest workers); this law was a general switch away from inclusionary policies towards language and cultural education. These policies reflected concerns about the rule of law, different customs, and general discussions about Dutch national identity.

The shift toward civic integration began in the late 1990s, as noted by Joppke (2007b), "[t]he new policy was first enunciated in the 1998 Newcomer Integration Law (Wet Inburgering Nieuwkomers), which obliges most non-EU newcomers to participate in a 12-month integration course consisting of 600 hours of Dutch language instruction, civic education, and preparation for the labor market" (p. 249).

The Civic Integration Act of 2007 was initiated because of neighborhood tensions between ethnic Dutch and non-Dutch migrants. As the numbers of immigrants increased in places like Brussels and Antwerp, ethnic Dutch people didn't recognize their neighborhoods anymore. Children of immigrants began to fill schools, and unemployment for immigrants became a problem as they had to rely on welfare benefits. Their children didn't learn Dutch and they fell behind in school as their families spoke Turkish at home. For many immigrants, they were in a situation where they didn't have to learn Dutch to be employed and many are unemployed.

The Netherlands has played a leading role in the development of integration policies that focus on civic integration. As we discuss in the following text, other countries have followed their lead, and this has become a focus for policy at the EU level as well.

Germany

According to government sources, most immigrants who come to Germany don't speak German (60 per cent to 70 per cent) unlike France or Britain where many immigrants already speak French or English. Integrating immigrants has become a priority for the German government since the Schroeder government emphasized that Germany is a country of immigration. The 2005 immigration law created the right to integration measures for new arrivals. This was the first time that integration had a legal basis.

There were no specific incidents in Germany, such as the riots in France, or the murder of Theo Van Gogh in the Netherlands, or the bombings in London that impacted the passage of legislation focusing integration policy on language acquisition and civic culture. However, these events and the passage of similar legislation in the Netherlands, France, and Britain clearly impacted the timing and nature of the new focus on language acquisition and civic education.

The government implemented the new integration law with a focus on language acquisition, and unlike many immigration related policies, implementation and funding is at the federal level. This language program is the most important and biggest federally run government program in Germany at approximately 215 million euros per year. Integration courses (language and civic training) are coordinated at the Federal level by the Federal Bureau for Migration in Nuremberg.

- Integration courses include 600 hours of language and 45 hours on culture and the legal system.
- Language courses can be extended to 900 hours or up to 1,200 hours for special groups.

The integration course is a big exception for Germany; most other policies like residence permits and citizenship are handled at the level of the communes and *Landesbehörden*. The federal government can't tell a commune who can be a citizen or who can get a residence permit. Another exception is asylum policy which is coordinated by the Bundesamt in Nuremberg.

Since the passage of the amendment to the 2005 immigration law in 2007, in the case of family reunification, the family member has to pass a language test in order to get a visa, but it is only required for non-visa waiver countries. There has been a 30 per cent decline in the numbers entering the country for family reunification since 2005.

In 2006 the government held its first integration summit which led to the development of a National Integration Plan. Many stakeholders were involved who committed to concrete actions, but there has been a problem with follow-through on commitments. Officials continue to focus on developing an action plan that will define clear goals and measures regarding integration. In recent years, these types of meetings have continued with stakeholders playing more of a role in the process of developing policies, particularly at the local level.

France

France has adopted policies on civic integration which are similar to those in the Netherlands and Germany. In 2003 France develop a series of policy proposals related to integration, known as *Le contrat d'accueil et d'Intégration* (CAI) – the integration/assimilation contract. The main proposals included requiring family members to take tests in their home country before joining family members in France, enhanced citizenship ceremonies, creating one minister to handle immigration and immigrant integration policy, and maintaining statistics on national origin (Mariani 2006). France doesn't put as much money into the language courses and requires a lower level of competence compared to Germany.

Since the early 2000s, France has experienced a series of devastating terror attacks perpetrated by "home grown" terrorists, which has led to questions about the country's ability to integrate immigrants from Muslim backgrounds. This has led to a variety of debates around integration and citizenship, and what it means to be French. Politicians have continued to pursue policies related to civic integration, while looking at new ways to address issues of alienation for immigrants and their children who have grown up in France yet feel that they are not accepted as French.

Antidiscrimination Policy

Ethnic and racial discrimination has been an issue for Europe throughout history, but given issues of growing minority communities and anti-immigrant violence in Europe today, antidiscrimination policy would seem a natural area for concern. It is important to note that antidiscrimination policy did not develop directly from demands by minorities in these countries as it did in the United States. The development of legislation in the U.S. came during a time of great social upheaval in the 1960s. The situation in Europe was quite different. As a response to the rise of anti-immigrant radical right parties, politicians in Europe drew upon policies that had been diffused from North America to Britain in the late 1960s. This approach ultimately led to the passage of the European Union's RED in 2000.

Beginning in 1965, Britain expressly recognized the role of race in British society because of immigration from former colonies with diverse populations which was increasing the numbers of ethnic minorities in the country. Drawing upon the American example, Parliament enacted a series of laws that prohibited racial discrimination. Parliament also established institutions specifically charged with their enforcement, including the creation of the Commission for Racial Equality (CRE). In many respects, the policies prescribed in the RED resemble these laws and institutions.

In the 1980s, increases in racist violence and entry of far-right parties into the European Parliament (EP) led to a response at the EU level. In 1984, the EP took the lead in dealing with racial discrimination, led by the British Labour party's Member of the European Parliament (MEP), Glyn Ford. The EP was seen as, and clearly was at that time, a secondary institution with little influence. However, given the outcome of the RED less than 20 years later, it is clear that the actions taken by the EP in the mid-1980s set in motion a series of reports and actions that would ultimately lead to the passage of the RED.

As the EU passed the Maastricht and Amsterdam treaties, advocates saw an opportunity to also expand the rights of ethnic minority groups and the European Commission became a partner in these efforts. The European Union declared 1997 the "Year against Racism." This declaration was clearly in response to the success of radical right parties, but it also signaled a shift in the approach that the EU would take to issues of racism and discrimination. First, it acknowledged that racism existed, and second, it helped to lay the groundwork for member states to take on this issue through policy change at the EU level. In the 1990s, there was a lack of institutions that could deal with discrimination issues. France's "color-blind" approach to discrimination made it difficult for ethnic minorities to prove disparate treatment. Germany's continued insistence that it was "not a country of immigration" made it difficult for Turks and other minorities to gain citizenship and be considered members of the community. Around this time, anti-racism organizations from around Europe formed the transnational ENAR to track and report on racist acts.

With the electoral success of the Austrian Freedom Party in 1999, it seemed that the EU's patience with these parties had come to an end. Left-leaning governments in the other 14-member states wanted to take action. One of the responses to the Freedom Party's success and entry into a coalition government in 2000 was the passage of the EU's RED. Antidiscrimination policy would now have to be passed into the national laws of all the current and future EU member states. The question was this: Would this translate into real change for ethnic minority communities in Europe?

All EU member states have transposed the RED into national law and created the equality bodies that were required by the legislation. However, the impact of the 2008 fiscal crisis, and changes in government led to a lack of support for these bodies. In a 2008 survey[4] by the EU Fundamental Rights Agency, the agency found that 57 per cent of immigrants and ethnic minorities were unaware of the existence of antidiscrimination legislation and 82 per cent of those who were discriminated against did not report it. In the spring of 2015, in a meeting with staff at ENAR, there was clear frustration at the lack of progress on antidiscrimination policy (Givens 2018). Despite the passage of the RED, Europe still needs to develop an environment where ethnic minorities are more aware of the resources available to them to deal with discrimination.

U.S. Anti-discrimination Policy

From its founding, race and law have been integral components of state- and nation-building processes in the United States. Slavery, in effect, transformed people into property, and elaborate rules governed the existence of blacks, free and slave, in the North as well as the South. Even after the institution of slavery was destroyed by a bloody civil war, whites continued to use law as a means of subjugating African Americans. As a result, an array of state and federal legal systems, often known by the euphemism "Jim Crow," codified various racial distinctions, often limiting the capacity of African Americans to vote or to enter into contracts, the two fundamental elements of participation in a Lockian democracy. In addition, under the common law, owners of property and capital essentially possessed a right to discriminate. They could thus refuse services, accommodations, and employment to individuals on any grounds. This right gave whites, particularly white men, considerable non-state power to shape communities.

The first antidiscrimination statutes date back to the Civil War era. They were part of an effort to incorporate free blacks into state and national polities. Unsurprisingly, the state of Massachusetts, an abolitionist stronghold, enacted the first such law on May 16, 1865. It prohibited discrimination on grounds of color or race in certain public places and provided that violations be punished by a fine not exceeding fifty dollars. At the federal level, antidiscrimination statutes were part of a state-building effort (Foner 1990). In 1875, just before the political demise of the Radical Republicans, Congress adopted "An Act to Protect All Citizens in Their Civil and Legal Rights" (hereafter referred to as the "Civil Rights Act of 1875"] (see Foner 1990, pp. 226–227, 233–234, 247). Although it was part of the Republicans' broader effort to reconstruct the American South, the Act applied to the entire nation, prohibiting discrimination on grounds of race, color, or previous condition of servitude in the use of inns, public conveyances, and other places of public amusement. Violators were liable to criminal and civil penalties in the federal courts, and aggrieved individuals retained the prerogative to seek redress under the common law or according to state statutes, where those existed. In the reactionary period that followed, however, the US Supreme Court struck down the Civil Rights Act of 1875, holding that

Congress had exceeded the scope of the federal government's powers under the Constitution. No further congressional action on racial discrimination was taken until 1957.

In 1954, the U.S. Supreme Court's landmark decision in *Brown v. Board of Education* made headlines around the world. In its wake, a newly galvanized civil rights movement emerged, culminating with the contrasting images of police brutality in Selma, Mississippi in 1965 and a peaceful gathering on the Washington Mall in 1963. The Civil Rights Act of 1964 and the Voting Rights Act of 1965 consolidated a patchwork of judicial and state-based reforms and articulated national civil rights standards enforceable through the federal courts.

Comparative Themes

In the U.S., the first antidiscrimination laws addressed racial discrimination, whereas gender discrimination was the subject of the EU's first antidiscrimination laws. In 1957, the founding document of the European Community, the Treaty of Rome, now Article 141 (formerly 119) of the present Treaty Establishing the European Community created a basic guarantee of equal pay for equal work between the sexes. At the time, French laws on equal pay were more advanced than its treaty partners. Fearing that those laws would put French industries at a competitive disadvantage within the common market, France insisted on the inclusion of this provision in the Treaty (Barnard 1996). Since then, EU efforts in the area of gender discrimination have been substantial. By contrast, Virginia Senator Howard W. Smith added gender as a protected class to the Civil Rights Act of 1964 in an attempt to divide the bill's supporters (Whalen and Whalen 1985).

Historically, the demographic composition of the European countries vis-à-vis the U.S. differs in important respects. America's African-American population is the legacy of slavery. To a lesser extent, the southwest contained Latino populations that were incorporated into the United States by virtue of the Treaty of Guadalupe-Hildago in 1848. By contrast, immigration flows into Europe from colonial sources did not accelerate until the 1960s. Thus, racially diverse groups comprise a smaller proportion of the population in European countries, with great variance among them in terms of both numbers and the origins of the immigrants, as we have already outlined in the first half of the book.

In the United States, strong civil society organizations had developed around the issue of race, for example, the National Association for the Advancement of Colored People, the Congress of Racial Equality, and the Southern Christian Leadership Conference were all formed to fight for equal rights for blacks, whereas women's organizations were still in a nascent stage by the mid-1960s. The European Starting Line Group (SLG) is similar in some ways to the coalition of American interest groups that lobbied for U.S. civil rights legislation in the early 1960s under an umbrella group known as the Leadership Conference on Civil Rights. However, the SLG did not have the same kind of support from a social movement. Although immigrant rights groups were involved with the SLG, immigrants themselves were not mobilized in the same way African-Americans and their white supporters were in the United States.

The EU and U.S. both confronted important constitutional issues in their pursuit of antidiscrimination legislation. The EP acted to put EU-wide anti-discrimination legislation on the political agenda in 1986 with its creation of the Parliamentary Enquiry Committee, charged with examining the rise of fascism and racism in Europe. However, at that time, the European Treaty did not provide a legal basis for the adoption of a legislative instrument addressing those phenomena. In 1992, the SLG began campaigning for both antidiscrimination legislation and the inclusion of an antidiscrimination provision in the European Treaty. The rise of radical right parties, anti-immigrant discourses, and violence against immigrants played a key role in motivating the actions of the SLG (Givens and Evans Case 2014).

The U.S. also experienced a reactionary movement against federal antidiscrimination laws. It erupted with the 1948 election. In response to President Harry S. Truman's signals of a new liberalism on civil rights issues, Strom Thurmond and a band of renegade Democrats, formally known as the States Rights Party, but colloquially known as the "Dixiecrats," ran their own presidential campaign. They won several Southern states, foreshadowing a breakdown in the New Deal Coalition. In 1964, U.S. Senator Barry Goldwater won some of those same states in his ill-fated contest for the presidency, and Alabama Governor George C. Wallace also enjoyed electoral success there.

There were several key factors that motivated policy in both Europe and the U.S. First, violence and discrimination against ethnic minorities and the development of anti-minority political groups clearly motivated policy developments in both cases. However, strategic litigation clearly played a greater role in the development of policy in the U.S., whereas it appears to be playing a greater role in the implementation of policy in Europe.

Immigrant integration has been an important issue that has developed over time in different countries and varies from a more passive approach to an approach that emphasizes language and culture training in an attempt to avoid problems that have been perceived to lead to immigrant alienation. The impact of these policies will need to be examined over time, as more recent immigrants become settled and their children become part of society. Socio-economic integration will continue to be an issue for low-skilled immigrants, and anti-discrimination policies will be important to ensure that immigrants who are ethnic minorities have the opportunity to succeed in the workplace.

Conclusion

Despite considerably divergent starting points, both new and old countries of immigration have been struggling with the task of integrating, socially and economically, their immigrant and foreign-born descendant populations. Unlike the United States, where "race" has never ceased to be the focal point of social division and the most prevalent form of discrimination, many European countries have tried to avoid a focus on race or religion in order to circumvent norms that have been advanced since the fall of the Nazi regime that for a brief time ruled most of the continent of Europe. The issues around racial discrimination in the U.S. are particularly distasteful to Western European sentiments, with governments in France and Germany going as far as to forbid any form of government sponsored statistics collection on the basis of race.

One can argue that religion and culture have become the new code words for "race" culminating in a situation where European countries are, however, faced with an unprecedented influx of immigrants of different cultures and religions. One could also argue that Europeans have not necessarily been "racist" in their discrimination because their societies have only recently contained a substantial racially distinct minority. Europeans may be considered more susceptible towards cultural and religious discrimination, something that may be on the rise today with the combination of a significant Muslim population and post 9/11 security concerns. The immigration policies of the countries outlined in this chapter illustrate how quickly race, religion, and culture became issues of concern beginning in the 1970s when the usefulness of post-World War II guest workers ended. It remains to be seen whether the juggling act of controlling the entry of any further "unwelcome" people while at the same time attempting to integrate them can continue in a productive way in Europe.

KEY TERMS

Assimilation   With assimilation, immigrants are expected to adapt to the language and culture of the host country, giving up their native language and cultural practices.

Civic Integration   A type of integration that became popular in the late 1990s which focuses on the immigrants' ability and need to know, understand, and even adopt their new home's civic values and "way of life." This often includes knowing their new country's history and political institutions and processes.

Integration   The processes that take place after an immigrant has moved to and settled in a new country. It involves both the immigrant adapting to their new home, as well as the native populations adapting to the new immigrant communities in their midst. Some states have formal integration policies to help facilitate this process, while others, such as the United States, do not.

Le contrat d'accueil et d'Intégration **(CAI)** A series of French policy proposals in 2003 that focused on the integration of immigrants. The contract requires any non-European foreigner who wishes to immigrate to France undertake civic and language training in order to promote integration into French society.

Multicultural The multicultural approach towards immigrant integration emphasizes the acceptance of immigrants who are encouraged to retain their cultural practices, while learning the language and civics of the host country. The term is sometimes used to describe immigrants, including those from Muslim backgrounds, who maintain their religious practices, and may be considered resistant to assimilation.

Racial Equality Directive (RED) Passed in 2000 by the European Union as a response to the entrance of radical right parties into European governments, this directive addresses racial discrimination in the areas of social protection, housing, education, and associations, as well as in employment.

NOTES

1 "Revised Executive Order Bans Travelers From Six Muslim-Majority Countries from Getting New Visas." *Washington Post* published 3/6/2017. http://wapo.st/2mXlFJW?tid=ss_mail&utm_term=.8c64148807f7, accessed 10/14/2019.
2 Carerra and Wiesbrock define it as "The term TCNs refers to those not holding the nationality of a member state and therefore not enjoying the status EU citizenship or derivative rights from it" (see Footnote 1).
3 ENAR Introduction http://www.enar-eu.org/Introduction-1301, accessed 10/11/2018.
4 EU MIDIS: European Union Minorities and Discrimination Survey http://fra.europa.eu/en/project/2011/eu-midis-european-union-minorities-and-discrimination-survey, accessed 10/13/2018.

REFERENCES

Bagley, Christopher. 1973. *The Dutch Plural Society: A Comparative Study in Race Relations*. New York: Institute of Race Relations/Oxford University Press.

Barnard, Catherine. 1996. "The Economic Objectives of Article 119." In Tamara K. Hervey and David O'Keefe, Editors, *Sex Equality Law of the European Union*. Hoboken, NJ: Wiley.

Bertossi, Christophe. 2011. "National Models of Integration in Europe. A Comparative and Critical Analysis." *American Behavioral Scientist*, 55(12): 1561–1580.

Caponio, Tiziana. 2018. "Immigrant Integration Beyond National Policies? Italian Cities' Participation in European City Networks." *Journal of Ethnic and Migration Studies*, 44(12): 2053–2069.

Carrera, Sergio and Anja Wiesbrock. 2009. "Civic Integration of Third Country Nationals: Nationalism Versus Europeanisation in the Common EU Immigration Policy." (Centre for European Policy Studies: Liberty and Security in Europe Series). Brussels: CEPS.

Castles, Stephen, Hein de Haas, and Mark J. Miller. 2014. *The Age of Migration: International Population Movements in the Modern World* (5th ed.). New York: Guilford Press.

Doomernik, Jeroen. 2003. "Integration Policies towards Immigrants and Their Descendents in the Netherlands." In Friedrich Heckmann and Dominique Schnapper, Editors, *The Integration of Immigrants in European Societies.* Stuttgart, Germany: Lucius and Lucius.

Doomernik Jeroen and Maria Bruquetas-Callejo. 2016. "National Immigration and Integration Policies in Europe Since 1973." In Blanca Garcés-Mascareñas and Rinus Penninx, Editors, *Integration Processes and Policies in Europe. Contexts, Levels and Actors.* (IMISCOE Research Series). Cham, Switzerland: Springer.

Favell, Adrian. 1998. *Philosophies of Integration.* London: MacMillan.

Foner, Eric. 1990. *A Short History of Reconstruction 1863–1877.* New York: HarperCollins.

Freeman, Gary P. 1979. *Immigrant Labor and Racial Conflict in Industrial Societies: The French and British Experience, 1945–1975.* Princeton, NJ: Princeton University Press.

Freeman, Gary P. 2004. "Immigrant Incorporation in Western Democracies." *International Migration Review,* 38(3): 945–969.

Freeman, Gary P. 2006. "National Models, Policy Types, and the Politics of Immigration in Liberal Democracies." *West European Politics,* 29(2): 227–247.

Givens, Terri. 2018. "Immigration, Race and Populism: Politics and Policy from Colonialism to Brexit." Paper presented at the 2018 UACES Annual Conference, Bath, England, September 3, 2018.

Givens, Terri and Rhonda Evans Case. 2014. *Legislating Equality: The Politics of Antidiscrimination Policy in Europe.* London: Oxford University Press.

Goodman, Sara Wallace. 2010. "Integration requirements for integration's sake? Identifying, categorising and comparing civic integration policies." *Journal of Ethnic and Migration Studies.* 36(5): 753–772.

Green, Simon. 2004. *The Political of Exclusion: Institutions and Immigration Policy in Contemporary Germany.* Manchester, England: Manchester University Press.

Howard, Marc Morjé. 2009. *The Politics of Citizenship in Europe.* New York: Cambridge.

Huddleston, Thomas, Jan Niessen, Eadaoin Ni Chaoimh, and Emilie White. 2011. *Migrant Integration Policy Index.* Brussels: British Council and Migration Policy Group.

Ireland, Patrick. 2004. *Becoming Europe: Immigration, Integration, and the Welfare State.* Pittsburgh: University of Pittsburgh Press.

Janoski, Thomas. 2010. *The Ironies of Citizenship: Naturalization and Integration in Industrialized Countries.* New York: Cambridge University Press.

Jiménez, Tomás R. 2011. *Immigrants in the United States: How Well Are They Integrating into Society?* Washington, DC: Migration Policy Institute.

Joppke, Christian. 1999. *Immigration and the Nation-State*. New York: Oxford University Press.

Joppke, Christian. 2007a. "Beyond National Models: Civic Integration Policies for Immigrants in Western Europe." *West European Politics*, 30(1): 1–22.

Joppke, Christian. 2007b. "Transformation of Immigrant Integration: Civic Integration and Antidiscrimination in the Netherlands, France, and Germany." *World Politics*, 59 (2): 243–273.

Kortmann, Matthias, and Christian Stecker. 2019. "Party competition and immigration and integration policies: A comparative analysis." *Comparative European Politics*, 17(1): 72–91.

Mariani, M. Thierry. 2006. "Rapport D'information Déposé par La Délégation De L'assemblée Nationale Pour Le Union Européenne, sur les Politiques D'intégration des Migrants dans l'Union Européenne (No. 3502)." Paris: Assemblee Nationale. http://www2.assemblee-nationale.fr/documents/notice/12/europe/rap-info/i3502/(index)/depots/(archives)/index-depots, accessed 10/11/2018.

Messina, Anthony M. 2007. *The Logics and Politics of Post-WWII Migration to Western Europe*. New York: Cambridge University Press.

Neureiter, Michael. 2019. "Evaluating the Effects of Immigrant Integration Policies in Western Europe Using a Difference-in-Differences Approach." *Journal of Ethnic and Migration Studies*, 45(15): 2779–2800.

Niessen, Jan. 2009. "Construction of the Migrant Integration Policy Index." In Thomas Huddleston and Jan Niessen, Editors, *Legal Frameworks for the Integration of Third-Country Nationals*. Leiden, The Netherlands: Martinus Nijhoff Publishers.

Penninx R., D. Spencer, and N. Van Hear. 2008. "Migration and Integration in Europe: The State of Research." COMPAS. https://www.compas.ox.ac.uk/fileadmin/files/Publications/Reports/Migration%20and%20Integration%20in%20Europe.pdf, accessed 4/19/2015.

Schain, M. A. 2008. *The Politics of Immigration in France, Britain, and the United States: A Comparative Study*. New York: Palgrave Macmillan.

Whalen, Charles and Barbara Whalen. 1985. *The Longest Debate: A Legislative History of the 1964 Civil Rights Act*. Washington, DC: Seven Locks.

Van Wolleghem, Pierre Georges. 2019. *The EU's Policy on the Integration of Migrants: A Case of Soft-Europeanization?* (Palgrave Studies in European Union Politics). London: Palgrave MacMillan.

10

CONCLUSION
The Ongoing Dynamics of Immigration Politics

Introduction

Perhaps the most important thing that we hope you get from this book is the understanding that the politics of immigration are complex and often don't fall in line with the mythologies that have become central to many countries' nation-building efforts. As we have explained in the chapters of this book, the paths that different countries have taken with immigration policy have been impacted by early nation-building efforts and more recently, the need for workers, as a country recovers from war or needs highly-skilled workers to fuel a tech boom. What is clear, is that immigration policy is a function of the political system and the electoral politics that define political party competition. For the conclusion of this book, we begin by examining the ongoing dynamics of immigration politics in the 21st century. We conclude with a discussion of the possibilities for regional and global governance that have developed along with trade pacts that focus on the flow of goods, yet only secondarily the flow of people.

The Ongoing Dynamics of Immigration Reform

The percentage of foreign born in the U.S. were close to 15 per cent in the first decade of the 21st century – very similar to the percentages at the beginning of the 20th century, a time when nativists and progressives were pushing for restrictions on immigration. Immigration has clearly led to major demographic changes around the world. Countries like the U.S., Australia, and Canada are becoming "majority minority," whereas European countries are facing declining birth rates and ongoing flows of immigrants and refugees from outside of Europe. This has led to growing concerns about cultural shifts and the importance of integrating young people, socially and economically, as these communities grow.

In our examination of the politics of immigration policy, we have seen that particular policies, such as quotas and preferences, have impacted the flow and integration of immigrants. However, what has dominated policymaking since the start of the 21st century is the focus on controlling immigration into the U.S. and Europe. Despite this focus, the desire to control immigration has not necessarily led to the passage of legislation.

In the U.S., since the 1990s, Congress has acted mainly as a veto point for immigration reform. As in the 1950s two patterns emerge: there is an increasing number of migrants and a growing sense that "something" must be done, yet the status quo cannot be overcome. When George W. Bush became president in 2001, there was great optimism that a new era of relations with Mexico and immigration reform would follow. President Bush was developing a strong relationship with Mexican president Vicente Fox when the 9/11 terror attacks took immigration reform off the agenda. As noted in Chapter 3, there was little change despite the effort to pass comprehensive reform legislation.

In 2010, undocumented immigration became the focus of policy, and in particular, children who had grown up in the U.S. College students who had been brought into the country as small children intensified their efforts to lobby congress to pass the DREAM Act. Jose Antonio Vargas, a respected journalist, wrote an article exposing himself as an illegal immigrant. In the meantime, immigration legislation languished in a starkly split Congress. President Obama was under fire from Hispanic groups for not following through on immigration legislation he had promised. By June of 2012, facing a tough election campaign against Mitt Romney, Obama issued an executive order allowing children who came to the United States as children to remain for at least two years without fear of deportation and apply for work permits.[1]

On June 25, 2012, the U.S. Supreme Court ruled invalid three key provisions of Arizona's SB 1070,[2] the state's attempt to regulate illegal immigration. This ruling once again reiterated the supremacy of the federal government in legislating and implementing immigration policy. Drawing on previous court rulings, Justice Anthony Kennedy, writing for the majority, noted that "[t]he Federal Government's broad, undoubted power over immigration and alien status rests, in part, on its constitutional power to 'establish a uniform Rule of Naturalization,' Art. I, §8, cl. 4, and on its inherent sovereign power to control and conduct foreign relations."[3] This ruling ensured that any reform in immigration policy would continue to be the prerogative of Congress and not the states.

The presidential election of 2012 did not revolve around the issue of immigration; rather, the economy was by far the top issue, but after Barack Obama's re-election there was a clear shift in approach from the

Republican party. Exit polls showed that Obama had won approximately seventy-five per cent of the Latino vote – and the vote was shown to be decisive, particularly in swing states like Ohio and Florida.[4] Within a few days, Republican pundits and politicians were talking about the need for immigration reform. Although it was clear that the economy was the most important issue for most Latinos, immigration came in a strong second. As the Republican party looked to explain why it had lost the presidency and control of the Senate, the focus shifted to their losing the Latino vote, and the impact this would have on the party's future.

Despite the loss of the 2012 election, with the election of Donald Trump in 2016, the Republican party would continue to move away from positions that might attract Latinx voters. Trump's policies, often considered cruel, were clearly anti-immigrant. The Muslim ban, family separations, restrictions on asylum seekers at the Mexican border, and ongoing anti-immigrant rhetoric placed U.S. policy in a very strict control mode.

The discourses around immigration policy in the U.S. have shifted from an emphasis on strict control to more open policies and back over our long history of migration (Tichenor 2002). Although the Democratic Party has been seen as the proponent of policies that would potentially lead to legalization (often referred to as *amnesty*), it was often Republican presidents who were champions of more open policies. Undocumented immigration has become the focus of policy, but we simply do not have enough visas to meet either the demands of employers or of immigrants.

It is striking that immigration is often described as a security issue, which focuses on the border, and yet there is little attention paid to the fact that there are somewhere between 10 and 12 million immigrants living in our country that we can neither document nor track. Which is the greater security issue? Many critics of immigration policy argue that illegal immigrants should be deported and made to "stand in line" to get back into the country. However, as advocates of comprehensive immigration reform often point out, there is no line to get into. This is why it is estimated that the majority of illegal immigrants come into this country on a valid (usually tourist) visa, and then overstay that visa, since they are able to get a job, housing, and make a living in the United States despite being out of status. Even with new programs to track visitors (e.g., US-VISIT), the government doesn't have the resources to track down every person on an expired visa.[5]

Globalization, the growth of the middle class, and other factors have enticed more people to attempt to enter the U.S. to find work and a better way of life.[6] Data show that the percentage of immigrants in the U.S. population in 2010 increased dramatically from the 1990s. According to the Migration Policy Institute's Datahub, between 2000 and 2010, the foreign-born population in the United States changed from 31,107,889 to 39,955,854, an increase of 28.4 per cent. In comparison, the foreign-born population changed from 19,767,316 to 31,107,889 between 1990 and 2000, a difference of 57.4 per cent. Immigrants as a percentage of the population also showed a significant increase with 12.9 per cent of the United States' total population as immigrants in 2010, compared to 11.1 per cent in 2000 and 7.9 per cent in 1990.[7]

As noted previously, the election of Donald Trump in the fall of 2016 has led to more deadlock in Congress. The main focus of the Trump administration has been to discourage immigration, with policies that focused on limiting migrants from Muslim countries and building a more robust border wall between the U.S. and Mexico. Detentions have been on the rise including the separation and detention of families. Little focus has been paid to immigration reform in terms of dealing with the DACA situation or the management of legal migration. The dilemma for politicians is how to address the issue in a way that can lead to solutions while keeping in mind the fears that immigration raises in the general population. Politicians have painted themselves into a corner by focusing on border security while being unwilling to pursue or compromise on policies that would deal with the real illegal immigration problem that is already inside of our borders.

The U.S. is an example of an approach to immigration which has also impacted Europe, in terms of the continuing focus on immigration control. The success of anti-immigrant far right parties and the Brexit referendum left politicians in Europe struggling to find common solutions for the flow of refugees coming from conflict areas and to escape economic hardship. It would seem to make sense that countries would want to increase cooperation to help those countries that need to develop economically, as well as finding ways to decrease conflict. However, as we will describe below, the prospects for global or regional governance of migration has its limits.

Immigration and the Prospects for Global Governance

Beyond issues of stalemate on the domestic political scene, confounding immigration policy even further are the catalysts for migration from the developing world that are rarely taken seriously by policymakers as challenges that can be taken on directly. The death toll of immigrants attempting to escape poverty and war in the Middle East and on the African continent have raised major humanitarian issues, yet it doesn't seem that immigration is a priority for regional or international governance. Zolberg (2012) noted that while Article 13(2) of the Universal Declaration of Human Rights expressly states that every human being has the right of exit from a particular state, "on the contrary, there exists a universal and unambiguous consensus on the very opposite principle, namely, that every state has the right to restrict the entry of foreigners" (p. 226). Therefore, the rights of sovereign states often overrule the human rights of individuals.

Unlike the flow of goods and finance, where states have established global institutions to coordinate their market-based policies, there have not been similar efforts to coordinate the flow of people across borders. Countries have traditionally avoided international obligations in this area of policy which has broad implications for employment and demographics. This is in contrast with the regional level where migration has increasingly been addressed in a cooperative manner (Lavenex, Jurje, Givens, and Buchanan 2015).

The growth in numbers of migrants has led states to work with each other to deal with these increasing flows in a more systematic manner. Koslowski (2006) pointed out some regimes already exist, "[t]here is an established international refugee regime, an emerging international travel regime and non-existent but potential international labor migration regime" (p. 107). The existing regimes, which are part of existing treaties or international human rights law, are part of what Betts (2011) referred to as "embedded institutions." An international regime related to the regulation of passports is not considered a migration regime but has a profound impact on migrants. Betts went on to note that much of this "embeddedness" is used to extend policies into the migration realm: "[r]ather than working towards the creation of a new UN migration organization, for example, the trend has been to work within the existing tapestry of international organizations and to develop a division of responsibility that can address emerging problems through existing organizations" (p. 17).

Along with the work of Betts and Koslowksi, much of the literature on migration governance has focused on global governance, but this also has implications for regional governance. Global governance of migration has tended to focus on refugee issues, particularly after World War II and the development of the UN High Commission for Refugees. For economic migrants, the post-World War II era was regulated through bilateral agreements, particularly for guest or temporary workers. As migration flows began to increase in the 1980s and 1990s, there were more calls for cooperation beyond refugee flows.

Started in 2007, The Global Forum on Migration and Development and the Global Migration Group are examples of the UN's attempts to bring a broader, global perspective to migration issues, particularly for developing countries. These forums for global governance seem to have had very limited impact on regional or national agendas on migration. In terms of policy impact, regional and bilateral relationships are more promising.

In their book which analyses international migration cooperation, Hansen, Köhler, and Money (2011) argued that "cooperation on migration issues will not develop unless there is a functional need" and when there is no need "incentives must exist for states to cooperate" (p. 10). Hansen et al. place the issue of regional cooperation squarely in the realm of international relations theory. Pointing out the roles of power, interests, and incentives, they develop a framework which explains the scope for cooperation. Reviewing a variety of case studies from the EU, to NAFTA, to South Africa, they conclude that, "there can be and is international cooperation over migration, but this cooperation remains limited and will only occur under very specific conditions." State interests must align, otherwise countries will act unilaterally (Hansen et al. 2011, p. 219).

Geddes (2012) was more skeptical of the potential for regional cooperation on migration in his analysis of regions and regionalism in migration policy. He found that regional organizations dealing with migration have limited scope, and "[a]side from the EU, it is often the case that migration and free movement provisions have been agreed upon and ceremonially signed, but then not implemented" (p. 590). In Europe, it has taken over 60 years of work toward integration to get to free movement. In South America and in Western and Southern Africa, where borders have been porous for a long time, states are trying to formalize rules that recognize and regulate their fluid borders. Put simply, in Europe, migration agreements preceded free movement. In South America and Africa, free movement preceded migration agreements. In the large Asian region, large-scale flows of low-skilled workers has been the focus, but attempts at regional coordination have been limited, again with porous borders preceding agreements in many areas. South America and Western and Southern Africa have made several ambitious attempts at establishing free movement agreements, but these agreements have remained mostly unrealized or have been watered down through amendments.

Free movement of workers has become a central element of the European Union treaties, even for new members after a seven-year transition period, and intra-EU migration has been relatively uncontroversial until recent years. Paraphrasing Meyers (2002), Geddes (2012) noted that Meyers argued that "agreement in Europe on free movement was attainable because of the relative absence of stark disparities and the limited potential for that movement" (pp. 579–580). The fiscal crisis which began in 2009 has created new pressures for migration from countries like Greece and Spain which had to be bailed out and are experiencing high levels of unemployment. Even prior to the fiscal crisis, the U.K. received large numbers of intra-EU migrants from the new member states of Eastern Europe, estimates are that anywhere from 700,000 to a million entered the U.K. between 2004 and 2012.

Geddes (2011) argued that "the development of EU migration and asylum is not indicative of states losing control or surrendering sovereignty, but of them trying to reassert control and seeking new 'venues' at supranational level that facilitate control efforts" (p. 87). The EU has worked to extend its control over migration flows by developing "Mobility Partnerships" (MPs) that focus on circular (temporary) migration from less-developed countries. These partnerships, however, were described as "insecurity partnerships" by Carrera and Hernandez i Sagrera (2011) in their analysis of these relationships. They argued that MPs "undermine the coherence of EU policy on labour immigration and increase the vulnerability of third country workers' human rights in Europe" (p. 97).

Several authors focus on the development of Regional Consultative Processes (RCPs) which are considered "the most important multilateral forms of consultation" (Köhler 2011, p. 100). Despite the skepticism of Geddes, RCPs are considered important more in terms of the processes they develop rather than binding outcomes. Köhler (2011) found in his analysis that "[t]he emphasis of RCP activities lies more with building trust through exchanging information than with promoting policy convergence by developing policy standards" (p. 119).

It may become necessary to accept the powerful exogenous pressures to cooperate as inevitable and to shift the level of governance over immigration from the national to the international, tying it more broadly with questions of poverty, disease, environmental degradation, and international and civil conflict. This is especially needed when we consider that discrimination towards immigrants in Europe is becoming a new "code" for racial discrimination. Many on the European Left, perhaps falsely, hope that increased development aid to the Developing World can "solve" the problem of immigration.

Comparing Immigration Policy – The Future

The politics of immigration is in constant flux. The rise of anti-immigrant populism in many countries around the world is an indicator of the contested nature of immigration policy. Despite the need for labor and the potential for the positive impact of immigrants in many countries, fear of change is driving many politicians to support policies to restrict immigration.

Although we are in a period of more restrictive policy, history shows that around the world, policy can go from more restrictive to more expansive in a short period of time. However, there are a variety of factors that will influence attitudes and policy toward immigration policy into the future.

One factor which we have not explored in detail in this book is climate change. Writing for the Washington, DC-based think-tank, The Brookings Institute, former presidential advisor John Podesta pointed to "[l]arge-scale human migration due to resource scarcity, increased frequency of extreme weather events, and other factors, particularly in the developing countries in the earth's low latitudinal band."[8] The threat of melting glaciers, rising oceans, and natural disasters has already led to the development of a new category of refugee: "environmental refugees." The UN has been reluctant to give those impacted by natural disasters official refugee status, but these movements are likely to increase as the impacts of global climate change intensify. The UNHCR stated that, "[a]n annual average of 21.5 million people have been forcibly displaced by weather-related sudden onset hazards – such as floods, storms, wildfires, extreme temperature – each year since 2008."[9]

Another ongoing risk for migration flows is conflict. Throughout history, migration flows have been connected to military conflicts, from world wars to regional conflicts. In fact, there is concern that the impacts of climate change may lead to military conflicts (Mach et al. 2019). The combination of ongoing regional conflicts and the negative impacts of climate change will contribute to an ongoing crisis of refugee flows within countries and beyond. This will put strains on the resources receiving countries can provide, and potentially lead to political issues over how to respond to conflicts.

With such large numbers of people at risk, it will be a challenge for countries around the world to manage flows and determine the status of people fleeing natural disasters and war. Differences across countries and history indicate that it is unlikely that a common approach will be taken. The study of immigration politics will continue to need a comparative lens. The ways that different countries approach immigration policy, and the politics that underpin them, will give us insights into the ways that a variety of factors are impacting our global society.

This book has examined the history of immigration policy, party politics, and policies from citizenship to immigrant integration. We have shown the different ways that countries have approached policies over time and drawn from the most important researchers in the field. There will always be more research to do, and the policies that are being made today will become the history that defines future policy. It is the hope of the authors that this book is only the beginning of your interest in this topic and that you will continue to follow developments in a field which has relevance beyond political science, including sociology, law, anthropology, and many more fields. There are many ways to contribute to the research and study of this complicated subject, and we hope you will share what you have learned far and wide.

NOTES

1 See "Obama to Permit Young Migrants to Remain in U.S." *New York Times* published 6/16/2012. http://www.nytimes.com/2012/06/16/us/us-to-stop-deporting-some-illegal-immigrants.html, accessed 10/19/2019. Details on the order posted on Homeland Security website: http://www.dhs.gov/ynews/releases/20120612-napolitano-announces-deferred-action-process-for-young-people.shtm, accessed 10/25/18.

2 See "Arizona Immigration Law (S.B. 1070)" https://immigration.findlaw.com/immigration-laws-and-resources/arizona-immigration-law-s-b-1070.html, accessed 1/15/2020.
3 See *Arizona v. United States* published 6/25/2012. https://www.oyez.org/cases/2011/11-182, accessed 10/25/2018.
4 See "2012 Election Eve Poll" *Latino Decisions* published 6/2012. http://www.latinodecisions.com/2012-election-eve-polls/, accessed 10/25/18.
5 See "Undocumented Workers Overstay Visas." *Arizona Daily Sun* published 5/11/2010. http://azdailysun.com/news/local/state-and-regional/article_825a9b53-c1f5-5451-a62b-db72b307c09d.html, accessed 10/25/18.
6 Studies from the U.S. and Mexico in 2011 indicated that migration was in decline and net migration was close to zero. http://articles.latimes.com/2011/nov/15/world/la-fg-mexico-migration-20111115, accessed 10/25/2018.
7 See MPI Datahub. https://www.migrationpolicy.org/programs/migration-data-hub, accessed 10/25/2019.
8 See "The Climate Crisis, Migration, and Refugees." *Brookings* published 7/25/2019. https://www.brookings.edu/research/the-climate-crisis-migration-and-refugees/, accessed 10/19/2019.
9 See "Frequently Asked Questions on Climate Change and Disaster Displacement." *United Nations, UNHCR* published 11/6/2016. https://www.unhcr.org/en-us/news/latest/2016/11/581f52dc4/frequently-asked-questions-climate-change-disaster-displacement.html, accessed 10/19/2019.

REFERENCES

*References marked with an asterisk are sources that can be used for further research and information.

Betts, Alexander. 2011. *Global Migration Governance*. New York: Oxford University Press.
Boucher, Anna K. and Justin Gest. 2018. *Crossroads: Comparative Immigration Regimes in a World of Demographic Change*. New York: Cambridge University Press.
Carrera, Sergio and Raul Hernández i Sagrera. 2011. "Mobility Partnerships: 'Insecurity Partnerships' for Policy Coherence and Migrant Workers' Human Rights in the EU." In Rahel Kunz, Sandra Lavenex and Marion Panizzon, Editors, *Multilayered Migration Governance: The Promise of Partnership*. London: Routledge.
Castles, Stephen, Hein de Haas, and Mark J. Miller. 2014. *The Age of Migration: International Population Movements in the Modern World*. New York: Guilford.
Geddes, Andrew 2011. "The European Union's Extraterritorial Immigration Controls and International Migration Relations." In Randall Hansen, Jobst Köhler, and Jeannette Money, Editors, *Migration, Nation States and International Cooperation*. New York: Routledge.
Geddes, Andrew. 2012. "Regions and Regionalism," In Marc R. Rosenblum and Daniel J. Tichenor, Editors, *Oxford Handbook of the Politics of International Migration*. New York: Oxford University Press.
Green-Pedersen, Christoffer and Simon Otjes. 2019. "A Hot Topic? Immigration on the Agenda in Western Europe." *Party Politics*, 25(3): 424–434.

*Guiraudon, Virginie and Gallya Lahav. (2000). "A Reappraisal of the State Sovereignty Debate: The Case of Migration Control." *Comparative Political Studies*, 33(2): 163–195.

Hansen, Randall, Jobst Köhler, and Jeannette Money. 2011. *Migration, Nation States and International Cooperation*. New York: Routledge.

Köhler, Jobst. 2011. "What Government Networks Do in the Field of Migration: An Analysis of Selected Regional Consultative Processes." In Randall Hansen, Jobst Köhler, and Jeannette Money, Editors, *Migration, Nation States and International Cooperation*. New York: Routledge.

Koslowski, Rey. 2008. "Global Mobility and the Quest for an International Migration Regime." In Joseph Chamie and Luca Dall'Oglio, Editors, *International Migration and Development. Continuing the Dialogue: Legal and Policy Perspectives*. New York: Center for Migration Studies.

Kunz, Rahel, Sandra Lavenex and Marion Panizzon. 2011. *Multilayered Migration Governance: The Promise of Partnership*. New York: Routledge.

Lavenex, Sandra, Flavia Jurje, Terri E. Givens, and Ross Buchanan. 2015. "Regional Migration Governance." In Tanja Boerzel and Thomas Risse, Editors, *The Politics of Regional Migration*. New York: Oxford University Press.

Mach, Katharine J., Caroline M. Kraan, W. Neil Adger, Halvard Buhaug, Marshall Burke, James D. Fearon, et al. 2019. "Climate as a Risk Factor for Armed Conflict." *Nature*, 571(7764): 193–197.

Peters, Margaret E. 2019. "Immigration and International Law." *International Studies Quarterly*, 63(2): 281–295.

Tichenor, Daniel J. 2002. *Dividing Lines: The Politics of Immigration Control in America*. Princeton, NJ: Princeton University Press.

Zolberg, Aristide. 2012. "Why Not the Whole World? Ethical Dilemmas of Immigration Politics." In Kavita Khory, Editor, *Global Migration: Challenges in the Twenty-First Century*. New York: Palgrave MacMillan.

INDEX

Made in the USA
Middletown, DE
18 January 2023